NOLO *Your Legal Companion*

"In Nolo you can trust." —**THE NEW YORK TIMES**

OUR MISSION
Make the law as simple as possible, saving you time, money and headaches.

Whether you have a simple question or a complex problem, turn to us at:

NOLO.COM

Your all-in-one legal resource

Need quick information about wills, patents, adoptions, starting a business—or anything else that's affected by the law? **Nolo.com** is packed with free articles, legal updates, resources and a complete catalog of our books and software.

NOLO NOW

Make your legal documents online

Creating a legal document has never been easier or more cost-effective! Featuring Nolo's Online Will, as well as online forms for LLC formation, incorporation, divorce, name change—and many more! Check it out at **http://nolonow.nolo.com**.

NOLO'S LAWYER DIRECTORY

Meet your new attorney

If you want advice from a qualified attorney, turn to Nolo's Lawyer Directory—the only directory that lets you see hundreds of in-depth attorney profiles so you can pick the one that's right for you. Find it at **http://lawyers.nolo.com**.

ALWAYS UP TO DATE

Sign up for NOLO'S **LEGAL UPDATER**

Old law is bad law. We'll email you when we publish an updated edition of this book—sign up for this free service at nolo.com/legalupdater.

Find the latest updates at NOLO.COM

Recognizing that the law can change even before you use this book, we post legal updates during the life of this edition at **nolo.com/updates**.

Is this edition the newest? **ASK US!**

To make sure that this is the most recent available, just give us a call at **800-728-3555**.

(Please note that we cannot offer legal advice.)

Please note

We believe accurate, plain-English legal information should help you solve many of your own legal problems. But this text is not a substitute for personalized advice from a knowledgeable lawyer. If you want the help of a trained professional—and we'll always point out situations in which we think that's a good idea— consult an attorney licensed to practice in your state.

1st edition

Every Landlord's
Property
Protection Guide

10 Ways to Cut Your Risk Now

by Attorney Ron Leshnower

FIRST EDITION	JANUARY 2008
Editor	JANET PORTMAN
Cover design	SUSAN PUTNEY
Book design	TERRI HEARSH
Proofreading	ROBERT WELLS
Index	THÉRÈSE SHERE
Printing	DELTA PRINTING SOLUTIONS, INC.

Leshnower, Ron
  Every landlord's property protection guide : 10 ways to cut your risk now / by
Ron Leshnower. -- 1st ed.
      p. cm.
  ISBN-13: 978-1-4133-0700-9 (pbk.)
  1. Rental housing--United States--Management. 2. Real estate management--
United States. 3. Landlord and tenant--United States. 4. Landlords--United
States. I. Title.
HD1394.5.U6L467 2008
333.33'8--dc22

                              200703179

Dedication

To my loving wife, Hillary, for her patience and encouragement, and to my son, Jacob, who has a world of reading to look forward to.

Acknowledgments

My heartfelt appreciation to Janet Portman, editor extraordinaire, for finding me at that conference and for everything since. My deepest thanks also go to Marcia Stewart for her inspiration and guidance, and to the entire Nolo staff for contributing their talents toward turning this idea into a reality.

About the Author

Ron Leshnower has written hundreds of informative, how-to articles for a national audience of landlords and property managers on a wide range of residential real estate topics, from compliance with the low-income housing tax credit program to premises liability issues. He is the founder and president of Fairhousinghelper.com, and is a communications analyst at a leading international law firm in New York. He is admitted to practice law in New York and Massachusetts.

Table of Contents

Your Property Protection Companion

Most rental property owners, at some time or other, find themselves awake at night, worrying about their investment. Do I have enough insurance, and the right kind? Did I repair the front porch railing properly, and can I put off the expensive rewiring job that I can't afford right now? When I showed the rental today to the applicant in the wheelchair, did I handle it properly? And what about my tax records and paperwork—oh, the paperwork—could I weather an inquiry from the IRS?

Short of sleeping pills, what can you do about these nighttime worries? Fortunately, you can do plenty, and this book can help. Experienced landlords will tell you that grief (lawsuits, property damage, higher insurance premiums, high turnover, bad publicity) is most likely to come not from out of the blue, but from well-known quarters. These owners can tick off the problems you're likely to encounter on two hands—they include bad tenants, repairs, fair housing claims, crime, hassles with employees and contractors, inadequate insurance, and, of course, taxes. It follows that by paying careful attention to just these ten issues, you can reduce most of the risk you face as a landlord.

Minimizing the risks in your business doesn't require a ton of money or a staff of experts. All you need to do is learn where you're vulnerable and then take commonsense steps to minimize that vulnerability. For example, it might surprise you to learn that a large number of fair housing lawsuits concern discrimination against people with disabilities, and that one way to prevent such a fate befalling you is to make sure you never steer a disabled applicant to a particular rental. (No matter how appropriate you might think your choice is, it's up to applicants to choose the rentals they like.) Now, how hard is that? A simple change in the way you do business will have a big payoff in the reduced risk of lawsuits.

To make low-risk landlording as easy as possible, this book is designed as a ten-step process—one for every common risk. We've organized the book to quickly get you the information you need. Here's how each chapter, or "Step," works:

1. First, you'll see a short explanation of the issue and what's at risk in a section called "What do You Have to Lose?" For example, in Step Six you'll learn that, contrary to what you might assume, you have a significant responsibility to keep your tenants safe from crime. Failure to do so might result in your being held partly liable for the consequences of a criminal's act.

2. Next, in "Is This You?" you'll find out whether you need to be concerned about the risk you just read about. You'll see a checklist of common mistakes landlords make in this area, and can scan it to see whether any of them describe your practices, too. For instance, in Step Seven's "Do You Think About Choosing Tenants Like These Landlords?" you'll be asked whether you automatically reject applicants who have any prior drug-related convictions? (Hint: This is a mistake.) If you don't find yourself on the list of risky business practices, great! You can move on to the next Step.

3. The third section of every Step, "Take Action!" tells you what you can do to minimize or even eliminate the risk. For example, in the course of making your property structurally sound, you'll want to do a thorough inspection and hire specialists if necessary.

Along the way, you'll see summaries of court cases or other real-life examples that illustrate what happened to landlords who experienced the risk addressed in the chapter. These "It Won't Happen to You" stories end with advice on how you can avoid the case's unhappy outcome.

To help you with your risk-lowering mission, each chapter ends with a handy list of actions to take. Use these lists as you tackle each risk, checking off each suggestion as you accomplish it. And when you're done with the ten Steps, be sure to give yourself the congratulations you deserve. You will have gone a long way toward protecting your business and your investment.

Now, here's a bonus. We know that low-risk landlording involves not just how you manage your property and tenants, but what you put in your leases and rental agreements. To help you out on this front, we've enclosed Nolo's lease-writing software, *LeaseWriter Plus*, which walks you through the creation of a lease or month-to-month rental agreement. Once you enter your state, *LeaseWriter*

Plus will automatically alert you to state-specific details, such as the limit of the security deposit and (for month-to-month agreements), the number of days' notice required to terminate the tenancy. The resulting document is in plain, clear English, so that both you and your tenants can understand the key rules that govern the tenancy. Using an understandable lease that complies with your state's law is a wise business practice—and one that will help you avoid legal problems. See, wasn't that easy?

Other Helpful Books from Nolo

Nolo publishes a comprehensive library of books written to help every landlord. Besides *LeaseWriter Plus,* Nolo offers:

- *Every Landlord's Legal Guide,* by Marcia Stewart, Ralph Warner, and Janet Portman, a comprehensive book that guides you through every rental event, from advertising to repairs, security deposit issues, access to the rental property, and terminating tenancies. The book includes charts for the law in every state, and dozens of forms (including a lease) on CD-ROM.
- *Leases and Rental Agreements,* by Marcia Stewart, Ralph Warner, and Janet Portman, includes a lease, rental agreement, and several other basic forms on CD-ROM.
- *Every Landlord's Guide to Finding Great Tenants,* by Janet Portman, focuses solely on advertising and showing your rental, evaluating prospects, and choosing and rejecting tenants, with dozens of forms on CD-ROM.
- *Every Landlord's Tax Deduction Guide,* by Stephen Fishman, includes all the information you need to take advantage of every deduction available to you.
- *The California Landlord's Law Book: Rights and Responsibilities,* by David Brown and Janet Portman, and *The California Landlord's Law Book: Evictions,* by David Brown, contain all the information California landlords need to run their business and handle an eviction in court by themselves.

Get the Right Insurance for Your Property and Business

nsurance is a complicated subject, made more so by the insurance industry's inability to explain its products in a way that the average person—or even the average business owner—can understand. Faced with an indecipherable policy squeezed into seven-point type on a flimsy brochure, most people toss the thing in a drawer and pray they'll never need to look at it. Indeed, if you implement the strategies suggested in this book, you'll probably never have to unearth your policy in a panic. But since some misfortunes are beyond your control, you should know what coverage you're paying for—or perhaps, should have bought.

Fortunately, you don't need to become an insurance professional in order to adequately and efficiently insure your property and business. In Step One, you'll learn the basics that will enable you to manage your risks, stay in business, and make your properties a success.

More Insurance Information

This Step gives you tips for choosing property, liability, and related coverage for your property and business. Insurance matters crop up in other areas, too.

- **Renters' insurance.** See Step Eight to learn about whether you should require tenants to get renters' insurance
- **Workers' compensation.** See Step Nine for information on handling worker's compensation issues with your employees, and
- **Your contractors' insurance.** See Step Nine to read about how to obtain adequate coverage when hiring contractors.

What Do You Have to Lose?

Everything. Almost every risk you'll read about in this book has the potential to ruin your business and leave you with attorneys' fees and settlements or judgments to boot. A tenant who falls on your just-washed lobby floor, for example, can sue you for medical expenses, lost wages, future loss of earning capacity, and more. These claims can quickly add up to several thousands of dollars. With the right insurance to cover these costs, you'll survive.

As you read through this chapter, you'll see how this dire scenario can play out. You'll read some real-life examples of landlords who found themselves in very hot water, owing a lot of money to tenants or their families after a tragic loss. But in each case, the landlords were able to settle claims and keep their business alive thanks to the fact they had adequate insurance in place to cover their risks.

It Won't Happen to You ...

What happened. A 23-year-old tenant in San Francisco died in an apartment fire. The tenant's family sued the landlord, a company that owned 60 properties, claiming that it negligently left a sofa over a floor furnace and didn't equip the apartment with functioning smoke detectors. The landlord settled for $1.5 million, and its insurer paid the full amount to the tenant's family.

How you can avoid it. Use good sense when placing furniture in furnished apartments. But understand that if you make a mistake—or if tenants move the furniture, and later claim they didn't—you'll need adequate insurance protection if someone is injured.

Is This You?

Very few readers can confidently skip this chapter. Unless you've had the good fortune to be working with an insurance agent or broker who understands the residential rental business *and* is familiar with your particular situation, you'll recognize yourself in at least one of the descriptions, below, of landlords who are courting disaster by not paying sufficient attention to the matter of insurance . Take a moment to scan the list of risky attitudes and behaviors and check off those that apply. If you finish with more than a couple of check marks, read on.

Do You Think About Insurance Like These Landlords?

☐ Each year, you renew your insurance policy without reassessing your coverage needs. In particular, you haven't looked at your policy limits (the maximum amount of money the insurer will pay out on a claim or per year) for a long time.

☐ You live in a geographic area that's prone to floods, hurricanes, tornadoes, wildfires, or heavy snowfalls, and you aren't sure to what extent your policies protect you from these disasters.

☐ You're renting out the home that belonged to your parents and have kept their homeowners' policy in place, figuring that's enough to cover your risks.

☑ You know insurance is necessary, but since you don't really understand the various kinds of coverage available, you trust your agent's recommendations about what you need.

☑ You've insured your rental business through the same agent who handles your car insurance—without learning whether he is familiar with your business and its specific risks.

☐ You've delegated most aspects of your rental business to a property management company, and you assume that its policies will cover you, too.

☐ Your building is brand new, constructed of fire-resistant materials, and so you think it's pretty safe.

☐ You screen your tenants carefully and trust that they'll keep an eye on things.

☑ Your business isn't organized as a limited liability company (LLC) or a corporation, which means that someone who secures a settlement or judgment against you can reach your personal assets (not just your rental properties).

☐ Figuring that because you run a tight ship and haven't been sued, you save some money by cutting back on coverage—but you haven't balanced the money you'll save in premium payments against the size of any uninsured loss.

☐ You have an excellent on-site manager who, you are confident, will nip problems in the bud.

☐ Your insurer has made certain recommendations for maintaining or repairing your property, but you've delayed or ignored them due to financial constraints, lack of motivation, or both.

☐ A friend who is a landlord is thrilled with the insurance policy she just bought, so you buy the same policy from her insurer without exploring other options.

☐ You've decided that your company's financial health determines how much money you're willing to spend on insurance premiums.

☐ Whenever you need to cut costs, your insurance policy is always the first item to meet the blade.

☐ You don't know whether your insurer will pay the full cost of replacing your building—or just its fair market value.

☐ You assume that your property insurance policy covers furniture, computers, and other valuable items you own inside your building.

☐ You use different vehicles for your business, but you haven't made sure they're all properly covered for use in your business.

☐ You assume that because you own three properties, you must buy three separate insurance policies.

☑ You don't know how to compare insurers or access ratings, so you rely on recommendations from your agent.

☐ You think it's smart to choose a low deductible so you can maximize your insurer's payments after a loss.

☐ You don't know whether your insurer will cover the rents you'll lose if tenants get displaced because of a fire, flood, or other loss.

☐ You worry about a terrorist attack, but you never thought to ask your insurer whether you're covered in the event an attack occurs and damages your property.

ion!

you recognize yourself among the landlords in the descriptions above? Even if you only remotely resemble one or two, consider the following strategies that will reduce the risks that each landlord is courting. These strategies will help you tackle insurance issues head-on and get the protection you need to achieve your goal of running a safe property and a successful business.

The chart below gives you a thumbnail sketch of the various policies available to landlords. Don't be overwhelmed—you probably won't need every one! But after you read about each insurance type in more detail in the rest of this chapter, you'll be well schooled in insurance for landlords. What's more, you'll be able to talk confidently with your broker about exactly which policies or coverage you need.

Insurance at a Glance	
Try to imagine an unpleasant scenario involving your property or your tenants—chances are, there's an insurance policy you can buy to cover your losses. Here are the main types of available policies or coverage.	
Insurance type	**What does it cover?**
Property insurance	Buildings and other physical structures on your property
Contents insurance	Items of personal property that you keep or store inside your buildings and structures, such as office equipment and furniture
Demolition insurance	Clearing debris or hauling away the remains of any destroyed structures on your property
Boiler and machinery	Losses that your boilers, air-conditioning units, compressors, steam cookers, electric water heaters, and other machinery in your buildings may cause
Inland marine	Outdoor fixtures, such as fences, signs, pole lights, and equipment such as lawn mowers, gardening tools, and snow plows

All Risk
Ad pol

wht f ?
empty.

Insurance at a Glance (continued)

Insurance type	What does it cover?
Builder's risk (cost of construction)	Losses that occur to parts of your building that are under construction or undergoing remodeling or repair
Basic coverage (a type of "named-peril coverage")	Named perils, typically including fire, lightning, explosion, windstorm or hail, smoke, aircraft or vehicles, riot or civil commotion, vandalism, and sprinkler leakage, sinkholes, and volcanoes
Broad coverage	Named perils included in basic coverage plus additional perils, most notably breakage of glass (from your buildings), falling objects, weight of ice, snow, or sleet, water damage (associated with your building's plumbing), and collapse from certain specific causes
Special form coverage ("all-risk coverage," "all-peril coverage")	All perils except for any exclusions, such as loss resulting from civil riot, war, earthquakes, and floods
Terrorism insurance	Losses your property suffers as the result of a terrorist act
Flood insurance	Property damage caused by water accumulation in your building (other than water blown in by wind)
Earthquake insurance	Loss caused by earthquakes and tremors
Sewer backup insurance	Damage that flows from clogged sewers
Ordinance or law insurance	The unexpected costs that compliance with new building codes can add when rebuilding or even repairing parts of your building
Liability insurance	Your legal obligations to pay for others' injuries and property loss that you cause
Commercial general liability insurance	All liability exposures (except for any exclusions), most notably, claims based on libel/slander, discrimination, unlawful and retaliatory eviction, and invasion of privacy
Loss of rents coverage (business interruption coverage, business income coverage)	Typically, the fair rental value of apartments that stay vacant due to a loss, for up to 12 months

Insurance at a Glance (continued)	
Insurance type	What does it cover?
Commercial automobile liability insurance	Accidents involving automobiles you own in connection with your business
Inflation guard insurance	The increase in construction costs in your area that are due to inflation
Blanket insurance	Allows for properties in different locations to be covered under one policy
Umbrella insurance (excess liability insurance)	Bolsters the limits of your liability insurance policy in return for a relatively small additional premium

Property Insurance: Protect your building and structures

You probably already have property insurance. It's not only the most basic and common type of insurance, but is required by banks and other financial institutions that lend you money or extend a mortgage. Property insurance covers the buildings and other physical structures on your property, such as stand-alone garages and storage sheds. It also covers "permanent fixtures," which are personal property items that have been bolted, screwed, nailed, cemented, glued, or attached to the property in any other way such that removing them wouldn't be possible without causing serious damage. Common examples of permanent fixtures include sinks, toilets, and installed appliances such as dishwashers and dryers.

Having a good property policy in place is essential, but it's not the end of the matter. It's important to have the right policy *limits*—the money available to you to satisfy a settlement or judgment. Ideally, you'll want insurance that covers the full cost of repairing or replacing your property. High policy limits are reassuring, but naturally they will cost you more in premiums. Lower limits are cheaper, but those savings may evaporate when you're facing a loss that the policy will only partially cover.

Property Insurance Policy Limits: How Much Coverage Do You Need?

Use this form to help you determine how much property insurance you need. Check off the descriptions that fit your situation, then take your conclusions to your agent or broker.

You may want lower policy limits—and lower premiums	Is this you?	You may want higher policy limits—and higher premiums	Is this you?
You've got a new building made with brick or fire-resistant materials	☐	Your building is an old wooden structure	☑
Your roof is fireproof	☐	Your roof is wood shingle	☐
Your property is located in an area that enjoys a very low crime rate	☐	Your property is located in an area with a high incidence of theft and other crimes	☐
Your building was built recently and is in pristine condition	☐	Your building is very old and hasn't been updated in the past 40 years	☐
Your building was constructed in such a way that it has a low replacement cost	☐	Your building has special design features and uses certain types of material that would make it very costly to replace	☐
Your property has fire hydrants in front of it and the nearest fire station is two blocks away	☐	Your property is located in an area with limited fire protection	☐
You or your business have excellent credit and you've never been sued	☐	You have poor credit and your business has been sued several times	☐
You haven't filed a single claim yet in your five years as a landlord	☐	You have already filed several claims or a few significant ones with your insurer	☐
Your property is located in an area that doesn't normally experience bad storms or natural disasters	☐	Your property is located in an area that's prone to certain types of storms or natural disasters	☐

Property Insurance:
Protect against what's likely to happen

You might think that a property insurance policy will spring to your rescue whenever—and however—your property is damaged or destroyed. Quite the contrary. The insurance industry limits coverage to damage resulting only from specific causes (called "perils") unless you request broader coverage, which you can purchase for a higher premium. If you check the wording in your policy, you're likely to find one of three types of peril coverages: "basic," "broad," and "special form" (also known as "all-risk"). What are the differences?

- **Basic coverage.** With basic coverage, your property is insured against only the "named perils" that are mentioned in the policy. These typically include fire, lightning, explosion, windstorm or hail, smoke, aircraft or vehicles, riot or civil commotion, vandalism, sprinkler leakage, sinkholes, and volcanoes. If you have basic coverage, read the policy carefully, looking for the definition of each peril so you understand any limitations. Don't assume the definitions are the same as everyday jargon or that they match the definitions in an older policy you once had with a different insurer. Also, if you choose basic coverage, make sure this limited coverage is all you need and that you can confidently do without coverage for unlisted perils such as falling objects (like broken glass falling from your building).

- **Broad coverage.** Broad coverage, like basic coverage, is a "named-peril" policy. The difference is that broad coverage includes more perils than basic coverage, such as breakage of glass (from your buildings), falling objects, weight of ice, snow, or sleet, water damage (associated with your building's plumbing), and collapse from certain specific causes. Again, make sure you understand how each peril in your broad coverage is defined and that you're covered for all the perils you need.

- **Special form or "all-risk," "all-peril" coverage.** Special form coverage will cost you more, but for good reason. Instead of covering you for loss resulting only from named perils, special form coverage takes the opposite approach: It protects your property against *all* perils—except for perils that are specifically excluded (such as nuclear hazards, earthquakes, and floods). Because there are so many ways your property can suffer a devastating loss or even a minor one, landlords should strongly consider all-risk coverage.

Contents, or Personal Property, Insurance: Insure what's inside

Landlords commonly assume that their property insurance covers "personal property," or items that they use or store inside their buildings. Alas, this is not the case. For example, should a fire damage the lobby of your apartment building, your property insurance may cover the costs of rebuilding the lobby, but you'd have to foot the bill for replacing any sofas, chairs, plants, mirrors, artwork, and other items of personal property destroyed by the fire.

It's often worthwhile to cover the contents of your buildings, especially if you have an on-site leasing office that houses your computers, desks, and filing cabinets. If you rent any furnished apartments (which contain couches, beds, and other furniture that you own), you'll definitely need to insure these contents separately.

Contents Insurance Policy Limits:
How Much Coverage Do You Need?

Use this form to help you determine how much contents insurance you need. Check off the descriptions that fit your situation, then take your conclusions to your agent or broker.

You may want lower policy limits—and lower premiums, if:

☐ You only rent unfurnished apartments

☐ You have a community room in your apartment building with nothing other than an old table and chairs

☐ You have a "study room" that's nothing more than a room with some old sofas where tenants may quietly enjoy a book

☐ There is no leasing office or non-rental space in your building

☐ Your leasing office has nothing but old furniture and framed posters on the wall

☐ You store your valuables in a safety-deposit box at the local bank

You may want higher policy limits—and higher premiums, if:

☐ Many of the apartments you rent are furnished

☐ Your community room has state-of-the-art audio-visual equipment, along with a kitchen containing top-of-the-line appliances

☐ You have a "business center" that houses brand-new computers, printers, faxes, and other expensive equipment for tenants' use

☐ You have a leasing office and other areas that are open to the public and see regular use

☐ Your leasing office has nice furniture and an expensive painting donated by a former tenant

☐ You store your valuables in a safe located in the model apartment on your property

Replacement Coverage: Get paid for the cost of a new building or item, not the market value of the destroyed one

If your apartment building is damaged beyond repair, don't assume your insurer will pay you to rebuild it—no matter how much property insurance you may have. Under some policies, insurers pay "actual cash value" (ACV) for destroyed property. ACV is the value of the property that was destroyed, taking into account its age and condition. In other words, it's the market value of the property just before it was destroyed, which is probably far lower than what it will cost you to rebuild.

An alternative payment approach, known as replacement cost coverage, is widely available and a much better option. With replacement cost coverage, your insurer must pay you for the cost of replacing your destroyed property with a new building. Yes, replacement cost coverage costs more than ACV, but it's usually worth it because you'll get paid what you need to rebuild after a catastrophe.

TIP

Replacement cost coverage doesn't cover the cost of clearing debris or hauling away the remains of any destroyed structures on your property. To get coverage for this, ask your insurer about adding a "demolition endorsement" to your existing policy.

The choice between ACV and replacement cost coverage also comes into play with a contents policy. Because an ACV policy takes depreciation into account, you won't get much compensation for computers and other equipment destroyed in a fire unless that equipment happens to be quite new. Choosing replacement cost coverage for your contents is wise because you'll get the money you'll need to replace your old equipment and other items with new products that rely on today's technology or standards.

TIP

If you get replacement cost coverage for your contents, make sure you're aware of any limitations. Very often, insurers cap recovery under a replacement cost policy for contents at a certain percentage, such as 40%, of the total value of your property.

Does Your Property Insurance Policy Include These Protections?

Don't trust your agent or broker to anticipate all your needs. Here are three types of coverage smart landlords include in their property policies. You probably won't find them in yours—unless you ask.

- **Boiler and machinery coverage.** A boiler explosion could throw your business into financial hot water. "Boiler and machinery" pays for losses that your boilers, air-conditioning units, compressors, steam cookers, electric water heaters, and other machinery in your buildings may cause. Your insurer may offer this coverage as a separate policy or as an endorsement to your property policy.
- **"Inland marine" coverage for personal property that's located or stored outdoors**. Don't be fooled by the name, which has taken on a much broader definition since the 1800s, when it referred to the nonocean part of a cargo transport. Items such as fences, signs, pole lights, and equipment including lawn mowers, gardening tools, and snow plows need to be covered under this separate endorsement or policy.
- **"Builder's risk" or "cost of construction" coverage for new construction.** When you add on to your building, repair, or remodel, you run the risk of a fire or other accidental damage, no matter how careful your workers are. This endorsement will cover you if damage occurs.

Flood and Earthquake Insurance: Depending on where you live, you may need it

Floods and earthquakes can cause serious damage to rental property across the country and are more widespread than you might think. Although California is widely known for bearing the brunt of earthquake damage, earthquakes have occurred in 39 states and have caused property damage in all 50 states, according to data from the Insurance Information Institute. Floods, which occur in all 50 states, are dangerous because even an inch of water can cause serious damage to your property. Because earthquake and flood claims are often huge, insurance companies minimize their own financial risk by typically excluding these perils from property insurance policies. (Many California landlords and other business owners learned this lesson the hard way following the 1989 Northridge earthquake.)

If you want flood or earthquake insurance, you must ask for it and buy separate policies. In certain situations, such as when your property has a mortgage from a federally regulated lender and is located in a high-risk flood area, your bank or other mortgage lender will require you to buy flood insurance.

- **Earthquakes.** If your property lies near a fault line, it's worth spending the extra money for earthquake insurance, which is available as an endorsement or separate policy from your insurer. Earthquake insurance provides protection from damage caused by the shaking and cracking that earthquakes cause. Note that you should already have coverage for other earthquake-related damage, including fire and water damage from burst gas and water pipes, under your regular property policy.
- **Floods.** If your property lies in a moderate or high-risk flood zone, give strong consideration to flood insurance. You can get flood insurance if your community is one of nearly 20,000 communities that participate in the National Flood Insurance Program (NFIP), which is administered by the Federal Emergency Management Agency (FEMA). If your community participates in the NFIP, it means it has adopted and enforces floodplain

management ordinances to reduce the risk of flood damage. In return, homeowners and businesses in these communities can get a standard, federally backed flood insurance policy through participating insurers.

For more information about earthquake insurance, check with your property insurance agent. Californians should visit the website of the California Earthquake Authority, a publicly managed, largely privately funded organization that provides catastrophic residential earthquake insurance (www.earthquakeauthority.com). For information on flood insurance, visit the National Flood Insurance Program on the Web at www.FloodSmart.gov. You can enter your property's address to learn its flood risk, find participating insurers and flood insurance agents, estimate your premium, and more. To check whether your community participates in the NFIP, visit www.fema.gov/fema/csb.shtm.

Don't Rely on FEMA

As many survivors of the Katrina disaster have learned, you can't rely on federal disaster assistance to bail you out. FEMA assistance kicks in only when the President of the United States declares a "major disaster"—but less than 10% of all weather emergencies are declared as such. And, even if you become entitled to federal disaster assistance, it's cold comfort—the assistance is usually a loan that must be paid back with interest.

FEMA itself shows you why you shouldn't rely on disaster assistance. It points out that for a $50,000 loan at 4% interest, your monthly payment would be around $240 per month ($2,880 per year) for 30 years. On the other hand, a $100,000 flood insurance premium would cost you only about $33 a month ($500 per year).

What About Terrorism?

You're far more likely to need insurance coverage because of a burst pipe or accidental fire than as the result of an act of terrorism. Still, depending on how much faith you have in the government's counter-terrorism efforts and the state of the world, and how prone you believe your part of the country is to a terrorist attack, you may feel that you need this coverage.

The huge losses caused by the events of September 11, 2001 produced a predictable response from insurance companies: They began writing liability and property policies that specifically excluded coverage for losses due to acts of terrorism. Congress reacted by passing the Terrorism Risk Insurance Act, or TRIA (15 U.S.C. §§ 6701 and following). Up to $100 billion in federal funds will be available to cover up to 85% of any loss (this is known as "gap" insurance), creating a deep pocket (the federal government) to help ensure that property owners have access to adequate terrorism insurance at affordable rates. Much like the federal flood insurance program, the law requires insurance companies to offer coverage (for an additional premium) for losses due to acts of terrorism committed "on behalf of any foreign person or foreign interest," and to void any clauses in existing policies that exclude coverage. If you want coverage under an existing policy for a loss due to acts of terrorism affecting your rental property, you can now buy it.

For more information about terrorism insurance, talk to your insurance broker or agent, or visit http://treas.gov/trip. Note that the federal law is set to expire on December 31, 2007. As this book went to press, the House and Senate each passed legislation to extend the law (to 2022 and 2014, respectively) and expand coverage to include domestic acts of terrorism. Despite differences between the two bills, industry observers expect Congress to reach a compromise that the President will sign into law before it expires.

Finally, be aware that flood insurance doesn't cover water damage when the water gets blown into your apartment building by the wind, such as from a hurricane or wind-driven rain. Fortunately, such damage (which the insurance industry calls "windstorm" damage, or damage from wind-driven rain) is normally part of a property insurance policy (unlike flood damage). Take a minute to look at your policy and make sure your policy will cover you.

- **Basic or broad coverage.** If you have this coverage, look for the term "windstorm" in the list of covered perils and read the definition.
- **All-risk coverage.** Read the section that describes what the policy covers, and make sure that "windstorm" (or something very similar) isn't identified as an exclusion.

> **TIP**
>
> **Ask about coverage for sewage backup.** Flood insurance doesn't cover the cost of fixing sewage backup problems, which can lead to costly damage. Your agent or broker should be able to add "sewer backup coverage" to your policy for a nominal charge.

"Ordinance or Law" Coverage: Cover the costs of rebuilding up to code

Hopefully, you'll never have to rebuild. But if you do, even if it's only to repair part of a building, the work must meet current building codes and other applicable laws. These probably impose tougher standards (which cost more to meet) than codes required when your building was first constructed.

Don't expect your property insurance policy to cover the costs that new building codes and other laws can add. Even replacement cost coverage won't take into account any additional costs needed to bring your property up to more stringent standards imposed by law.

For a small additional premium, you can remove this risk by getting an "ordinance or law" endorsement that covers the added cost of rebuilding or repairs that comply with new applicable laws.

Make sure the endorsement also covers you with respect to rebuilding and recouping the value for any *undamaged* parts of your buildings that are affected. Very often, local building codes require that if a significant portion of a building is destroyed (for example, 50% or 80%), the entire building must be demolished before being rebuilt. Also, as a practical matter, you may need to reconstruct certain undamaged portions of your building along with the damaged parts to meet new code requirements or comply with other laws.

Ordinance or law coverage is tricky to understand, there's no doubt about it. Perhaps an example will help. Suppose a fire ravages 40% of the stand-alone clubhouse at your property. Your local building code doesn't require you to demolish the clubhouse, but the code was amended recently (following a particularly damaging hurricane season) to require structures to be built with at least six feet of clearance from the ground. If repairing the damaged portion of the clubhouse in compliance with the new code while keeping the undamaged portion out of compliance is unrealistic, you'll want to make sure your "ordinance or law" endorsement covers you for the expense.

Liability Coverage: Don't let a "slip-and-fall" wipe you out

You've probably heard about victims of accidents or crimes who have won staggeringly high judgments or settlements against landlords or other business owners. Astronomical verdicts and settlements are not the norm—most of the time, such cases are resolved for far less. That's not to say that you can weather them without cost, however.

Fortunately, you can protect your business and personal assets by purchasing liability insurance, which covers you against claims from tenants, their guests, and other visitors who suffer injury or loss or damage of personal possessions while on your property. It also covers the cost of defending and settling personal injury claims, including attorneys' fees.

How much coverage do you need? Understand that liability exposure is not tied to the value of your property. So, if your property is worth $800,000, you'll have different *property* insurance needs than if your property is worth $8 million. But a tenant who is paralyzed after falling from a collapsed deck could win a million-dollar judgment against you regardless of the size or value of your property. Play it safe by getting a high level of liability insurance coverage. Ask your agent or broker about the typical coverage level for a business and property like yours.

It Won't Happen to You ...

What happened. After a 19-year-old tenant drowned in a swimming pool at her New Jersey apartment complex, her family sued the landlord, claiming the two lifeguards on duty weren't paying attention. One lifeguard allegedly was sitting in a lawn chair ten feet from the pool and the other was repairing a car. The landlord settled with the family for $900,000, which was paid by the landlord's insurer.

How you can avoid it. This tragedy could have been avoided by properly training and supervising the lifeguards. But even with the best practices, accidents can happen. Make sure that the type and extent of your insurance meet the risks at your residential rental.

Commercial General Liability Coverage: Cover all your liability exposures

Personal injury and damaged property lawsuits brought by tenants, guests, or others aren't the only sources of liability lawsuits. A landlord can be sued for libel or slander, invasion of privacy, and retaliatory or unlawful eviction. Charges of discrimination, in particular, can have very expensive consequences. Does your liability policy cover you in these circumstances? The narrow liability policy described above won't.

You can get broad protection under a commercial general liability (CGL) policy (also known as "comprehensive general liability coverage"). With a CGL policy, your coverage won't be limited to claims arising from physical injuries to people and their personal property. Instead, like its "all-risk" property policy relative, it will cover all your liability exposures except for any that are specifically excluded.

Make sure you understand and accept any exclusions listed in a CGL policy before you sign on the dotted line. Don't be like the Pennsylvania landlord described in "It Won't Happen to You," below.

It Won't Happen to You ...

What happened. A tenant's ex-boyfriend illegally entered the tenant's apartment at a Pennsylvania complex, assaulted the tenant with a knife, and threw the tenant to her death from her fourth-floor window. The deceased tenant's family sued the landlord, claiming that the landlord failed to protect its tenant from the attack. A judge ruled that the landlord's commercial general liability policy specifically excluded claims based on assault and battery by *any* person—not just by the landlord (as the landlord tried to argue).

How you can avoid it. Read your policy and discuss any questions with your broker. Make sure you understand what each exclusion covers. For example, ask whether an assault-and-battery exclusion applies to claims based on others' criminal acts. In all cases, if you learn that you are lacking coverage, find out what it will cost to add it and decide whether you need it.

Limits of Liability: Do you have enough coverage?

It's one thing to have the right kind of liability coverage, but you'll be disappointed if your policy won't cover the size of any claims or judgments. In a money-saving move that must be sadly familiar to you by now, insurance companies have designed their liability policies so that they have two dollar limits:

- a limit for each occurrence or claim—for example, the policy will stop paying after a claim exceeds a specified amount, such as $400,000, and
- a total limit for the policy year—for instance, the company will stop paying when the sum of all the claims made on the policy in that year exceeds $1.5 million.

Here's how the limits described above play out: Suppose you submit four $500,000 liability insurance claims to your insurer within one policy year. To avoid exceeding the per-occurrence limit, your insurer pays $400,000 of the first three $500,000 claims, or $1.2 million. To avoid exceeding the per-year limit, your insurer can then pay you no more than $300,000 for the fourth claim (even though the per-occurrence limit is $400,000).

CAUTION

Don't confuse "policy year" with "calendar year." Unless the term of your policy happens to begin on January 1, your policy year will be different from the calendar year. For example, your policy year may run from April 25 through midnight April 24 the following year. This is important to keep in mind because annual limits and deductions are based on the policy year.

It Won't Happen to You ...

What happened. A 22-year old California tenant suffered serious burns after criminals threw Molotov cocktails from the street into her apartment. Although she managed to get her babies out the window safely, she remained trapped in the living room because she couldn't find her key or escape through the barred windows. The tenant sued the landlord, claiming that she couldn't escape the fire because the landlord violated building codes by having an illegal double-keyed deadbolt lock on the apartment door and nonrelease security bars over the windows. The tenant settled with the landlord for $1 million, the amount of the landlord's policy limit.

How you can avoid it. First, be sure you know and comply with local building and safety codes. If you mistakenly violate them (this landlord probably thought he was doing his tenants a favor by giving them secure apartments), have enough insurance to cover a claim.

Extra liability coverage doesn't have to mean sky-high premiums. You probably don't want to pay for a $5 million liability policy if $1 million is all the coverage you're likely to need. For those rare (but still possible) very large losses, consider getting an umbrella policy (also known as an "excess liability policy"). Umbrella policies kick in only after a liability policy has been exhausted. Claims under umbrella policies are rare, so the premium for the extra coverage is less than you would pay for the same coverage under a liability insurance policy. With an umbrella policy, you can add $1 million, $2 million, or more in coverage without breaking the bank.

Understanding the Deductible

Your policy's deductible is the amount you pay for a loss before your insurance will kick in. The higher the deductible, the more you agree to pay before your insurer opens its wallet. For example, if the cost of repairing your property is $10,000, but you have a $1,000 deductible, you'll get only $9,000 from your insurance company. It may seem like you'll save money by choosing a lower deductible, but a higher deductible is often the better choice because your premiums—which, unlike your deductible, you know you must pay each year—will be lower. It's always wise to consider a higher deductible, after you've settled on the appropriate policy limits.

Loss of Rents Coverage: Keep your business going after a loss

When there's a fire or other loss at your property, your property insurance should cover it. But property insurance won't compensate you if tenants must live elsewhere during the repair period and stop paying rent. The last thing you want is an interruption in your rental income stream.

Prepare for this situation now by purchasing "business income coverage" (formerly known as "business interruption coverage"). For landlords, this is more commonly known as "loss of rents coverage," and it normally covers the fair rental value of apartments that remain vacant due to a loss for up to 12 months. Your agent or broker can tell you how much of a premium you should expect to pay, based on factors such as the number of apartments covered, your apartments' fair rental value, and the desired number of months for coverage.

Automobile Liability Insurance: Cover the vehicles your business uses

If any vehicle that you use—or let others use—in connection with your business gets involved in an accident, the victims can sue you for the harm they suffer. If you don't have the right automobile liability insurance coverage, you could be on the fast track to financial ruin. Evaluating your auto insurance involves:

- looking at the policy you currently have for personal use (will it suffice?)
- making employees authorized drivers for any policy that covers vehicles they use, and
- supplementing employees' policies (when they use their own cars while doing your business).

The sections below explain these concerns.

Determine whether your personal insurance will suffice

If you use your car only occasionally in connection with your business, and don't require employees to use any vehicles for your business, then your personal automobile insurance policy might very well provide you with all the protection you need. To be sure, though, you should run your situation by your agent, who can tell you whether your personal automobile policy will do the trick. However, many landlords find they rely on one or more vehicles so much for their business that they need to buy a commercial automobile liability insurance policy to ensure adequate coverage.

Commercial automobile liability insurance covers cars, trucks, and other vehicles you own that you use primarily for your business. Unlike the case with a personal auto policy, having a commercial policy means you don't risk having a claim denied simply because you were using the vehicle for business purposes when you got into a serious accident. Your insurer can advise you on how much auto liability coverage you need. A $1 million limit is standard for businesses, but you should not go under $500,000.

If you own multiple vehicles that you use in connection with your business, you can cover them all under the same commercial auto policy. Your policy must identify all the vehicles along with coverage amounts, so if you start or stop using certain vehicles primarily for business, notify your insurer immediately to update your policy.

Make your employees authorized drivers

If you let any of your employees drive any company-owned vehicles for business purposes, provide your insurer with their names, ages, and driver's license numbers so they may be listed on your policy as authorized drivers. Employees should also be covered if you let them use such vehicles for personal use, but confirm this with your insurer before granting your employees permission to do this.

Never let anyone operate your vehicles until you know they have a valid license and a good driving record. If you don't check an employee's driving record and he gets into an accident while using your car, the accident victims may sue you for negligence (entrusting the car to a poor driver)—on top of any loss they suffered from the accident itself! To check an employee's driving record, talk to your employee screening company or search the National Driver Register (NDR). To search the NDR for an employee, visit the National Highway Traffic Safety administration at www.nhtsa.gov. Type "National Driver Register" in the search box and follow the instructions.

Beef up your insurance when employees use their own cars

Do you rely on employees to drive their own cars for your business? For example, does a maintenance employee drive her car—and not a vehicle that you or your business owns—to pick up tools or supplies for your property? Or, does your resident manager routinely transport files from your office to an off-site storage facility? Don't assume that because these drivers have their own insurance, you'll never face a problem.

Here's what might happen. Suppose your manager drives her van to the hardware store to pick up a part for a repair at your property. On the way, she causes an accident. The accident victims sue the manager and you, as the manager's employer, for their injuries. You'll want to refer this problem to your insurance company—but will they handle it?

To be confident that your insurer will step up, you'll need to add a "non-owned auto liability endorsement" to your commercial auto policy. This coverage will mean you won't have to hire a lawyer in a lawsuit brought by someone injured by an employee driving his own car (your insurance company will supply the lawyer). It will also help you if you're found partly at fault. If you wish to cover this situation (at the price of a small additional premium), ask your insurer to add coverage for "employees as additional insured."

TIP

Make sure your business will be covered. If title to a vehicle you own and use in connection with your business is in your name, you are the only person covered by the policy. If a claim is filed against your business, however, you'll want to make sure the business gets covered, too. Ask your agent to add your business's name (assuming it's different from your name) as an "additional insured" to the policy. Adding an additional insured to a policy is a common request that insurers typically honor at no additional charge.

Inflation Guard: Automatically update your policy limits

Because of inflation, the cost of products and services rises nearly every year. This means that it will cost more each year to, say, repair your building after a fire. Over time, the rising cost of labor and materials can creep dangerously close to, or even surpass, the limits of your insurance coverage. To make sure your coverage limits rise with the cost of repairs, consider adding "inflation guard" coverage to your policy. It will automatically adjust your coverage limits to reflect the increase in construction costs in your area that are due to inflation.

Loss-Control Recommendations

Insurance companies often make "loss-control recommendations" after reviewing your claims history and inspecting your property. These recommendations are aimed at improving maintenance, housekeeping, and safety issues at your property.

Take your insurer seriously when it makes these recommendations. If you get a written list of recommendations and don't follow through with suggested work, your insurer may be entitled to cancel your policy. Also, putting off needed repairs means you'll risk more costly repairs down the road, and you'll increase the chance of injuries and lawsuits.

If you can't afford to follow your insurer's recommendations, ask whether there's a less costly way to address your risks. This gesture will show your insurer that you take its recommendations seriously, which will help you maintain a good relationship with your insurer and avoid policy cancellation.

Buy Smart: Be a savvy insurance consumer

You want nothing less than the best insurance coverage for your property and business—and you want to get it at the best price. You can be a savvy insurance consumer by

- paying for coverage you really need, and
- not trying to cut costs by declining coverage you do need.

You can be a smart consumer even when you're already insured. Although you may believe you have adequate coverage, it doesn't hurt to explore options with other insurers, especially when renewal time comes around. You may find that you need different or greater coverage. Sharing the results of your shopping with your current insurer may help you negotiate lower premiums. Or, you might decide to do business with that more attractive competitor. If you switch, be sure that your coverage periods overlap—it's too risky to let yourself be exposed for even a day or two.

Use a highly rated insurer

Insurance companies are rated according to their financial strength. A low-rated insurer is likely to face financial trouble if the marketplace changes and competition heats up. A low-rated company may need to limit the types of coverage it provides or may even become insolvent, leaving you suddenly unprotected. Your homework isn't hard when it comes to researching an insurance company's rating—first you need to understand how the ratings game works, then it's time to check out the rating for any company you're considering.

Five major outfits, whose websites and rating range are described below, do insurance rating. Companies such as A.M. Best, Standard & Poor's, Fitch Ratings, Moody's, and TheStreet.com Ratings (formerly Weiss Ratings) each have their own system for rating insurers. Ratings companies may have different opinions of an insurer's financial strength, so check at least two companies' ratings to get a more accurate picture of a particular insurer.

Fortunately, you may be just a minute away from getting the ratings you need about a particular insurer you're considering. Each ratings company lets you search for ratings on a particular insurer through its website (listed in the chart above). Searches are free, but you may need to register first. Another useful third-party Web resource, http://info.insure.com/ratings, lets you search Standard and Poor's ratings and Fitch Ratings without registration or charge.

Who Rates the Insurance Companies?

These are the five top outfits that rate insurance companies. You can learn more about them and their rating scheme by visiting their websites.

Ratings company	Website	Ratings range	Accept nothing less than this grade
A.M. Best	www.ambest.com	A++ (Superior) to B and lower (Vulnerable)	A-
Fitch Ratings	www.fitchratings.com	AAA (Exceptionally Strong) to BB+ and lower (Vulnerable)	AA-
Moody's Investor Service	www.moodys.com	Aaa (Exceptional) to Ba1 and lower (Vulnerable)	Aa3
Standard & Poor's	www.standardandpoors.com	AAA (Extremely Strong) to BB+ and lower (Vulnerable)	AA-
TheStreet.com Ratings (formerly, Weiss Ratings)	www.thestreetratings.com	A+ (Excellent) to D+ and lower (Vulnerable)	A-

Compare insurance offers

Don't take shortcuts when vetting insurers. Take the time to consider a few companies, ask questions, talk about your needs and options for your property, and negotiate. Use a worksheet like the one shown below to record and compare the various companies' positions on each type of insurance coverage you intend to purchase (such as property, CGL, and so on).

Begin by making sure you're talking with companies that have experience insuring residential landlords. These companies may already have package deals that will fit your needs and have attractive prices. Then, tell the agent or broker about your business—its size (how many properties do you own? How many tenants live there?), its location, and the challenges you've faced in the past (for example, you may have a recurring problem with burglaries, vandalism, or flood damage). Although you don't want to paint a negative portrait of your property or give the impression that your business is claims-prone, you do need to be honest and complete. Accurately describing your business's needs will allow the insurer to assess your risk and recommend appropriate coverage; hiding the ball could result in no coverage where you need it.

Once you're satisfied that you're talking with a company that regularly does business with residential landlords, and appears willing to design an insurance package that fits your profile, consider the following issues.

Deductible

You can save a lot on premiums by increasing your policy's deductible, which is the amount you must pay toward claims before your insurer will. For more information, see "Understanding the Deductible," above.

Discounts

Ask insurers about any discounts they may offer. An insurer may give you a break by packaging together multiple policies (into a "business owner's policy" or "landlord's policy," for example). Or, by increasing your coverage (and premium) on one policy, your insurer may give you a discount on another policy. You may also be eligible for a discount if you insure multiple vehicles (such as more than one or more than five vehicles) under your commercial auto policy.

Discounts vary among insurers and are subject to change. So, don't miss out on possible savings—ask your insurer about what discounts it offers that may apply to you and your business.

Blanket insurance for multiple properties

If you own more than one rental property, ask your insurer about buying one blanket policy that covers all of them. By pooling all your properties together in this way, there's more of a chance you'll have enough coverage if a loss occurs at any one of them.

The following examples show how you can save with a blanket policy. Suppose you own two buildings with a coverage limit of $150,000 and $350,000, respectively. You suffer a $400,000 loss at the second building. If you had separate policies for each building, you would be covered for only $350,000 of the loss. If you had one blanket policy covering both buildings for $500,000 ($150,000 + $350,000), you would be fully covered for the $400,000 loss.

In addition to providing more coverage, a blanket policy can save you money because you'll pay only one premium (which should be lower than the total of two separate premiums). You'll also have only one deductible to meet for all properties covered under the blanket policy.

It Won't Happen to You ...

What happened. In 2001, Tropical Storm Allison flooded a 23-unit Pennsylvania apartment complex. As the floodwaters rose to the ceiling in the basement laundry room, a gas dryer became dislodged, triggering a gas leak. The building exploded, killing and injuring several tenants. The injured tenants and the estates of the deceased tenants sued the landlord, claiming that the explosion could have been avoided had the landlord used just a few more bolts to properly secure the dryer's gas line. The landlord settled for $27.5 million—all of which was reportedly paid by the landlord's insurer.

How you can avoid it. This owner may have cut corners by having untrained workers install his appliances. The explosion undoubtedly resulted in multiple insurance claims, for injuries and property loss.

Advance payment options

Instead of paying your premiums by the month, find out whether you can pay in lump sum payments covering, for example, a six-month period. Lump sum payments may save you money, because many insurers charge a processing fee for individual monthly payments. Paying in advance is also more convenient and helps ensure continuous coverage (there are fewer opportunities to forget to write that check).

Insurance Comparison Form

Policy type _____

Company	_____	_____	_____
Date	_____	_____	_____
Contact	_____	_____	_____
Rating	_____	_____	_____
Recommendations	_____	_____	_____
	_____	_____	_____
	_____	_____	_____
Experience underwriting residential landlords	_____	_____	_____
Customer service	_____	_____	_____
Policy limits	_____	_____	_____
Deductible	_____	_____	_____
Premium	_____	_____	_____
Notes	_____	_____	_____
	_____	_____	_____
	_____	_____	_____
	_____	_____	_____
	_____	_____	_____

What *Not* to Do When Buying Insurance

Keep these rules in mind when talking with agents or brokers:

- **Never say yes to any coverage unless you understand why it's important for your property or business.** If every landlord needed identical insurance, this chapter would indeed be quite short. Most agents understand that each landlord's needs are unique, but you may encounter an agent who promotes certain coverage, insisting, "Every landlord needs it." It's not necessarily so—for example, some types of problems, such as earthquakes, are likely to occur only in certain geographic locations. If you buy coverage for problems that are a long shot, you're wasting money. Remember that, unless your lender requires it, coverage decisions are always yours to make. If an agent's explanation of why you need certain coverage doesn't add up, don't agree to it. You can always keep the questionable coverage in mind and update your policy later if your needs change.

- **Be wary of agents and brokers who offer coverage at remarkably lower premiums than those offered by others.** If it looks too good to be true, it probably is. Rather than being quick to believe you're getting a fantastic deal, ask the agent why the premiums are so low. Try scrutinizing the policy on your own to determine what coverage, if any, is being denied in return for the low premium. Consider asking a competitor agent about the low premiums. The competitor can either call the first agent's bluff or—better yet—beat the first agent's offer.

- **Don't work with agents you feel are pressuring or steering you toward purchasing certain policies or adding coverage.** You can be sure that agents who do this are putting their own financial interests ahead of yours. You need an agent who is willing to take the time to understand your property and your business's needs and craft a policy that addresses those needs—and only those needs.

1

Insurance: My To-Do List

With a little time and patience, you can find out whether your current insurance coverage is really a good fit for your property and your business. If it's not, you can use what you've learned and make the changes that will give you the protection you need. Use the list below to guide you through the steps that will result in a thorough review, showing you where your current coverage may be lacking.

☐ **Property insurance:** Consider full-cost replacement coverage.

☐ **Property insurance:** Check for appropriate policy limits.

☐ **Property insurance:** Determine reasonable deductible/premium balance.

☐ **Property insurance:** Get overage for both structures and contents.

☐ **Property insurance:** Confirm coverage for floods and earthquakes, if needed.

☐ **Property insurance:** Consider "Ordinance or Law" coverage.

☐ **Liability insurance:** Be sure to cover all liability exposures.

☐ **Liability insurance:** Check for adequate coverage.

☐ **Loss of rents insurance:** Avoid interruptions in my rental income stream.

☐ **Automobile Liability insurance:** Is a personal or commercial policy needed?

☐ **Automobile Liability insurance:** Are all my vehicles and drivers covered?

☐ **Insurance shopping:** Check insurer ratings.

☐ **Insurance shopping:** Compare insurance offers, check insurer ratings, and seek ways to reduce premiums.

☐ **Inflation guard:** Keep policy limits updated.

☐ **Insurer's recommendations:** Review suggestions and design a plan for implementation.

☐ **All policies:** Read the fine print to learn, for example, what I may need to do to lessen the damage in the event of an accident or emergency (see Step Five, "Prepare for and Handle Disasters and Emergencies").

Make Your Property
Physically Sound

n Step One, you read about how important it is to have the right insurance to protect your business after a loss—especially a loss that's caused by physical hazards lurking at your property or forces beyond your control, such as the weather. Now, you'll focus on lowering the chances that you'll have to resort to insurance in the first place. Step Two covers physical problems at your property that may result in injury-causing accidents, citations for not complying with building or safety codes, or tenant rent withholding.

Fortunately, there's a lot you can do to make your rental property physically and legally sound. First, you can learn what the law has to say about minimum safety, health, and structural requirements for properties like yours. Then, you can use your common sense to bring the property up to snuff, such as making sure that you or your manager take care of all maintenance problems and legitimate tenant repair requests.

What Do You Have to Lose?

A physically unsound property—whether due to structural or managerial problems—poses a number of risks to landlords. Here's the rogue's gallery of unpleasant consequences:

- **Disgruntled tenants.** Your tenants aren't likely to appreciate a building that's not maintained, and they may move on at the first opportunity. "Turnover" (the rate of rerenting) will cost you two months' rent on average.
- **Uninterested prospects.** When deficiencies are major or widespread, they'll be obvious to prospects. This will stymie your marketing efforts by making it hard to convince good prospects to apply for an apartment, prolonging turnover time.
- **Tenants who withhold the rent, use "repair and deduct," or move out.** In many states, tenants may withhold the rent—or fix problems themselves—when their landlord fails to maintain a fit and habitable rental. They can even move out without further responsibility for rent. These interruptions in your rental stream pose huge headaches.

- **Injured tenants, guests, or other visitors.** If someone is injured on your property, you'll need to call on the insurance you've judiciously purchased. But the more you need to use your insurance, the more it will hurt your wallet. A large claim, or many small ones, can lead your insurer to increase your premiums or even cancel your policy.
- **Citations for code violations.** Inspectors who find code violations will issue fix-it orders, which may be backed up with fines or, in extreme cases, orders to vacate the building while repairs are made. This is a disaster.
- **Expensive repairs instead of minor ones.** A minor issue, left unattended, can turn into a major problem that's much more difficult and costly to address.

It Won't Happen to You ...

What happened. At the hotel and casino Trump Taj Mahal in Atlantic City, New Jersey, an elderly woman was seriously hurt when the toilet she was sitting on broke away from the wall. Eighteen months later she fell again, and claimed in a lawsuit that the injuries she suffered from the first fall caused the second one. She argued that the casino should be held liable for all her injuries, and finally settled for $1.2 million.

How you can avoid it. This case just goes to show that even the richest property owners of famed resorts aren't immune to risk. You can minimize the chance that this sort of thing will occur at your property by performing regular maintenance inspections and promptly fulfilling repair requests. If you ignore this responsibility, you too may have to pay a large sum to an injured tenant—and watch your profits go down the toilet.

Is This You?

As a conscientious landlord, you may be working hard to make your property as safe as possible. Is there more you can do? Unless you're already following the strategies laid out later in this chapter, you may have some catching up to do. Even if no one has been injured by a physical hazard or you've never received an unwelcome visit from housing inspectors, you may very well recognize yourself in at least one of the following descriptions of properties that are particularly vulnerable to accidents or inspectors' code violations.

Do You Think About Your Building Like These Landlords?

☐ Your property is old and hasn't been thoroughly renovated in a long time.

☐ Your building was constructed on the cheap and has already experienced lots of structural problems.

☐ You know about certain problems but haven't fixed them.

☐ Because no one has complained to the authorities, you're hoping that inspectors won't come to your property and discover code violations.

☐ You don't have an on-site manager, and rely on reports from tenants and your occasional visits to spot problems.

☐ You have a lot of senior tenants or families with young children.

☐ You've made mostly "Band-Aid repairs" over the years, putting off addressing the underlying causes of structural or other problems.

Take Action!

Are any of the landlords described above familiar? If so, take a moment to read the following strategies. Each one is aimed at helping you make your property physically sound and code-compliant. This can be a tall order, because physical hazards come in all shapes and sizes. But if you adopt the strategies outlined below, you'll greatly reduce the risk that a structural problem with your rental property will lead to injuries, high tenant turnover, fix-it orders, or a lawsuit.

Comply with basic state legal requirements

To be a successful landlord, you must follow the law when it comes to repairing and maintaining your property. Don't rely solely on your contractor's advice or even your own common sense. Start by knowing the basic legal requirements for keeping your property physically sound. If you don't know what they are, your property might meet your own standards but fall short of what the law actually requires.

Virtually every landlord must comply with a legal rule known as the "implied warranty of habitability." This means you must make sure your rentals are in a "fit" and "habitable" condition when tenants move in, and you must maintain this condition throughout the tenancy. For example, you can expect the law to require you to maintain electrical, plumbing, sanitary, heating, ventilating, air-conditioning, and other facilities in working order. The same goes for supplying adequate amounts of water, hot water, and heat at reasonable times.

In addition to the implied warranty of habitability, you must also comply with health and safety laws. For example, most states require smoke detectors, and some require specific door and window locks. Some local governments have added more requirements, too.

Knowing that your rentals must be "fit" and "habitable" is a good first step—but what exactly do these terms mean? You'll have to do a bit of homework to learn. In some states, the laws are very specific, telling you that the hot water, for instance, must be a certain temperature. But other states are intentionally vague, leaving it up

) the courts or housing inspectors to fill in the details. To learn the ecifics that apply to your property, you'll need to consult your state's ndlord-tenant statutes and look for the code sections that have to do with the condition of rental property. Use the "State Landlord-Tenant Statutes" chart in the appendix, and once you're in the codes, look for code sections that are titled "Landlord's Duties," "Landlord's Obligations," and so on.

Comply with local building, health, and safety codes

Most landlords are familiar with the phrase "up to code," yet few really know what those standards are. In truth, many landlords happily go about their business without ever encountering the fine print that dictates everything from the minimum number of outlets per room to the placement of smoke detectors and the construction of handrails. These days, however, your chances of remaining blissfully ignorant are dwindling, not because code-related problems are necessarily on the rise, but because you may get found out: Many cities have established periodic residential rental inspection programs, designed to ensure landlords' code compliance (and generate revenue via the fees charged).

The consequences of having a noncompliant rental property vary greatly, from nothing to an order from the city or an agency to cease operations and relocate your tenants to an off-site location (at your expense) until the problem is fixed. In extreme cases, you can be fined and even charged with a crime. Aside from the government's enforcement efforts, if code noncompliance is a major factor in a tenant's injury or damage to your building, the fallout can be huge. For example, suppose a small fire starts in your boiler room while employees are working, and spreads to consume half your property. Because you don't have a fire extinguisher installed near your boiler room, as your local code requires, your employees aren't able to prevent the fire from spreading. In situations like this, your insurer might refuse to cover a claim.

Your first step is to learn which codes apply to your property, where you can find them, and what they say. Chances are, you

can conveniently read codes on the Internet by visiting y
or municipality's official website. (You can find the offici
typing your state's, county's, or city or town's name in an
search engine.) Once you're on the website, look for an option
entitled "Laws," "Ordinances," or something similar. If your state or
municipality doesn't post its laws on its website, call the informational
number listed on the site and ask how you can get a copy. Some third-
party websites, such as www.statelocalgov.net, http://municipalcodes.
lexisnexis.com, and www.reedfirstsource.com/codes/index.asp, are
also good sources for finding state and local codes on the Internet.

Don't feel overwhelmed once you get a copy of the code. Most
parts of the code don't pertain to residential housing, which means
you can safely ignore them. Also, be aware that the codes won't
necessarily be organized in a user-friendly way—often the housing
parts are scattered around, and you have to use some creativity when
searching the tables of contents (don't be shy—consider calling your
mayor or city manager for help in finding what you need). When
reviewing a code's table of contents, look for "Housing" but also for
headings such as "Buildings," "Health and Safety / Sanitation," and
"Fair Housing / Civil rights / Human rights / Discrimination." The chart
below lists some common code topics or subtopics you're likely to find
in your code's table of contents (with examples of what they cover).

Inside the Codes	
Topic or subtopic	What it talks about
Fire	Installation of extinguishers or indoor sprinkler systems, use and storage of fireworks
Health and safety	Preventing pest infestation, number and placement of smoke detectors, garbage removal
Structural and mechanical requirements	Heating, electrical equipment, ventilation
Common areas	Adequate lighting, no obstructions in passageways

As you read through the various code sections, you'll naturally picture your property and start making mental notes of items that need your attention. For example, you may discover that you don't have the requisite number of smoke detectors in your multi-story single-family rental, and the bathrooms don't have the required type of ventilation. Use a worksheet like the Code Compliance Worksheet shown below to note the issues as you discover them, and take a stab at setting priorities, deciding which problems need your attention right away, and which can wait. For instance, you'll want to buy and install fire extinguishers now, but getting all your door and window lintels in tip-top shape might need to wait.

Code Compliance Worksheet

Use a worksheet like this when checking your property for compliance with relevant building, fire, and health and safety codes. When you're done, assign a priority to your work based on the seriousness of the risk of damage or danger.

Date	Priority	To-do	Code section	Target fix date	Fixed
5/1/08	High	Buy three more fire extinguishers	Civil Code § 10.862(b)	5/5/08	5/4/08
5/15/08	Low	Fix heating in clubhouse (by end of summer)	Civil Code § 6.76(d)	9/1/08	8/12/08
8/17/08	High	Check batteries on smoke detectors and replace, if necessary	Civil Code § 10.869(c)	8/20/08	8/19/08

Take reasonable steps to prevent injury or losses

As you know, landlords must comply with state and local laws regarding proper maintenance and repair of their buildings. In addition, you're also legally required to take care of your tenants and their guests when it comes to foreseeable accidents or injuries. In a nutshell, if you know (or should have known, given the circumstances) that an accident is waiting to happen, you have a duty to take reasonable steps to warn tenants and guests and fix the problem. If you don't take these steps and someone gets hurt or suffers losses, you could find yourself owing a hefty sum to compensate victims for their injuries or property loss.

Let's take a moment to see how this situation can develop. Suppose your resident manager tells you about a problem with your pool's diving board—it's wobbling and making unusual sounds when people bounce on it. A prudent response would be to keep people off the board, with barriers or caution tape, until you can get it checked out by a specialized maintenance person. If you don't take these steps, it's only a matter of time until someone gets hurt and asks a court to make you pay.

As you can see, unlike the need to put specific kinds of locks on doors and windows, your duty to take care of tenants and guests isn't spelled out with specific instructions. It's a general legal principle that you have to apply each day and in every aspect of your business. Looking around your property, ask yourself whether you can identify risky situations that could lead to injury. If you can, then think about whether you're proactively taking steps to warn tenants and their guests about these situations as you proceed to fix problems. The minute you stop asking yourself these questions is the minute you let risk back in the door.

Make repairs: Identify problems and fix them promptly

When you learn that something at your property needs repair—whether it's a broken-down elevator or a burnt-out lightbulb—act promptly (or immediately, if it's an emergency) to fix it or arrange to have it fixed. Unless the problem can be fixed immediately, warn tenants and others who might encounter the hazardous situation by using caution tape, traffic cones, posted warnings, or taking other appropriate measures.

Most problems don't jump up and announce themselves. Usually, you have to do a bit of work to learn about them. Your own inspections, information you get from your tenants, and inspectors' reports (assuming your city has a regular inspection program for residential rental properties) are the three main ways to get the information you need.

It Won't Happen to You ...

What happened. After the window screen in his family's Philadelphia apartment fell out, a three-year-old boy fell to the concrete below, sustaining severe head trauma. The family sued the landlord, claiming that it knew there was a problem with window screens in the building and that it should have warned tenants and installed window guards. After a two-week trial, a jury awarded the family $7 million.

How you can avoid it. Respond promptly when you learn of a dangerous problem on your rental property. If necessary, make a temporary fix and post appropriate warnings until you can do the job right. (In this case, the landlord might have warned the tenants against opening the windows until new window guards could be installed.)

Perform your own inspections

Perform a visual inspection of your buildings and property on a regular basis—at least twice a year. This way, you'll have the chance to discover obvious defects before they can develop into serious hazards. For example, if your buildings have balconies, inspect them for signs of rust (if metal) or decay (if wooden). Loose nails, screws, or bolts could also act as a red flag that a railing or other part of a balcony needs to be repaired or replaced.

Sometimes your own inspection won't be sufficient, particularly if you're not sure that you'll recognize every warning sign. Even if you have the eyes of an experienced contractor, you may not have the specialized knowledge (or tools) needed to inspect and evaluate certain aspects of your building, such as its furnace, elevators, or roofing. To supplement your own efforts, consider scheduling regular inspections by experts who can tell you whether you have latent problems that should be nipped in the bud.

Leave Specialty Maintenance to the Pros

When it comes to maintaining and repairing your boiler, elevators, and other major machinery at your property, leave it to the pros. It usually pays to buy a maintenance plan for these items and equipment, because fixing them requires certain parts, tools, and know-how that you or even your maintenance employees probably don't have.

Be sure you understand the particulars of your warranties and maintenance plans. The warranty or plan may be voided if you try to fix the machinery yourself. Also, your efforts may trigger more damage if you're not sure what you're doing.

Aim High With Elevator Maintenance

You surely know never to skip or delay your state-mandated periodic inspections of your elevators. But we all know that problems can arise in spite of regular inspections. If you learn there's a problem with an elevator, take it out of service immediately and call your maintenance company for repair. Minor problems such as buttons losing their illumination shouldn't be ignored, but they're not immediate cause for alarm. When serious issues short of a breakdown occur—such as a sticky door or a wobbly carriage—play better-safe-than-sorry and take the elevator out of service until it's fixed. Never let other people ride an elevator that you wouldn't feel confident riding yourself.

It Won't Happen to You ...

What happened. A real estate agent was struck by a malfunctioning elevator door at a California apartment house while showing apartments to prospects. She suffered a severe concussion and sued the landlord and the current and prior elevator maintenance companies. For 20 years, the landlord had failed to address the elevator's serious mechanical problems, ignoring the maintenance companies' recommendations. The landlord, along with the two maintenance companies, settled with the defendant for $475,000.

How you can avoid it. Regular elevator maintenance is a must. Engage a reputable contractor and follow through with any recommendations. You can bet that 20 years of proper maintenance would have cost this landlord much less than $475,000.

Listen to tenant repair requests or complaints

Many landlords are quick to view tenant requests as a source of annoyance. True, some tenants are unreasonable and demanding, asking for frequent cosmetic work or insisting on unnecessary upgrades. But many tenant complaints or requests are legitimate, especially when a landlord doesn't practice steady maintenance. It's important to take these requests seriously. In fact, savvy landlords encourage tenants to be conscientious and keep them in the know.

When tenants make requests, it's helpful to write down information about each request so that you and your staff can track your efforts to fulfill them. Creating a "paper trail" will also come in handy if a tenant stops paying rent on the grounds that you didn't perform a needed and important repair. When you try to evict that tenant for nonpayment of rent, you'll be able to show a judge that you promptly and properly handled the request.

A well-kept repair log can also fend off unfounded discrimination claims, because it will show that you handle repair requests in the order in which you receive them (with the sole exception of emergencies). So, for example, if a tenant accuses you of racial discrimination because her repair was completed after another tenant's later request, your log can show that the complaining tenant's repair was addressed first but took longer because you had to order a replacement part. Be sure to jot down the reason you can't fulfill a tenant's request promptly, or at all, in the "Notes" section of the log. Consider keeping a Tenant Repair Request Log like the one shown below.

Tenant Repair Requests: Keep a Log to Track Progress

Here's a sample log you can use to keep track of your efforts to fulfill tenant repair requests. Hang on to your log—you may need it later to show that you promptly handled a certain request or that you take all tenant repair requests seriously.

Tenant Repair Request Log

Date of Request	Tenant Name	Unit	Phone Number	Staff member contacted	Description	Completion Date	Notes
2/4/08	Alice Smith	5G	(410) 555-0100	Mark B.	Leaky faucet in kitchen	2/5/08	Visited 2/4/08 but couldn't fix; sent outside plumber to fix on 2/5/08
2/12/08	John Washington	11R	(410) 555-0101	Sara K.	Possible electrical problem affecting all outlets in bedroom		Arranged repair visit for 2/15/08 but tenant not home; tenant did not return two subsequent phone messages; problem possibly went away

It Won't Happen to You ...

What happened. A New York City tenant complained to her landlord repeatedly about a leak in her apartment's bathroom, but the landlord didn't fix the problem. One day, the tenant's foot fell through a water-damaged floor, tearing a shoulder ligament and requiring surgery. She sued her landlord, and settled the case for $70,000.

How you can avoid it. Never brush off a repair request that has the potential to become a very serious problem down the road. Here, a simple repair would have avoided a lot of property damage, not to speak of the injury the tenant suffered.

Go beyond code compliance

Just because your buildings are in compliance with state and local codes doesn't mean they're accident-proof. Always look for ways to minimize the risk of injury, even if it means exceeding the law's requirements. For example, if you have a step or two in your lobby or hallways that tenants and guests can easily miss, put bright-colored safety tape along the steps' edges to prevent falls or install a light nearby—even if your state and local codes don't require it.

Warn of dangers that aren't yet fixed

When you can't fix a physical hazard immediately, you must warn tenants and visitors so they may steer clear. Doing so will not only help them avoid the danger, but it will shield you from liability if tenants or visitors ignore your warnings and get hurt. For example, if you mopped up a spill in the lobby and an area of the floor is still wet, barricade the area and post a warning sign. If you made a temporary fix to your clubhouse's refrigerator door, tape a warning on the door cautioning people to open and close it carefully. Similarly, if a pothole erupts in your parking lot, surround it with traffic cones until you can arrange to get the hazard paved over. You get the idea.

TIP

Keep safety and warning devices on hand. Traffic cones, barricades, safety tape, signs, and other safety devices are not just inexpensive—they can save you a bundle by preventing liability-triggering accidents. You can find these handy items in home improvement stores such as Home Depot and Lowe's, or on the Internet at websites such as johnmwarren.com, TrafficSafetyExperts.com, TrafficSafetyStore.com, and ULINE.com.

Don't Set Traps for Trespassers

Plagued by persistent trespassers, such as a homeless person who uses your side entryway as a place to sleep or teenagers who try to break into your pool area at night, some landlords get angry and set traps or create other hazardous situations for them. While it is true that trespassers aren't guests and have no business being on your property, you're not at liberty to treat them as you wish. But unlike the case with guests (where you must worry about negligently causing harm), the duty you owe a trespasser is minimal, and boils down to this: You mustn't intentionally harm a trespasser on your property.

Refrain from taking matters into your own hands, because the last thing you want is a trespasser suing you for injuries sustained on your property—and winning. (Besides, how would you know for sure that traps intended for trespassers won't cause harm to guests or even to your tenants?) Instead, contact local law enforcement if you need help with a trespassing problem.

Keep your property's pool, playground, or other extras clean and safe

If your rental property includes attractive "extras" such as a pool, playground or play set, or even something as elaborate as a fitness center, you're counting on these features to enhance your property's appeal to prospects and keep good tenants from having a reason to move. But, if you're not careful, your pool or playground can become a double-edged sword, posing a serious threat of harm to tenants and their guests. It's a sad fact that more than 200,000 children in the United States are treated in emergency rooms each year for injuries sustained in playgrounds alone, according to the U.S. Product Safety Commission. If people who get hurt using your property's pool or playground believe that you didn't make them safe, they're likely to sue you for their injuries.

You shouldn't have to put your business on the line in return for providing attractive extras. Here are tips smart landlords follow to keep their extras safe and their risks to a minimum.

Use "House Rules" to Communicate Important Policies

Many of your safety-related policies won't be part of your lease or rental agreement—they're simply too detailed. Furthermore, putting them in the rental document hampers your ability to change them or add to them. (You may have to wait until the lease is up to do so; and with a month to month agreement, you'll have to give proper notice before changing them.)

For maximum flexibility, place your policies in a set of house rules or regulations, and refer to them in your lease or rental agreement. Use a clause that specifies that the tenant has received the rules, agrees to follow them, knows they can be changed from time to time, and understands that significant violations will be grounds for terminating the tenancy. Be sure that you don't slip significant policies (such as a late fee) into these house rules. They're meant for more day-to-day issues such as proper use of your playground, pool, laundry room, and other common areas.

Fence in outdoor facilities

Erect a fence around outdoor facilities such as your playground and your pool. In many areas, your local law will require you to add a fence of a specified height and to install a self-closing, latching gate. Consider these requirements to be your starting-point—don't hesitate to erect a taller fence and take additional safety steps, such as limiting access to those with keycards or keys, to further reduce the chances that a child will wander into a potentially dangerous area without an adult.

Set appropriate age limits

It's illegal to discriminate against families with children. This means that you can't, for example, ban children from using the pool or clubhouse because you want adult-only facilities. But it's okay to create rules that single out children if the point of the rules is to protect their health or safety. So, you can require that children under a certain age (such as 12) use your pool or playground only with adult supervision, and you can ban children under a certain age (such as 16) from your fitness center or sauna (even with adult supervision).

Ban alcohol use and rowdy behavior

It's quite risky to let tenants use alcohol while supervising children in play areas or while using your pool or fitness center. As a practical matter, you can't control the amount of alcohol that tenants consume, which means their judgment and physical coordination may become impaired. If an accident were to happen, you might end up sharing some responsibility on the grounds that you allowed a dangerous situation to develop at your property.

For similar reasons, prohibit rowdy behavior and horseplay from *all* your facilities. Don't limit this rule to children—not just to avoid discrimination complaints, but because you really don't want adults acting irresponsibly or causing problems either.

Though you can't police what people will do every hour of the day while on your property (and indeed, no law in this country requires landlords to do so), an announced (and enforced) policy against drinking and roughhousing will go a long way toward shielding you from liability.

Make it easy to call for help

Because pools and other athletic facilities are among the places where accidents are most likely to occur, include a pay phone in the area or as close as possible so that a witness to an accident can conveniently call 911. Although many people today carry cell phones, understand that calling 911 on a cell phone can result in significant delays. (Often, the call gets routed to a responder who's many miles away.) By contrast, when you dial 911 on a landline, the call goes to the nearest responder. Providing a pay phone to call 911—and posting a sign telling users that they should use that phone in case of an emergency—can make the difference when it comes to saving lives and keeping you out of court.

Provide first-aid and life-saving equipment

Have a large first-aid kit ready in case someone gets hurt at your facilities. This way, if there's a serious incident, witness can actually help, rather than just wait for the paramedics. Keep life-saving equipment such as life vests, ring buoys, shepherd's crooks, and throw lines poolside or in a nearby shed that you keep unlocked and accessible during pool hours.

TIP

Post your rules in a prominent place, even if they're already in your lease or house rules. Don't expect that tenants will remember them, and realize that guests don't get copies of your lease with attached house rules. Post facility rules, including the hours a facility is open, near the entrance to a facility or in a prominent spot inside. Make it clear that you reserve the right to deny the use of your facility to anyone at any time. If you decide to bar someone from using a facility, make sure it's for a legitimate business reason—such as the safety of your tenants—and not the fruit of illegal discrimination.

> ## Guidance From the Government on Pools and Playgrounds
>
> The U.S. Consumer Product Safety Commission offers free information on how to remove physical hazards from your property's facilities. At www. cpsc.gov, use the search box to find the following useful pamphlets:
> - *Guidelines for Entrapment Hazards: Making Pools and Spas Safer.* This 32-page booklet includes guidelines, a hazard checklist, and more.
> - *Handbook for Public Playground Safety.* This publication includes extensive guidelines for owners of public playgrounds, including those located at apartment complexes.

Keep common areas free of tenants' belongings

Some tenants drive landlords crazy by chaining bicycles to the stairwell's railings, parking strollers outside the front door, depositing umbrellas and boots near their entryways, and even placing a storage unit in the hall. When tenants leave items in your common area, it's not just an annoyance—you run the risk that someone will get hurt by tripping over items or veering to avoid them. Many local codes require landlords to keep common areas clear to ensure that firefighters can reach a fire and occupants can evacuate a building safely.

To prevent problems, bar tenants from storing any items of their personal property in your common areas in a house rule or lease clause. Include a list of common items that tenants like to store, such as bicycles, strollers, toys, furniture, shoes, wet clothing, and umbrellas. A smart landlord will figure out how to accommodate tenants' storage needs by making space available in safe and secure areas. If you just can't offer storage space at your property, talk to the owner of a nearby self-storage facility about offering tenants a discount in return for the added business.

Remove snow and ice to avoid natural accumulations

A snowfall can be beautiful, but when a tenant or visitor slips and falls on natural accumulations of snow and ice on your property, it's not so pretty. Of course, you can't be held responsible for creating a storm, and you're not expected to erect a dome over your property to protect your tenants from stormy weather. That said, you're not completely off the hook for Mother Nature's physical hazards. Because tenants and others who slip and fall on icy rental property regularly sue landlords, it's worth your while to remove those hazards.

First, follow your state or local law's requirements for snow and ice removal. If your state or municipality has such requirements, you can find them identified in their codes' table of contents. Also, check your county, or city or town's website as winter approaches. In addition to posting useful tips and winter storm information, many municipalities take the opportunity to remind property owners of snow and ice removal requirements. Local removal laws can vary significantly, as you can see in the chart below.

Suppose your state and local laws don't include snow or ice removal requirements (because your region seldom sees snow, for instance). If your property gets hit with a winter storm, use common sense and act diligently—just as you do whenever you discover any dangerous condition on your property. You're not expected to shovel or plow *during* a snowstorm, but be ready to remove snow from major pedestrian paths on your property and abutting public sidewalks as soon as it's feasible to do so after a snowfall ends. The longer you wait, the higher the risk that someone will slip and fall on your property and convince a judge or jury that you were at least partially at fault.

When the Weather Outside Is Frightful

Many cities have snow removal ordinances specific to residential landlords. If your rental property is in a snow-prone area, check for laws like these.

- In West Lafayette, Indiana, landlords must remove snow from sidewalks six hours after daylight and after a snowfall has ended.
- In Ann Arbor, Michigan, landlords must remove snow and ice that has accumulated on sidewalks before 6 a.m. by 12 p.m. Right after the accumulation of ice, landlords must treat sidewalks with sand, salt, or another substance to prevent them from becoming slippery. Within 24 hours after the end of each accumulation of snow greater than one inch, landlords must remove the accumulation from sidewalks.
- In Cambridge, Massachusetts, landlords must remove snow within 12 hours after it stops falling in the daytime, and before 1 p.m. the day after an evening snowfall. Landlords must remove all ice or cover it with salt, sand, or a similar substance within six hours after the sidewalk becomes icy.
- In River Falls, Wisconsin, landlords have 24 hours after a snowfall ends to remove snow and ice that has accumulated on sidewalks. However, if ice or packed snow is so compact that it can't be removed, landlords must keep it sprinkled with a nonskid material that will prevent the sidewalk from posing a hazard.

Limit use of the roof to official business

Apartment building rooftops are typically full of equipment, wires, vents and other hazards, and often host ongoing construction projects. When you need to make repairs, your staff or contractor navigates the roof carefully and probably doesn't take pains to cordon off a construction site, as they would if the work were being done to part of your lobby. But all too often, tenants and their guests use rooftops for stargazing, sunbathing, or partying. If you allow access to a roof that hasn't been made safe for such uses, you're exposing people to dangerous situations—and you could be liable if an accident occurs.

Unnecessary use of your roof also adds wear and tear that can bring costly repairs. If your roof becomes defective, water can seep into top-floor apartments after it rains, further damaging your property as well as the personal property of the tenants below. Finally, letting tenants use your roof may void your roof's warranty, interfere with your contract with a roof maintenance company, and cause your insurer to raise your policy premiums.

With so much at stake, lower your risks by restricting your roof to employees for business purposes and to everyone else in cases of emergency only. Don't go so far as to lock the entrance to your roof. Tenants may need to flee there in case of a fire or other emergency (and, in fact, your local fire code may bar you from doing this). But you can arm the door with an alarm that sounds when it's opened (along with a helpful warning about the alarm). Adding an alarm to your door may cost you a few bucks, but it should prove highly effective in deterring people from accessing your roof for the wrong reasons.

It Won't Happen to You ...

What happened. On a sunny afternoon in June 2001, Ryan Corbin, singer Pat Boone's 24-year-old grandson, fell through a skylight on the roof of his Brentwood, California, apartment building where he had been sunbathing. Ryan landed on a concrete floor three floors below, and almost died. He sued his landlords, claiming they should be held liable for his injuries because they knew tenants visited the roof to sunbathe and watch fireworks, yet didn't warn them that the skylight opening was a hidden trap, concealed by corrugated fiberglass. In 2004, the landlords settled with Ryan for over $10 million.

How you can avoid it. Limit roof access to employees and contractors and to others only in emergencies. If you learn that tenants are using the roof for recreational purposes, take prompt steps to stop this practice— or at least make sure the areas used don't pose a danger.

Control traffic on your parking lot and roadways

Circular driveways, roadways, and parking lots on your property can become serious liability traps if drivers are free to go as fast as they like. Tenants who get hit by a speeding vehicle on your property may sue you for their injuries, claiming you didn't make your property safe for pedestrians. You can lower your risks by taking two smart steps to limit motorists' speed:

- **Add signs restricting speed.** You can post your own speed limit or stop signs on your private property. For example, post signs that say, "Stop," "Yield," "Slow," and "Speed Limit 10 MPH."
- **Add pavement modifications.** Also known as "traffic calmers," pavement modifications force drivers to reduce their speed or even come to a complete stop. The most common pavement modifications are speed bumps and speed ridges (patches of indentations in the road that make tires vibrate, alerting motorists to reduce their speed).

> **CAUTION**
>
> **Make sure drivers can see any speed bumps you install.** If they don't know what's coming and, having driven over the bumps fast, sue you for damage to their vehicles, you'll have lowered one risk only at the expense of adding another. Post a sign saying, "Speed Bumps Ahead" and paint speed bumps a bright yellow or other color to ensure they stand out.

Light your property as required by law and common sense

No matter how structurally safe your parking lot, lobby, or other common areas may be, if lighting becomes inadequate, nearly everything can turn into a potential hazard. How much light is enough? You'll need to satisfy any applicable local codes, and then use your common sense.

Lighting required by law

Your local codes may require parts of your property to maintain a certain intensity of illumination, which is often measured in "foot-candles." A foot-candle is the amount of light a single candle generates from one foot away. Foot-candles are measured with special handheld digital light meters that any professional lighting contractor should have. If you believe your lighting isn't up to code, hire a lighting contractor to check the sufficiency of your interior and exterior lighting. If you feel confident about measuring foot-candles on your own, you can buy a meter and do it yourself. Light meters are available on the Internet at prices starting at around $100. Just search for "light meter."

Lighting dictated by common sense

If your local laws don't address rental property lighting, take advantage of the experience of professionals. The Illuminating Engineering Society of North America (IESNA) publishes its own standards for lighting apartment complexes, which you may wish to follow in the absence of (or in addition to) local law. You can get more information about the IESNA and its lighting standards by visiting www.iesna.org.

Finally, use your own common sense. Walk around your property at various times of the day and night, and determine whether you can see adequately. If it's hard to see where you're going on outdoor walkways, add more lamps or increase the intensity of the existent lighting, if possible. When you formally inspect your property and each time you walk through it, look for burnt-out bulbs and dirty lenses on floodlights and replace or clean them promptly. Also, pay attention to tenants' suggestions for better lighting. If you notice that automatic timers aren't properly set, fix them immediately.

It Won't Happen to You ...

What happened. A Los Angeles tenant walked down a dark stairway in her apartment building, slipped on broken eggs, and fell. After requiring two surgeries to fix her broken ankle at a total cost of $27,000, the tenant sued the landlord for negligence, claiming the automatic timer on the stairway lights wasn't working properly and caused the lights to come on too late. The landlord settled for $105,000—even though he wasn't responsible for putting the broken eggs on the stairway.

How you can avoid it. "Smart" devices such as automatic timers don't live up to their name if a (smarter) human being doesn't monitor them. In this case, the landlord undoubtedly had some idea that the timer was amiss. His apparent failure to fix the timer and, in the meantime, override it, led to this expensive settlement.

Lower the risk of fire

In 2005, fire departments responded to 381,000 fires at apartment buildings and other types of homes in the United States, according to the National Fire Protection Association. These fires caused 13,300 civilian injuries, 3,030 civilian deaths, and a whopping $6.7 billion in direct damage.

Although fires sometimes can't be avoided, there's much that landlords can do to lower the risk of a fire occurring at their property. Here are strategies you can follow to prevent fires.

Require tenants to keep smoke detectors in working order

Your state or municipality probably requires you to install smoke detectors in your apartments. But, according to a study by the Public/Private Fire Safety Council based on 2003 data, an estimated 20% of homes in the United States have smoke detectors that aren't working (typically, because the batteries are either dead or missing). This figure translates to roughly 21 million apartments and other homes across the country. Not surprisingly, nearly half of the households interviewed in the study admitted that they disabled the smoke alarm because the sound annoyed them.

Having working smoke alarms at your property is essential for saving lives and minimizing property damage. When smoke triggers a detector's alarm, tenants have extra time to escape a fire and find safety—especially if the fire starts when tenants are sleeping.

Smoking: A Major Cause of Apartment Fires

According to the National Fire Protection Association, which analyzed smoking-related fires, injuries, and deaths between 1980 and 2003, in most years, smoking materials were the leading cause of *all* fire deaths in the U.S. Trash, mattresses and bedding, and upholstered furniture were the items most often ignited by smoking materials in home fires, and together they accounted for half of fires, three-fourths of associated deaths, and two-thirds of associated injuries. Fires in apartments constituted 22% of all smoking-material fires, 24% of all deaths, 29% of injuries, and $129 million in direct property damage. Clearly, smoking-related fires are a huge risk to multifamily rentals. And statistics for such fires in single-family homes are even higher, showing that these structures accounted for 54% of all smoking-material fires, 69% of the deaths, 57% of the injuries, and $288 million in property damage. ("The Smoking-Material Fire Problem," 2006.)

Rental property owners have begun to take notice, as have municipalities throughout the country. Many landlords have adopted a policy of "no smoking" on their property, and cities, including several in California, have passed ordinances banning smoking in multifamily housing. For more information on smoking and apartments, see the Smoke Free Housing Consultants at www.s-fhc.com.

Make sure you understand what your state or local law requires you to do when it comes to installing and maintaining smoke detectors. At the least, you probably must make sure that smoke detectors are placed outside each bedroom on or near the ceiling, and that they are in working order at the time tenants move in. Replace detectors periodically—even with regular battery replacement, expect smoke detectors to work properly for no more than ten years.

If a tenant reports a malfunctioning smoke detector, respond promptly. If you take your time to investigate and a fire occurs, tenants may claim you're responsible for their harm.

Limit space heater usage

Space heaters pose a fire risk—especially if they're not used properly. In 2003, space heaters were involved in 73% of deaths from home heating fires, according to the National Fire Protection Association (NFPA). They were also responsible for 58% of injuries in home heating fires and 51% of property damage from these fires. You can minimize these risks by limiting tenants' space heater usage. Here are some suggestions:

- If you let tenants use space heaters, limit them to electric space heaters. Kerosene and other nonelectric heaters pose a serious risk of fire and carbon monoxide poisoning. Not surprisingly, they're even illegal in certain parts of the country.
- Require tenants to place space heaters at least three or four feet away from combustible items such as books and clothes. The NFPA notes that space heaters pose a greater fire risk than central heating systems in part because they are often placed close to household combustibles.
- Make sure tenants' space heaters contain a mark of approval from an independent testing laboratory, and that tenants follow the manufacturer's instructions and safety precautions.
- As part of your house rules, specify that tenants may not leave space heaters unattended. For example, they should turn off space heaters when leaving their apartment.

Consider banning halogen lamps

Halogen lamps were all the rage in the 1990s, but when the fires started to rage, the halogen lamp's hidden danger became all too apparent. Halogen lamps may look sleek, effectively light up a room, and cost less than traditional lighting, but they pose a serious fire risk because the bulbs operate at a much higher temperature than regular incandescent light bulbs. The classic torchiere-style halogen lamp, which is the most popular type, is also the most dangerous type. These lamps tip over easily and can ignite a fire when the bulb touches combustible materials.

To make matters worse, some people misuse halogen lamps as coat racks or clothes dryers, adding to the risk they pose. Although lamp manufacturers now include a wire guard surrounding the halogen bulb, many people have older lamps that don't have this safety device.

The best way to remove the risks that halogen lamps pose is to adopt a strict policy banning their use at your property and include your ban in your lease or written house rules. Also, consider refraining from using halogen lamps yourself at your property. A halogen lamp in your lobby, leasing office, or community room has the potential to cause the same—if not greater—damage as tenants' halogen lamps inside their apartments.

It Won't Happen to You …

What happened. Among the many reports of fires and deaths caused by halogen lamps, the most notable is the January 1997 fire in jazz legend Lionel Hampton's New York apartment. No one was killed when his bedroom lamp tipped over and ignited his bed, but 250 firefighters tackled a blaze that injured 11 people, forced a hundred people to evacuate, and caused the building to sustain serious property and smoke damage.

How you can avoid it. Create a rule that bars tenants from having halogen lamps in their rentals. When you or your employees visit rentals for repairs or other legitimate reasons, keep your eyes peeled and note whether tenants are violating your rule. Act quickly to enforce it, if needed.

Let tenants use fireplaces—if they follow your rules

Do you offer working fireplaces as an amenity for tenants? If you do, make sure the fires stay in their fireplaces by requiring tenants to follow certain safety procedures. Here are fireplace safety rules you should adopt at your property:

- **If you can't attend to a fire, put it out.** Tenants must never leave a fire unattended. Tenants who start a fire should extinguish it before leaving their apartment.
- **Don't close the flue until the fire is long gone.** To avoid carbon monoxide buildup, tenants should open the flue before starting a fire but should not close the flue until the fire is done smoldering. (Carbon monoxide is covered at length in Step Four.)
- **Surround fire with screen.** A good fire screen surrounding a fire is essential for preventing sparks from escaping the fireplace.
- **Burn only dry, seasoned wood.** Forbid the use of other substances, such as loose paper, charcoal, coal, garbage, plastic materials, and flammable liquids. This helps prevent the buildup of creosote, an oily deposit that can catch fire inside the chimney or flue. By using only dry, seasoned wood, you'll also avoid creating toxic fumes or create a fire that can rage out of control.
- **Keep flammable materials a comfortable distance from the fireplace.** Require tenants not to place anything, such as magazines, pillows, clothes, toys, and holiday decorations near a fireplace.
- **Keep small children away from fireplace.** Tenants—and any nurse, au pair, or babysitter they hire—should be sure to keep babies, toddlers, and other small children several feet from an active fireplace to avoid harm from sparks or flames.
- **Notify you of problems.** If tenants believe their fireplace might not be working properly, they should alert you to the potential problem immediately.

Be sure to inspect and clean your building's fireplaces regularly (at least once a year). This type of routine maintenance will prevent fires as well as carbon monoxide poisoning that can result when smoke gets backed up due to a blockage. (See the discussion on carbon monoxide in Step Four.)

Ban consumer fireworks

The 9/11 attacks spawned a surge of patriotism across the country, which has led to an increased interest in traditional patriotic displays such as fireworks (and not just on Independence Day). Open spaces in rental properties are prime locations to tenants who wish to set off their own fireworks. Although the personal injuries associated with fireworks are well known, only five states—Delaware, Massachusetts, New Jersey, New York, and Rhode Island—currently ban all consumer fireworks. (Many cities, however, have their own bans or limitations on use.)

Even if your state and local government haven't banned fireworks, you still need to pay attention to the risks they pose. Remember, as a landlord you're responsible for taking steps to minimize the chances that people will be hurt from foreseeable harm. Fireworks are unquestionably "foreseeable harm."

To help ensure tenants comply with the law—and to protect yourself against liability if they don't and people get hurt—add language to your lease that bars tenants from using fireworks or letting their guests use them on your property. If tenants understand that using fireworks can get them evicted, they may think twice about using them.

What Are "Consumer Fireworks"?

Regulations from the U.S. Department of Transportation define "consumer fireworks" as cone fountains, cylindrical fountains, roman candles, sky rockets, firecrackers, mines and shells, helicopter-type rockets, certain sparklers, and revolving wheels. List each type of consumer fireworks in your lease or house rules, to be sure you've covered all your bases.

 TIP

Tell tenants about public fireworks displays near your property.
Also, take the opportunity to remind them that using fireworks of any kind on your property poses a serious danger to people and property, constitutes a major violation of their lease that could lead to eviction, and is illegal (if that's true where your property is located).

Maintenance: My To-Do List

In Step Two, you've learned how to take a good look at the physical condition of your rental property, and review your systems and approach to maintenance. Use the list below to guide you as you proceed to lower the risk that something broken, old, or not up-to-code will result in damage or injury.

☐ **Inspections:** Inspect my property for physical hazards on a regular basis.

☐ **Inspections:** Walk through my property and notice things that are loose or broken, and fix them.

☐ **Safety:** Pay serious attention to safety issues even if my business has excellent insurance coverage and I've never been sued.

☐ **Maintenance:** Get a maintenance contract for the boiler, elevator, or other machinery at my property.

☐ **Repairs:** Put a system in place for written tenant requests, including my response.

☐ **Code compliance:** Learn what's required on major issues, such as smoke detectors, lighting, and safety devices on doors and windows.

☐ **Code violations:** If my building gets cited for code violations, promptly take steps to make my building compliant again.

☐ **Safety:** Keep signs, traffic cones, safety tape, or other items ready in case I need to warn people of danger and block off an area that suddenly becomes hazardous.

☐ **Rules:** Make sure all safety-related policies are written down, in my leases or rental agreements, or in my house rules that are referenced by the lease or rental agreement.

☐ **Extras:** Post rules and warnings at facilities such as my property's swimming pool, playground, or fitness center.

☐ **Common areas:** Don't let tenants store bicycles, strollers, and other belongings in my building's hallways.

Maintenance: My To-Do List (continued)

☐ **Snow and ice removal:** Learn what my state and local law requires when it comes to removing snow and ice from my property after a storm.

☐ **Roof:** Restrict access to authorized individuals and for emergencies only.

☐ **Parking lot:** Equip the parking lot with appropriate traffic calmers to prevent people from driving their vehicles too fast.

☐ **Lighting:** Confirm that the lighting in the lobby, parking lot, and other common areas is adequate and code-compliant.

☐ **Fire safety:** Limit tenants' use of space heaters in their apartments.

☐ **Fire safety:** Bar tenants from using halogen lamps or require them to follow rules for proper usage.

☐ **Fire safety:** Require tenants to keep smoke detectors in working order.

☐ **Fire safety:** For apartments that offer working fireplaces, require tenants to follow safety rules when using them.

☐ **Fire safety:** Don't let tenants or their guests use consumer fireworks on the property.

Make Your Rental Property Accessible to Disabled Tenants

I n Step Two, you set about discovering and removing physical hazards and code noncompliance from your property. In this chapter, you'll learn how to go one step further and make your property accessible for people with mobility impairments and other disabilities. First, you'll want to make sure that your structures follow legally enforceable accessibility guidelines (known as "design and construction" requirements). Then, you'll want to be sure you understand your responsibilities should a disabled prospect or tenant ask you to modify your building in order to meet that person's needs.

Aside from requests for physical modifications to your building, prospects and tenants often ask landlords to make changes to their rules, practices, policies, and services to accommodate a disability. For example, if you normally ban pets from your property, a visually impaired prospect might ask you to let her keep a guide dog in her apartment. As is the case with modifications, you must take all accommodation requests seriously and grant them if they're reasonable. For more information about reasonable accommodations, see Step Seven.

Many federal, state, and local laws set out various rules for making apartments, common areas, and other parts of your property accessible. For example, the entrance to your leasing office must be wide enough for wheelchairs to pass through, and you may need to design a certain number of spaces in your parking lot that are extra-wide and have accessibility features such as curb ramps and access aisles. This chapter also helps you evaluate requests for modifications, such as a hearing-impaired tenant's request for a light-activated doorbell system to accommodate his disability.

What Does "Disabled" Mean?

The laws that require you to maintain an accessible building, or grant reasonable modification requests, are designed to help prospects and tenants who are disabled. According to the law, a disabled person is someone who has a physical or mental impairment that substantially limits one or more major life activities. Prospects and tenants are also protected if they have "a record of having such an impairment" (they have a history of having an impairment or have been misclassified), or are "regarded as having such an impairment" (their impairment incorrectly appears to others to substantially limit major life activities).

Common qualifying disabilities include cerebral palsy, autism, cancer, diabetes, mental retardation, HIV infection, drug addiction (other than addiction caused by current, illegal use of a controlled substance), and alcoholism.

Ignoring accessibility laws is very risky—just one complaint can lead to fines, private lawsuits, and retrofitting, all of which can prove very costly.

What Does "Accessible" Mean?

The essence of the Fair Housing Act's protections involves the requirement of "accessibility." This concept is aimed mainly at ensuring that a person in a wheelchair can move about an area or use a certain feature of an apartment. Making your rental property accessible also means making sure it's safe for and usable by people with other disabilities.

What Do You Have to Lose?

Landlords who don't take accessibility seriously have a lot to lose. First, understand that unlike building and fire codes, accessibility guideline noncompliance isn't usually discovered by regular troops of inspectors who examine new construction and renovation and check up on existing buildings as part of local inspection programs. Instead, a building's noncompliance with federal, state, or local accessibility standards (or a landlord's refusal to modify a rental) is likely to come to light when a disabled prospect or tenant complains to the Department of Housing and Urban Development (HUD), a fair housing advocacy group, or a civil rights attorney.

Once a complaint has been made, as the examples in "It Won't Happen to You" illustrate, you're in for it. At best, you'll probably need to spend time and money retrofitting one or more parts of your apartments, common areas, or public-use areas that a prospect or tenant complains about. If a prospect or tenant sues, it can be worse. The court may order you to pay penalties and damages to prospects or tenants who prove they're the victims of discrimination, get fair housing training, and submit records—on top of requiring what could prove to be even more extensive (and expensive) retrofitting. To add insult to injury, your reputation will surely suffer, as colleagues, tenants, prospects, and—often enough—the press learn of your situation.

> **TIP**
>
> **Accessible properties give you a marketing edge.** Making your property accessible increases the pool of prospects to fill your vacant apartments. This can prove particularly helpful during slow economic times.

Is This You?

Even if you know for sure that your rental property complies with accessibility laws, don't stop reading just yet. There's a good chance you may need to make additional modifications to your apartments— or even to your common or public-use areas—if tenants request them on account of their disabilities. See if you recognize yourself in any of the descriptions below.

Do You Think About Accessibility Like These Landlords?

☐ You didn't construct the rental property you own, and do not know whether it meets accessibility guidelines.

☐ You don't worry about accessibility issues because your staff follows a policy—written or unwritten—of renting only to people who aren't disabled.

☐ No disabled tenants rent at your property and you've never encountered a disabled applicant, so you haven't thought much about accessibility issues.

☐ You're not sure who should pay for a physical modification—you, or the tenant who requests the modification.

☐ You're afraid you'll be sued for discrimination if you ask tenants to give you something in writing from a doctor or other third party that shows they need a modification for their disability.

☐ You don't accept modification requests from prospects, reasoning that you have no obligation to accommodate them in this way because they haven't yet signed a lease.

☐ You own a few properties that were built in different years over the past few decades, and you don't know how that affects accessibility compliance.

Take Action!

Did you see yourself in any of the descriptions of landlords above? If you do, or if you don't feel that you have a firm grip on what you're required to do as a landlord when it comes to accessibility compliance, read the following action steps carefully. Each strategy is aimed at helping you comply with accessibility laws by having an accessibility-compliant building to begin with and treating prospects and tenants fairly. If you adopt the suggestions we discuss below, you'll also gain the confidence to handle situations that are likely to arise when a prospect or tenant asks you to modify their living quarters to make them accessible.

The FHA's design and construction requirements: Do they apply to your property?

There's a good chance that a building you own or are considering purchasing is covered by the FHA's design and construction requirements, which are the legal guidelines for fair housing/disability structural compliance. Not all buildings are in this group. Your building is covered if:

- **The building has four or more apartments.** The design and construction requirements apply only to "multifamily dwellings," which means that a building must have at least four apartments to be covered (even if the apartments are detached from each other by means of a breezeway, stairwell, or other similar feature). Community rooms, game rooms, business centers, and fitness centers don't enter the equation—to be covered, the building must have at least four rental units.
- **The building was "designed and constructed" for first occupancy after March 13, 1991.** This means the building was not used for any purpose on or before this date. If, for example, even one tenant lived in your building on or before March 13, 1991, then your building isn't covered and doesn't need to meet the FHA's design and construction requirements.

- **The last permit for the building was issued after June 15, 1990.** If your building was designed and constructed for first occupancy after March 13, 1991, the FHA's design and construction requirements don't apply if the last building permit (or renewal) is dated after June 15, 1990. (This rule gave developers time to factor the requirements into the design and construction phases of their buildings.)

And Then There's the ADA

The Fair Housing Act doesn't apply to every rental building—your property may be exempt due to its size or age. But don't stop reading if your property isn't covered by the FHA. Another federal law, the Americans with Disabilities Act (ADA), may affect your property instead. Title III of this law applies to public areas and some common areas of the property—known as areas of "public accommodation." The ADA protects people with disabilities from discrimination when using goods, services, and facilities in such areas.

For landlords, this could include your rental office and any facilities, such as your clubhouse or other rooms that you rent out to the public. For example, if you advertise your clubhouse for use as a wedding reception venue, that area must comply with the ADA.

Understanding what's required under the ADA is tricky. For help, contact the toll-free ADA Information Line at the Department of Justice (DOJ) at 800-514-0301 or consult the DOJ's website dedicated to ADA compliance at www.usdoj.gov/crt/ada. You may also want to hire a consultant—search for "ADA consultants" using your favorite search engine, or ask a colleague for a recommendation. Don't take this lightly—a single Title III violation could trigger a $55,000 penalty, with a $110,000 penalty for subsequent violations.

CAUTION

Extensive renovations to an exempt building can themselves be nonexempt. If your building isn't covered by the design and construction requirements, renovations you make to the building normally won't affect its exempt status. But if you add a wing or other new section to your building, and this addition includes four or more apartments, the new section isn't exempt and must be built in compliance with the requirements.

Low-Income Housing and FHA Design Requirements

Many landlords mistakenly believe that the design and construction requirements apply only to buildings that get federal assistance or participate in an affordable housing program. Not so—unless your building is exempt, as explained above. If your building does get federal assistance, you may also need to comply with an additional set of access standards (Section 504 of the Rehabilitation Act of 1973). For example, you may need to provide a certain minimum number of accessible apartments in your building.

The FHA's design and construction requirements: Determine which apartments must comply

If you determine that your rental property is covered by the FHA's design and construction requirements, you'll next need to know which apartments must meet the requirements. The answer depends on whether your building has an elevator:

- **Multiple floors with an elevator.** All apartments in the building must comply.
- **Single-story buildings or buildings with multiple floors but no elevator.** Only the ground-floor units must comply.

It Won't Happen to You ...

What happened. In September 2005, the Department of Justice settled with a major housing developer and several architectural firms in Michigan, Indiana, Illinois, Ohio, Wisconsin, Virginia, and Nebraska, after claiming that they all discriminated against people with disabilities by not complying with the Fair Housing Act's design and construction requirements. The developer and architectural firms agreed, among other measures, to retrofit 49 multifamily properties and pay a total of $1,060,000—$950,000 to the victims of the alleged discrimination, and $110,000 as a civil penalty.

How you can avoid it. It's hard to imagine how big operators like these failed to learn and apply the accessibility rules. You don't have to imagine the same fate befalling you. Instead, take the time to learn what's required and comply (see the suggestions in "Putting the FHA accessibility rules into practice," below).

The seven principles of the design and construction requirements

Although the FHA's requirements are packed with details only an engineer or architect would be expected to understand, you can quickly determine, with a fair amount of certainty, whether your property and apartments measure up. The seven rules explained below capture the essence of the accessibility rules (for convenience, we'll call them the Seven Rules). If you're not sure that your building complies, you may need to hire an architect to visit your property and assess what, if any, steps you must take to meet all the requirements. Contact the architect that designed your building, or use the American Institute of Architects' online "Find an Architect" feature by visiting www.aia.org/architect_finder. Fixing violations before you're "caught" is a smart way to remove risks, and it may prove to be less costly than you think.

Rule 1: There must be an accessible building entrance on an accessible route

Buildings must have at least one accessible entrance on an accessible route, unless the terrain or other factors make this impractical. Let's take this apart a bit:

- An "accessible entrance" is a door or other entryway that complies with detailed specifications. It must be at least 32 inches wide, have a low (or no) threshold with clear maneuverable space inside and outside the door, and be equipped with a door that requires little force to open, contains accessible hardware, and has a safe closing speed.
- An "accessible route" is a continuous, unobstructed path connecting accessible elements and spaces within a building or property, such as parking spaces, transportation stops, loading zones, public streets, and sidewalks. The route must be easy to navigate and safe for someone using a wheelchair.

Rule 2: Common and public use areas must be accessible

Common use areas, such as such as a mailroom, laundry room, storage area, and hallways, must be accessible. This means, for example, that your laundry room should include front-loading washers and dryers with side-hinged doors or assistive devices (such as reachers) that let disabled tenants use top-loading machines. In addition, if you have public use areas, like your rental office or rooms you rent out for special occasions (such as parties or wedding receptions), these too must be accessible.

Rule 3: Doors must be usable by a person in a wheelchair

All entrance doors and those within your building must be wide enough (generally, at least 32 inches in width) for wheelchairs. This requirement applies to doors that lead to walk-in closets, but it doesn't apply to doors for linen closets (which have shelves in easy reach) and any other situation where the door isn't intended for passage.

Rule 4: There must be an accessible route into and through an apartment

Routes that tenants take from the entrance to their apartment to decks and patios must be accessible for wheelchairs. This means they should be at least 36 inches wide (except when the route passes through interior doors, at which point they need be only 32 inches wide), so that tenants can comfortably make 90-degree turns with their wheelchairs. You must also comply with specifications for minimum height or headroom, and you must make sure that accessible routes are free from protruding objects. Level changes are also restricted, usually to no more than 1/4-inch (or 1/2-inch, if tapered). Finally, if you have special design features, such as split-level entries, sunken living rooms, and loft areas, you must follow requirements for making sure they have accessible routes.

Rule 5: Light switches, electrical outlets, thermostats, and other environmental controls must be in accessible locations

Tenants using wheelchairs must be able to comfortably reach electrical switches, outlets, and thermostats. Thermostats must be low enough not only to reach but to read, and there must be clear knee space below a countertop to allow a tenant in a wheelchair to reach an outlet on the wall above it. This rule does not, however, cover controls on moveable appliances, range hoods, garbage disposals, special-use wall outlets (a rarely used outlet that's dedicated for a specific appliance), circuit breaker panels, and telephone/television jacks.

Rule 6: Bathroom walls must be reinforced for later installation of grab bars

Installing grab bars isn't part of the FHA's design and construction requirements, but it may be required if a tenant requests grab bars as a reasonable modification under the FHA, as discussed in greater detail below. This means that bathroom walls must be reinforced, often with solid-wood backing that's securely anchored to studs, so that the bars can be safely added to the walls.

Rule 7: Kitchens and bathrooms must be usable by a tenant in a wheelchair

A tenant using a wheelchair must be able to move about kitchens and bathrooms, and operate their fixtures and appliances. For example, kitchens must have clear floor space at ranges, stovetops, and sinks so that there's ample room for a tenant in a wheelchair to make a parallel approach. Similarly, bathrooms must offer enough maneuvering space to permit such a tenant to enter and close the door, then reopen the door and leave.

Putting the FHA accessibility rules into practice

As straightforward as the Seven Rules appear to be, their implementation is not so obvious. How will you know, for example, that the light switches are within adequate reach, or that the turnaround spaces in the kitchen and bathroom are sufficient? To answer these questions, consult one of eight HUD-approved design manuals. HUD calls them "safe harbors," which means that if you follow any one of these manuals' specifications, HUD will consider your property to be in compliance with the FHA's design and construction requirements.

CAUTION

Your state or local law may impose more stringent accessibility requirements. For example, the FHA generally requires that at least 2% of parking spaces be accessible and located on an accessible route. State or local law may require a higher percentage, or specify that a certain number of parking spaces be made accessible. If you don't already know what your state or municipality requires, review the law to check whether your property complies. For help in accessing state and local laws online, see Step Two.

HUD-Approved Safe Harbors for Accessibility

HUD has approved the following eight design and construction standards that builders and developers may follow to ensure compliance with accessibility requirements.

- HUD *Fair Housing Accessibility Guidelines* (published March 6, 1991) and the *Supplemental Notice to Fair Housing Accessibility Guidelines: Questions and Answers about the Guidelines* (published June 28, 1994)
- HUD *FHA Design Manual*
- ANSI A117.1 (1986), used with the FHA, HUD's regulations, and the Guidelines
- CABO/ANSI A117.1 (1992), used with the FHA, HUD's regulations, and the Guidelines
- ICC/ANSI A117.1 (1998), used with the FHA, HUD's regulations, and the Guidelines
- *Code Requirements for Housing Accessibility 2000* (CRHA)
- *International Building Code 2000* (as amended by the 2001 *Supplement to the International Codes*), and
- *International Building Code 2003* (with a condition).

The HUD *FHA Design Manual* is written in plain English and is full of useful illustrations to help you understand these very technical requirements. You can download a copy of the manual for free by visiting www.huduser.org/publications/destech/fairhousing.html. If you would like a hard copy of this 334-page document but don't wish to print it yourself, you can click a link to order a copy from HUD for only $5.

WHAT IS AN ACCESSIBLE ROUTE ?

An accessible route is a continuous, unobstructed path through sites and buildings that connects all accessible features, elements, and spaces. It is the critical element that allows the successful use of any site or building by a person with a disability. Such a route is safe for someone using a wheelchair or scooter and also is usable by others.

Accessible routes on a site may include parking spaces, parking access aisles, curb ramps, walks, ramps, and lifts. Accessible routes within buildings may include corridors, doorways, floors, ramps, elevators, and lifts. Specifications for accessible routes are found in ANSI 4.3. Certain elements of accessible routes which must be given careful attention are:

- width of route
- ground and floor surfaces
- headroom
- protruding objects
- slope of route
- cross slope
- curb ramps
- lift/elevator design

These elements are discussed in detail in Part Two, Chapter 2.

Stairs and Accessible Routes

Stairs are not an acceptable component of an accessible route because they prevent use by people using wheelchairs and others who cannot climb steps. ANSI specifications for accessible stairs (4.9) make stairs safer and more usable by mobility impaired people who can climb stairs.

accessible routes must connect covered dwelling units with accessible site facilities (and at least one of each type of recreational facility when more than one of each is provided at any location)

accessible mailbox kiosk

accessible play area

accessible bus stop shelter with wheelchair parking space *and seating for people with limited stamina*

curb ramp that complies with ANSI 4.7 provides benefits for other users

Route with No Abrupt Change in Level to Provide Access to Dwelling Units and Site Amenities

HUD's helping hand to landlords: The "Fair Housing Accessibility FIRST" initiative

It would be a mistake to dive into the design standards described above, or turn the whole project over to an expensive team of engineers and contractors, without first using the free help offered by HUD. HUD's program, called the "Fair Housing Accessibility FIRST" initiative, offers a comprehensive training curriculum, free Internet resources, and a toll-free information line for technical guidance and compliance support. You can also get information about attending live seminars, offered throughout the country. For more information, visit www.fairhousingfirst.org or call 888-341-7781.

It Won't Happen to You ...

What happened. The landlord of an apartment complex in East Moline, Illinois, refused to rent an apartment to a couple because the man needed to use a wheelchair. The landlord told the couple that they had a "no-wheelchairs policy." After being slapped with a fair housing complaint, the landlord agreed to pay the couple $35,000, modify apartments as needed to make them more accessible, get fair housing training for staff, advertise a nondiscrimination policy, and submit the next three years of rental records to the Department of Justice for monitoring.

How you can avoid it. Understand that the ban on disability discrimination bars you from making rules that keep any disabled prospects off your property. Having a "no-wheelchair policy" may imply that you'll rent to people who have less serious mobility impairments or other types of disabilities. But it still violates the law because prospects who use wheelchairs have a right to fair housing, too.

Modification Requests: Take all requests seriously and grant the reasonable ones

Once you determine that your property is either not covered by the FHA design and construction rules or is in compliance with these rules, you may think you're done with thinking about accessibility. That would be a mistake. Regardless of whether your property is exempt from or perfectly in compliance with FHA rules, you may still need to respond to a disabled person's special request for physical modifications of your rental property. For example, although your single-family residence isn't covered by the requirements, a disabled applicant or tenant may expect you to install grab bars. Or, an applicant for your completely accessible ground-floor apartment may still ask you to consider a unique modification, for instance by asking you to widen an interior door beyond what HUD's safe harbors recommend. When prospects and tenants request modifications, take each request very seriously.

Common Modification Requests

The following common requests are usually considered reasonable:

- installing grab bars in bathrooms
- lowering kitchen cabinets
- widening entryways to rooms
- modifying sidewalk pavement to allow easy wheelchair access from your parking lot, and
- adding a ramp to the door of an apartment.

Verifying disabled status

Now, suppose an applicant or a tenant asks for one of the modifications mentioned above. Are you automatically required to supply it? No—unless the tenant is legally "disabled," as described above in "What Does 'Disabled' Mean?" You have the right to ask the prospect or tenant to give you a statement from a physician or other medical professional that says the prospect or tenant is legally disabled and needs the modification in order to live safely and comfortably on your property. Do not, however, ask prospects and tenants for more information about the nature or extent of their disabilities. For example, you might respond to a modification request by saying, "We'll definitely consider the request. To do so, I just need to ask for written confirmation from a professional, such as your doctor, that you're disabled and that you need this modification. The doctor should not explain what your disability is or why you need the modification."

If the disability is obvious—such as when a prospect is in a wheelchair and asks for a ramp—skip the verification request altogether. (If you proceed with it, you risk that the prospect will accuse you of harassment.)

Deciding whether to grant the request

Once you have the verification you need from prospects and tenants about their disabled status, consider the requests on a case-by-case basis and grant them if they're reasonable. Requests are likely to be unreasonable if they would cause damage or stress to your building, pose a threat to other tenants, change the fundamental nature of your building, or present a serious architectural challenge. For example, you'd be on solid ground if you denied a request to reconstruct the apartment so that the kitchen is on the other side.

CAUTION

You can't deny a modification request that simply asks you to conform to construction and design standards. If a tenant requests a modification that wouldn't be needed had you properly constructed your building in compliance with the FHA's design and construction requirements, then you must make the modification—at your own expense. Why? In such a situation, it's not a true modification request but a matter of retrofitting your building to correct your violation of the requirements.

You're not required to come up with alternatives if you deny a prospect's or tenant's modification request because it's unreasonable. But if you think of another modification that you believe would work, you may certainly suggest it. For example, if a tenant who uses a wheelchair asks you to double the size of his bathroom, you can offer instead to widen the doorway to ensure access, if that is the issue. Even if prospects and tenants reject your suggestions, the fact that you've taken this extra step could help you if you ever need to make the case that you take modification requests seriously.

TIP

Keep records to show how you handle modification requests. It's a good idea to keep written records summarizing your prospects' and tenants' modification requests and your responses to them. Doing so will help you remember why you rejected a request if a prospect or tenant later sues you for discrimination. Also, if you must deny a modification request because you believe it's unreasonable, your records can help you show that you've consistently denied all similar requests that tenants at your building have made. Use a log like the Modification Request Log shown below, which recounts a landlord's resolution of a modification request on a property that was not covered by the FHA's design and construction requirements.

It Won't Happen to You ...

What happened. In August 1991, a woman renting an apartment in Florida asked her landlord for a permanent ramp built at her expense as a reasonable modification for her disability. After the landlord denied the tenant's request, she built a temporary ramp so she could finally access her apartment, but the landlord promptly ordered her to remove it, claiming, "Ramps displace landscape." The tenant sued the landlord and settled for $60,000. The landlord agreed to let the tenant add the ramp, as well as having its property inspected for accessibility compliance and getting training for its staff.

How you can avoid it. This landlord didn't understand that fair housing compliance trumps landscaping concerns. Consider whether modification requests place an undue burden on your business or property—not whether they adversely affect your property's overall aesthetic appeal.

Modification Request Log

Property: <u>1240 Marilyn Avenue, Akron, Ohio</u>

Date of request	Unit	Tenant making request	Modification requested	Granted? (Yes/No; include date)	Explanation
May 1, 2008	5B	Peter Smith	Grab bars added to bathroom walls	Yes, on May 9, 2008	Tenant supplied letter from doctor attesting to tenant's disabled status and need for modification. Cost to install bars: $400. Tenant agrees to remove grab bars at end of tenancy

Who pays?

Generally, tenants who make modification requests are responsible for paying for them, whether the modifications are to the tenant's own living space or to common areas. But before you breathe a sigh of relief, note that if your building is federally financed, then you must pay for your tenants' reasonable modifications. If your building gets only state or local assistance, it too may be subject to this same requirement. The compliance officer you deal with at your state or local housing agency can tell you whether you have such a requirement. Also, your state may require you to pay for modification requests under certain circumstances. For example, if your property is located in Massachusetts and has ten or more apartments, then you must pay for your tenants' reasonable modifications.

> **CAUTION**
> **Don't require tenants to pay a higher security deposit to compensate you for the extra time and effort you and your staff may spend handling a modification request.** Doing so will expose you to an expensive charge of discrimination. You can, however, expect the tenant to undo the modification when the tenancy ends, as explained below.

Undoing the modification

When considering requests for modifications inside apartments, you may condition your approval on the tenant's written promise to restore the rental to its original condition when the tenant moves out (reasonable wear and tear excepted). However, you may do this only if it's reasonable to restore the unit. For example, if you let a tenant remove a storage cabinet under the sink in her bathroom, it's usually reasonable to require her to replace the cabinet when her lease ends and before she vacates her apartment.

You're entitled to more than the tenant's promise. To ensure there will be funds available to pay for restorations at the end of a tenancy, you may require a tenant to put money (not exceeding the cost of the restoration) into an interest-bearing escrow account. The interest belongs to the tenant.

Ensuring against a problem with the modification

Not all modifications are simple or without risk. For example, constructing the modification may involve getting into plumbing, electrical, or structural systems. If the work is done poorly, you could have a problem. To reduce the risk you run every time someone aims a hammer, saw, or even a screwdriver at your property, get some concrete proof that the work will be done well. You can require your tenant to give you a description of the modification and reasonable assurances that the modification will be made in a workmanlike manner and after receiving any required building permits. For example, you can request a statement to this effect from a licensed contractor.

Got Accessible Apartments? Market Them!

If you've equipped some apartments with accessible features, let the people who are looking for such features in your area know that you've got them. The National Accessible Apartment Clearinghouse (NAAC), sponsored by the National Apartment Association (NAA), the National Multi Housing Council, and the Virginia Housing Development Authority, host a free, searchable database of thousands of accessible apartments in more than 155 major metropolitan regions, at www.accessibleapartments.org. The database currently holds more than 80,000 apartments across all 50 states, according to the NAAC.

You can register your property and market your accessible apartments at no charge. Prospects who find your property through a search can use the contact information you provide to get in touch with you and visit your available apartments.

Accessibility: My To-Do List

In Step Three, you learned about basic accessibility requirements for buildings that are covered by the Fair Housing Act's design and construction guidelines, and you learned how to handle modification requests. Use the checklist below to help you systematically evaluate your property and your business approach to this important area.

☐ **Compliance:** Determine whether my property must comply with the FHA's design and construction requirements.

☐ **Compliance:** Become familiar with the design and construction requirements, and figure out whether my property complies.

☐ **Retrofitting:** If my property doesn't comply with the design and construction requirements, take steps to retrofit the property, as needed.

☐ **Parking:** Make sure there are enough parking spaces designated for disabled tenants.

☐ **Common areas:** Check to see that common and public use areas are accessible to people with disabilities.

☐ **Reasonable approach:** Take physical modification requests seriously and grant them if they're reasonable, even if I rarely encounter prospects who have noticeable disabilities.

☐ **Cost:** Understand who pays for a physical modification.

☐ **Verification:** Know how to ask tenants for a statement in writing from a third party that verifies their disabled status and shows their need for a requested modification.

☐ **Undoing modifications:** Understand how to ensure that tenants will remove their requested modifications when they move out of their apartment.

Remove Environmental Hazards From Your Property

Providing a physically sound rental property (covered in Step Two) involves more than ensuring adequate lighting or safe staircases. There's one type of physical hazard that's in a class all by itself: environmental hazards. These hazards are the result of naturally occurring elements that have been left unchecked and may cause serious health problems (and, in some cases, property damage).

Removing environmental hazards is a little trickier than removing other physical hazards. Why? Generally speaking, physical hazards are visible, even though the risk they pose may not be so obvious. For example, you can see that an alley between two buildings on your property is too dark because of broken light bulbs, or there's a loose step on the front stairs (an accident waiting to happen). It's not too much of a stretch to conclude that a dark alleyway invites crime, and that a loose step can lead to a slip-and-fall. When hazards can be spotted, either by you or a tenant who brings a repair issue to your attention, they somehow seem more manageable.

Environmental hazards, on the other hand, are hazards that typically can't be seen. Often, it's not until these hazards cause injury or property damage that they become apparent—for example, you may first learn of lead paint dust on your property when your tenant gives you his child's medical results showing elevated levels of lead in his blood. What's more, in some cases environmental hazards remain invisible even once they've caused damage, as with carbon monoxide or radon.

Fortunately, you don't need to wait until environmental hazards cause serious damage before you can address them. Step Four is dedicated to letting you know about the most common types of environmental hazards that may lurk at your property, and showing you practical ways that you, your employees, and your tenants can keep your property and everyone on it safe.

Environmental Hazards: A Rogue's Gallery

Environmental hazards are often hidden, shifty, and deadly, and oddly enough, they may be better left alone. You'll read all about these nasty characters in this chapter. But first, here's a thumbnail sketch.

Hazard	Where does it come from?	What does it do?	How do you deal with it?
Lead paint dust	Deteriorated paint that was manufactured before 1978; lead can also leach from lead water pipes and lead solder	Causes serious health problems such as brain damage, attention-deficit disorders, and hyperactivity, especially among children	Disclose lead paint hazards and provide information to tenants; encapsulate, enclose, or remove deteriorated lead paint
Asbestos	Insulation around heating systems, in ceilings, and in other areas (common before the mid-1970s); building materials, such as vinyl flooring and tiles (common before 1981), and sprayed-on acoustic ceilings	Increases risk of cancer	Avoid disturbing asbestos-containing materials; follow OSHA regulations to protect tenants and employees
Mold	A microscopic organism with several varieties, mold grows on porous substances and thrives under warm, humid conditions	Believed to be responsible for a wide range of health ailments, such as asthma, rashes, nausea, and chronic fatigue syndrome	Prevent buildup by promptly fixing leaks and providing adequate ventilation; clean up suspected mold promptly
Carbon monoxide (CO)	A colorless, odorless, lethal gas, it's the by-product of fuel combustion	When inhaled, causes problems ranging from dizziness, nausea, confusion, and fatigue to unconsciousness, brain damage, and even death	Practice regular maintenance to check for malfunctioning appliances, and clogged vents, flues, and chimneys
Radon	A naturally occurring radioactive gas, it's found in buildings built on uranium-rich soil that have tight insulation	Causes lung cancer	Take steps to ventilate the building

What Do You Have to Lose?

Environmental hazards are serious matters. Certain hazards, such as carbon monoxide, have the power to ruin people's lives, if not take them instantly. Others, such as some molds or lead paint dust, can cause serious illness or other medical problems over time. To add insult to injury, mold can also cause property damage. And even if an environmental hazard on your property doesn't actually cause harm, chances are its presence is a violation of a federal, state, or local law, especially if you're aware of the hazard and do nothing about it.

The consequences to you, in terms of dollars, time, and energy, range from inconvenient but minor repairs, to major repairs and then, if someone is hurt, to expensive insurance claims or even lawsuits. The money you'll spend to settle a simple slip-and-fall at your property is insignificant compared to the cost of a child's lead-poisoned and impaired mental development.

Is This You?

Environmental hazards are a fact of life for every landlord, even those who promptly take care of repair requests and problems they discover on their own. You'll be one step ahead of the game if you've completed Step Two's "To Do" list and addressed physical hazards on your property—for example, making sure your downspouts are functioning properly will not only remove the chance that people will slip in a puddle, it will also take away moisture that mold needs in order to flourish behind a wall. But because some environmental problems are so downright sneaky, even conscientious landlords often miss them. See if you recognize yourself in any of the following descriptions.

Do You Think About Environmental Hazards Like These Landlords?

☐ You can't confidently say you're following all federal, state, and local laws regarding lead paint.

☐ You don't know whether you must follow any lead paint disclosure rules when making renovations or repairs to your buildings.

☐ You think mold is just an aesthetic issue, and that as long as you don't notice any mold at your property, you don't have a mold problem.

☐ You wait until tenants complain about mold before taking any action to address or prevent it.

☐ You don't require tenants to let you know about all leaks and flooding— even the water problems they claim to have fixed on their own.

☐ You don't know whether your building contains asbestos.

☐ You don't want to get your building tested to determine whether it has asbestos because you're afraid it will mean you must tear parts of it down.

☐ You know or suspect that your building has asbestos in it, but you nevertheless make repairs to your building without hiring specialized contractors who are trained to deal with the presence of asbestos.

☐ You don't know whether owners of other buildings in your area are dealing with a radon problem.

☐ You haven't thought about installing carbon monoxide detectors, or you're not sure where they should be located.

☐ You think there's only so much you can do to prevent or control environmental hazards as compared to physical hazards.

Take Action!

If you see yourself or your property in any of the portraits described above, it's time to take action. In the sections below, you'll learn practical strategies to follow right now that cover each of the major environmental hazards you're likely to face as a landlord. Understanding these approaches will ensure that you're aware of the harm that each environmental hazard poses. And adopting them will let you succeed in minimizing, if not eliminating, environmental hazards from your property.

Lead paint dust: Avoid creating it, clean it up

Before 1978, lead was quite commonly used in apartment buildings, primarily in paint but also in other materials, such as solder on copper water pipes. As the paint deteriorates, it creates flakes or dust laced with lead. Children ingest the lead when the dust travels from floor or windowsill to toys, hands, and finally mouth. Today, we know that lead paint exposure can lead to learning disabilities, hyperactivity, hearing loss, and even serious brain damage and mental retardation.

The Residential Lead-Based Paint Hazard Reduction Act (enacted in 1992 and commonly known as "Title X" [Ten]), applies to most properties constructed before 1978. If you own such a property, the law presumes that your property contains lead, with a few exceptions. Most notably, you needn't comply with Title X if your building is certified as lead-free by a state-accredited lead inspector, or you run a senior housing community or housing for people with disabilities, unless children under six may occupy any of your apartments. (If your buildings fit into one of these exceptions, you can confidently skip this section. However, check your state law for requirements that may apply.)

Fortunately, if Title X applies to your property or you know that your property contains lead, you don't need to tear down walls or rebuild. But there are some things you need to do.

Almost all states also have laws protecting people from lead. In addition to banning lead-based paint, the laws usually require landlords to monitor and maintain existing lead-based paint and building materials that contain lead. Often, states require lead abatement projects to be performed by licensed contractors. Some states require additional types of notifications. For example, West Virginia requires landlords to notify the state health department before undertaking lead abatement projects, and Maryland requires landlords to register their properties.

Disclosure rules: Tell tenants about lead and what you know about your property

If you own a pre-1978 property, you must tell tenants and applicants about the dangers of lead paint dust, and you must disclose what you know about the presence of this hazard on your property (for example, if you're certified lead-free, you need to show tenants and applicants a copy of a state-certified lead inspector's report). This disclosure rule comes from Title X—among other requirements, the disclosure rules require you to give tenants the U.S. Environmental Protection Agency (EPA) pamphlet, *Protect Your Family From Lead in Your Home* at lease signing and at each renewal. You must also give tenants a lead paint disclosure form in or with your lease and have them initial it to acknowledge receipt of both the form and the EPA pamphlet.

To get a copy of the pamphlet in different languages and formats, visit www.epa.gov (type the name of the pamphlet in the home page search box). You can also request copies be sent to you in the mail by visiting www.epa.gov/lead/pubs/nlicdocs.htm or calling 800-424-LEAD. To get a copy of the disclosure form, visit www.epa.gov/lead/pubs/lesr_eng.pdf.

Disclosure rules: Inform tenants when renovating

Many landlords who own pre-1978 buildings don't realize they must comply with additional disclosure rules when renovating their buildings, even when doing small renovations. For lead paint disclosure purposes, a "renovation" is any activity that disturbs two or more square feet of paint on a wall or any other building component. So if you must open a wall to make repairs to your electrical or plumbing system, you'll probably have to comply with the notification requirements.

To comply, you (or your contractor) must give the EPA pamphlet to tenants in all affected apartments. If renovations are to your common area, make the pamphlet available to tenants and give them a renovation notice that describes the nature and location of the work, along with the dates. You must either start the work within 60 days or send a supplemental renovation notice.

For a helpful compliance tool, including a sample renovation notice you can use, read the EPA pamphlet, *The Lead-Based Paint Pre-Renovation Education Rule*. To download a copy of this pamphlet, visit www.epa.gov/lead and type the name of the pamphlet into the home page search box.

Maintenance: Monitor lead paint

If you know your building has lead or even think that it might, it's important to monitor your apartments and common areas to make sure lead-based surfaces don't deteriorate. If you perform annual or semi-annual inspections of your apartments (which is highly advisable for spotting all types of hazards and other maintenance issues), look for lead dust and signs of deterioration, such as chipping, peeling paint. Take steps such as cleaning up dust with a high-efficiency particulate air ("HEPA") vacuum and repainting with a fresh coat of non-lead-based paint.

It Won't Happen to You ...

What happened. In a case involving a child's brain damage due to lead poisoning, a New York landlord was ordered to pay $4.5 million in damages. Rejecting the landlord's claim that this was a case of "genetics," the jury found that the landlord ignored repeated requests for repairs concerning the lead paint by both the tenants and a city health agency.

How you can avoid it. This landlord knew full well that he had lead on his property, yet he failed to take prompt, remedial action (such as covering or removing the aging lead-based paint). Once you learn that lead is an unwanted resident at your property, you can lessen the chances that someone will be hurt (and you'll be sued) by taking these steps.

Cleanup or removal: Hire qualified workers

Most states and some cities require a license or certification to perform lead abatement work, and offer a training program for this purpose. You may find it helpful to have someone on your staff become licensed or get licensed yourself. Otherwise, hire a contractor who's licensed with your state or city. If your property is in a state and city that doesn't require a license or certificate for lead abatement work, try to find a contractor who's licensed in another state. If not, hire a contractor who's been trained to conduct lead-based paint inspections and risk assessments, preferably based on coursework created by the EPA or your state. Also, check the references of the last few lead inspections or risk assessments the contractor performed.

To find qualified contractors, consider a trusted recommendation or contact your regional EPA office for assistance. Visit www.epa.gov/epahome/locate2.htm for more information.

Tenant education: Support your tenants' efforts

Help your tenants control and clean up any lead dust that may be present in their apartments. Instead of just handing them the disclosure and EPA pamphlet, encourage tenants to communicate with you about the state of the paint on their walls, windowsills, and door thresholds. If the paint peels or chips, tell tenants to remove the chips and dust and notify you promptly so that, using a HEPA vacuum for proper cleanup of any remaining lead dust, you can make sure all the pieces are removed.

Record keeping: Keep good records to prove you've complied with the law

Keep records of your compliance with lead paint laws by saving the disclosure form receipts and documenting your renovation activities. (In fact, federal law requires you to keep disclosure form receipts, as well as a list of available lead-related records and reports, for three years from the start of the lease.) Also keep renovation notices you send to tenants, along with receipts (or self-certification of delivery) and certificates of mailing, for three years. A complete file for every apartment will enable you to show that you followed the law, if tenants later claim that you're responsible for their child's elevated blood-lead level.

Asbestos: Don't let it get into the air

Asbestos is a microscopic mineral fiber that was used for years to strengthen building products such as pipes, flooring, and siding, and to insulate heating ducts. Asbestos was popular because it was not only strong, but provided effective fire resistance and heat insulation. In houses and apartment complexes, asbestos is most likely to be present in insulation, vinyl floor tiles, hot water and steam pipes, and roofing and siding shingles, among other places (see the list below).

As asbestos-containing building materials aged over the years or became damaged, asbestos showed itself to be a very serious environmental hazard. Microscopic asbestos fibers become airborne when asbestos is disturbed by renovation or even wear and tear. When people inhale these fibers, they can develop serious health problems, most notably mesothelioma (a rare form of cancer affecting the chest and abdominal cavity lining), asbestosis (lung scarring from fiber irritation), and lung cancer. Tenants and other asbestos victims may not develop symptoms of any disease until 20 or even 30 years after first exposure to asbestos fibers.

Fortunately, few products today contain asbestos. Although asbestos was widely used in textured paint and in patching compounds, this use was banned in 1977. Federal law now requires that any asbestos-containing products made in the United States today be properly labeled. Although it's quite unlikely you'll buy asbestos-containing products, it's still worth making sure you and your contractors keep an eye out to check that products you buy don't carry this label. Also check any products you recently bought but haven't yet used. If you discover they contain asbestos, exchange them for a safer replacement.

If you own a property built in the 1980s or earlier, there's a very good chance that your property contains asbestos. See "Where is Asbestos Found?" below, for a listing of the most likely places.

Where Is Asbestos Found?

According to the Environmental Protection Agency, these items are among the most common to contain asbestos.

acoustical plaster	fire curtains
adhesives	fire doors
asphalt floor tile	fireproofing materials
base flashing	flooring backing
blown-in insulation	heating and electrical ducts
boiler insulation	high-temperature gaskets
breaching insulation	HVAC duct insulation
caulking/putties	joint compounds
ceiling tiles and lay-in panels	laboratory gloves
cement pipes	laboratory hoods/table tops
cement siding	packing materials (for wall/floor
cement wallboard	penetrations)
chalkboards	pipe insulation (corrugated air-cell,
construction mastics (floor tile,	block, etc.)
carpet, ceiling tile, etc.)	roofing felt
cooling towers	roofing shingles
decorative plaster	spackling compounds
ductwork (flexible fabric	spray-applied insulation
connections)	taping compounds (thermal)
electric wiring insulation	textured paints/coatings
electrical cloth	thermal paper products
electrical panel partitions	vinyl floor tile
elevator brake shoes	vinyl sheet flooring
elevator equipment panels	vinyl wall coverings
fire blankets	wallboard

If you know or suspect that your property has asbestos, it's not necessarily a cause for alarm. As with lead paint, if asbestos is intact (with no fibers sloughing off), you may be better off just leaving it alone and monitoring its condition. Or, your best course may be to cover it up, again as with lead paint. Let's go through the steps a conscientious landlord will take to discover the condition of asbestos-containing items, and learn what to do about what you find.

Detection: Find out if your property has asbestos-containing materials

First, you'll need to determine whether your property contains materials with asbestos. If your building was built before 1981 and you suspect it contains asbestos, you should operate under the presumption that it does. The only way to know for certain is to have the building tested by a qualified inspector who has EPA- or state-approved training and is licensed by your state or city (if your state or city has a licensing requirement). Testing is not required by law.

Some parts of your building that might contain asbestos aren't likely to pose a health risk because they're hidden or difficult to access, such as hot water and steam pipes. Likely culprits, however, may include items such as the backing on vinyl sheet flooring and adhesives for installing floor tiles, an asbestos blanket or paper tape insulating your boiler, and textured paints and patching compounds on your walls.

Assessment: Is your asbestos intact, or airborne?

If you know or even suspect you have asbestos in your building, it's no cause for alarm. But it is time to commit to a course of action to avoid a situation where your asbestos starts creating problems for you and your tenants.

Asbestos isn't dangerous if the material that houses it is in good condition, so rest easy knowing that the best thing to do with such materials is to simply leave them alone. Materials that get disturbed, however, pose a health risk because they're likely to release dangerous fibers into the air. Look for signs, such as tears, cracks, abrasions, and water damage, that indicate materials have been disturbed.

Keep watching out for disturbed asbestos, and with any luck, you won't discover any problems. But if you do encounter materials that you suspect may be releasing fibers, you need to take action to minimize the risk of harm.

Intact asbestos: Watchful monitoring

Having checked materials such as your cement pipes, boiler insulation, and vinyl floor tile, for asbestos, suppose you conclude that the asbestos in them hasn't been disturbed. What next? In most situations, you'll want to use common sense and avoid disturbing these materials. For instance, refrain from activities that can trigger the release of asbestos fibers, such as sanding your walls or drilling through shingles. If asbestos-containing insulation surrounds your furnace, think twice before moving your furnace, as even this could create a problem.

Adopt a watchful "wait and see" program, and take a look at suspect materials every few months or so to check for signs of deterioration. If materials do begin to deteriorate, you'll be ready to either have them removed or covered up.

Deteriorated asbestos: Take action

Your assessment efforts may have revealed that the asbestos on your property is in bad shape. For instance, you may have noticed that cement pipes are rotting, heat insulation is coming apart, or floor tiles are broken. Or, you may have concluded that other items, such as door gaskets and stovetop pads, probably contain asbestos and these items are in poor condition. If this describes your situation, you should take action by appropriately alerting your tenants, and then addressing the problem.

- **Protect your tenants.** If you know or suspect that you have an asbestos problem, whether in a common area or in certain apartments, promptly warn your tenants. Also, be prepared to temporarily relocate tenants (ideally to vacant apartments in another part of your building) until their apartments are once again safe for occupancy.

- **Block off access to the asbestos.** Block access to an affected common area with a warning sign, traffic cones, safety tape, and a lock (if the problem affects an entire room). Don't try to cover up the problematic material or "fix" it in any way—you must leave that part to the professionals.
- **Hire an "asbestos professional" to fix the problem.** The EPA offers asbestos training, and many states require it, for contractors who undertake such work. Depending on the damage, the professional will either repair the material or remove it.

Your professional will probably take one of two approaches to the job. Asbestos material is often repaired by "encapsulation," a method that seals the material so that asbestos fibers bind together and can't become airborne. Another method is "enclosure," which involves carefully covering the material (for example, with a protective jacket) to prevent the fibers from being released. There is a third method, "removal," but this is an expensive option that actually poses an increased risk of fiber release, and so should be considered only as a last resort.

Hire the Right Asbestos Professional

When it comes to fixing an asbestos problem or having work done involving material that you know or suspect contains asbestos, don't hire just any contractor. Make sure the contractor you hire is a trained, if not licensed, asbestos professional. This person will use special equipment and wear protective clothing, such as respirators and gloves. Here are some pointers on finding a good asbestos professional for your building:

- **Insist on specific training.** Ask asbestos professionals about their training and background. The federal government offers courses for asbestos professionals throughout the country. Many state and local governments also offer training and licensing programs.

- **Get proof of training and licensing.** Ask the people you interview for documentation that proves they completed federal or state-approved training and earned a license from your state or local health departments.

- **Check references.** If possible, follow a recommendation from a friend or colleague or from a trusted contractor. If not, ask the professional to provide references so you can find out if other landlords were satisfied with the professional's services.

- **Comparison shop.** Don't be tempted to hire the first asbestos professional who looks good. Because fees can vary considerably, take the time to interview or meet with more than one professional.

Repairs and renovations: Be ready to deal with asbestos

A landlord who has identified, monitored, covered, or encapsulated asbestos might still have to deal with it in another situation—when performing repairs or renovations on asbestos-containing materials that, prior to your work, were in fine shape. For instance, suppose you decide to upgrade your building's plumbing or electrical system, or you're planning to tear down some interior walls to make a one-bedroom apartment into a two-bedroom apartment. Now you're about to disturb those insulated pipes and asbestos-containing ceilings or floors—and you have to deal with the airborne asbestos fibers that your work will create.

If your building was constructed before 1981 and you don't get it inspected to rule out the presence of asbestos, you'll need to comply with OSHA regulations on disclosure and maintenance. Most importantly, make sure the contractor you hire has asbestos training, as well as any licenses required by your state or city. Hiring a contractor who doesn't have this training and isn't familiar with the risks associated with airborne fibers can itself be a serious risk. The contractor's work might result in a very unhealthy, if not deadly, situation for your tenants and the contractor's employees. In addition, anyone who gets sick from asbestos fibers may sue you for not hiring a qualified asbestos contractor. You may also be subject to state fines for violations of their asbestos regulations.

For more information about dealing with asbestos and finding a qualified contractor, read the EPA's "Asbestos in Your Home," which is available at www.epa.gov/asbestos/pubs/ashome.html.

It Won't Happen to You ...

What happened. In 2005, a Cleveland landlord got caught for violating regulations governing the proper disposal of asbestos. When renovating his apartment building, the landlord and his contractor didn't give the Ohio EPA the required five days' notice before starting the renovation, didn't wet friable asbestos materials during removal and processing, and didn't dispose of the material at a landfill licensed to accept asbestos-containing waste. The landlord settled with the Ohio EPA by agreeing to pay a $10,000 penalty.

How you can avoid it. When doing renovations, work with an experienced, licensed asbestos-removal contractor. (A licensed professional is not likely to ignore the rules, given that his license is at stake.) Always follow proper removal and disposal practices.

TIP

Get the best deal. Make sure that the professional who performs the asbestos inspection isn't the same person whom you hire to do the work. If they're one and the same, there's a risk that you'll pay too much because the "inspector" has a financial incentive to have the "fixer" do a lot of work.

Radon: Move it out

Radon is a colorless, odorless, tasteless gas formed by the natural radioactive decay of uranium in rock, soil, and water. Although certain areas of the country are more likely than others to contain higher levels of radon, radon gas can be found in all areas. Radon gets into buildings by moving up from the ground through cracks and other holes in a building's foundation. Once inside a building, radon can get trapped and become a serious hazard. Although radon from soil gas is the main cause of radon problems, radon can also enter buildings through well water.

According to the EPA, radon is the second-leading cause of lung cancer in America, claiming more than 20,000 lives annually. It's also the leading cause of lung cancer among nonsmokers—even deadlier than second-hand smoke. Here's what you need to know about how to find radon and get rid of it.

Detection: Find out if your rentals have dangerous amounts of radon

According to the EPA, any level of radon exposure carries health risks, but the agency recommends that property owners fix radon levels if the property's occupants' exposure will average four picocuries per liter (pCi/L) or higher. (A picocurie is a measure of the rate of radon's radioactive decay.) If you don't know whether your property has high levels of radon, it's a good idea to get it tested. Although you can buy do-it-yourself tests at a home improvement store such as Home Depot or Lowe's or a hardware store, you'll probably want to hire a qualified professional to test your property to ensure accurate results, depending on the size of your property and how much may be at stake. Your professional will likely start with a short-term test, which involves leaving items such as charcoal canisters and charcoal liquid scintillation detectors on your property for a couple of days. The professional may decide to follow up with a long-term test, using devices known as alpha track and electret ion chamber detectors, which stay on your property for more than 90 days.

To find a qualified radon service professional, get in touch with your state radon contact, available at www.epa.gov/iaq/whereyoulive.html. Or, contact the National Environmental Health Association (NEHA) at 800-269-4174 or www.neha-nrpp.org, or the National Radon Safety Board (NRSB) at 866-329-3474. These two private companies have their own nationally recognized certification program for radon professionals. The EPA also has a National Radon Information Line at 800-SOS-RADON (800-767-7236).

TIP

To discover the highest concentrations during the year, test for radon when it's cold outside. During cold winter months, the difference between outdoor and indoor air pressure is greater than when it's warm, which is likely to lead to a higher level of radon entering a building. And apartment buildings and other homes are typically not as ventilated on cold days as they are when it's warm, thus trapping the radon inside.

Removal: Disperse high levels

If your professional tester informs you that your property has a dangerously high level of radon, it's time to take action. Ask the tester about what type of radon reduction techniques would be best for your situation. Keep in mind that there are several techniques, aimed at either preventing radon from entering your building or lowering the levels of radon after it has entered. Not surprisingly, the EPA recommends techniques that fit into the first category (such as "soil suction," which vents radon from the ground through pipes into the air surrounding your building, where it's quickly diluted). If you tested for radon on your own, make sure you hire a qualified radon service professional (see above) to perform any needed mitigation work at your property. Never attempt to get rid of radon on your own.

For help in finding the right qualified contractor for your property, including which questions to ask and how to get the best price, read the EPA's "Consumer's Guide to Radon Reduction" by visiting www.epa.gov (type the name of the pamphlet into the search box). You may also want to read "A Citizen's Guide to Radon," which is a useful general overview.

If you discover high levels of radon at your property, let tenants know about your proactive efforts to fix the problem promptly and your commitment to following your contractor's recommended radon reduction techniques to ensure levels remain low. To educate tenants about radon, offer them a copy of the EPA's "A Radon Guide For Tenants," which is available at the website mentioned above.

Help for Landlords Who Rent to Low-Income Tenants

If you rent to low-income tenants, your property may qualify for funding to reduce high levels of radon in apartment buildings. Federal programs that offer this funding include the Community Development Block Grant (CDBG) program, which is administered by HUD, and Environmental Justice Grants, administered by the EPA's Office of Environmental Justice. Your state may also provide loans for radon reduction work in limited income housing. To learn more about programs or assistance that your state may offer, contact your state radon office. You can access a directory of offices by visiting www.epa.gov/iaq/contacts.html.

Mold: Prevent it, get rid of it

Mold has been in buildings for as long as buildings have existed, but until recently, the unsightly discolorations around windows and in bathrooms were viewed as little more than aesthetic issues. Today, mold is recognized as a potentially serious health threat to tenants, employees, and even guests. And mold litigation—tenants suing landlords who let their buildings get or stay moldy—has become a lucrative legal subspecialty. For this reason alone, it's too risky to ignore this issue.

Mold spores are microscopic and reproduce easily by feeding on porous substances (such as wood, paper, carpeting, and foods) under moist, warm conditions. As they grow, certain molds produce substances that at least some people may find irritating or harmful. Medical science is not of one mind when it comes to understanding the effects of mold spores on people, and it's very difficult for doctors to say for certain whether a person's symptoms are clearly traceable to exposure to a particular mold. Nonetheless, mold has been successfully blamed in court for causing several health problems, including head-aches, nausea, asthma, bronchitis, sinusitis, infections, vertigo, and skin disease. As far as landlords are concerned, the question isn't whether a particular mold did or didn't cause the problems a tenant is complaining about—your job is to try to never get there, by doing your best to prevent and remove any mold, however innocuous you think it is.

Apart from mold's real or imagined effect on health, it can also cause substantial property damage, costing you a tremendous amount of money in professional removal efforts. Very often, mold grows out of sight behind walls, floors, and ceilings. By the time it's discovered, it may be so widespread that it's no longer possible to remove it. Instead, the only way to fix the problem is to remove the affected walls, floors, and ceilings themselves and replace them with new parts and materials.

Prevention: Maintain plumbing and fix leaks

Your first step toward diminishing the risk of mold in your rental property involves simple maintenance. Mold needs moisture to grow. If you maintain your plumbing and drain systems, including roof runoff, you've gone a long way toward making this problem nonexistent at your property. Careful property owners will regularly check their building systems and promptly remedy any problems. You'll want to be particularly attentive when you ready a new apartment for occupancy, and you should tell your maintenance workers to be on the lookout for problems when they enter tenants' apartments to perform any type of maintenance.

You'll need to follow your state's rules regarding tenant privacy when scheduling an inspection of their rental. Unless it's an emergency, tenants have the right to reasonable notice before you enter their apartments to make repairs. Depending on your state law, you may need to give up to 24 to 48 hours' notice (see the appendix for a list of your state's laws). If tenants agree to a shorter notice period or say it's fine to come right over, you of course may do so.

 TIP

Most tenants will cooperate by letting you make repairs to their apartment. After all, it's in their best interest to do so. But if you have trouble, keep a copy of your written notice or a log documenting any oral notice you give tenants before you enter. This will help show tenants you respected their privacy and abided by the law.

Prevention: Enlist your tenants' help

Even the best maintenance system can't completely anticipate and prevent accidents or sudden equipment failure. Your tenants are often in the best position to alert you to these occurrences—after all, they live there. Be sure your house rules tell tenants to alert you after a leak or flood occurs—even if they believe they've fixed the problem and cleaned up the water themselves. Tenants should also contact you if they observe any mold on walls, ceilings, or other parts of their apartment.

When you (or your contractor) investigate, make sure that there are no lingering or unseen problems. Despite a tenant's cleaning efforts, you may discover there's enough moisture to pose a mold threat. And even if all the moisture is gone, you may still need to determine the cause of the leak or flood, so that the problem doesn't reoccur. You may want to send a periodic reminder to tenants (for example, seasonally, as the weather starts to get warm) about the importance of promptly reporting leaks and floods.

It Won't Happen to You ...

What happened. In 2006, a group of Maryland tenants sued their landlord for failing to maintain the property in a reasonably safe condition. Although the tenants notified the landlord about a water problem, the landlord didn't respond to their repair requests. The ensuing mold caused serious injuries, requiring multiple hospitalizations and significant out-of-pocket expenses. The tenants won a $270,000 verdict.

How you can avoid it. Never ignore a tenant's request to repair a leak. At best, you'll face property damage that will grow worse along with the mold, and at worst, you'll be hit with a personal injury lawsuit, as happened here.

Detection: Trust your eyes and your nose

It can be painfully obvious that your property has a mold problem. You'll see the stains and discolorations that accompany many types of mold. But don't assume mold isn't present simply because you can't see it. Mold may be lurking behind walls and other parts of your building that are out of sight. If tenants report a strange, musty odor, or if many of your tenants suddenly get sick, take it as a sign that you may have a mold problem in your building and investigate promptly.

Mold buildup: Remove it

Because mold can spread so easily and quickly, acting fast is key to preventing serious property damage and health risks. If tenants, employees, contractors, or visitors report seeing mold, hire a professional with solid references to test for mold and then follow the tester's recommendations for fixing the problem immediately. Unlike the case with lead and asbestos, there are no federal or state licenses for mold remediation companies. However, organizations such as the National Mold Institute (www.nationalmoldinstitute.com), the National Association of Mold Professionals (www.moldpro.org), and the Environmental Solutions Association (www.esaenviro.com), among others, offer training and certification programs. When interviewing a company, make sure you learn that it follows EPA recommendations, the American Industrial Hygiene Associates (AIHA) guidelines, or other industry standards and has experience removing mold from your type of building. To avoid a conflict of interest, make sure the tester you hire isn't the same person or company you hire to perform remediation work.

Carbon Monoxide: Detect it instantly

It's known as "the colorless, odorless gas," and it can kill within minutes. This scary environmental hazard is carbon monoxide (CO), and it can be a major problem in an apartment building. According to the *Journal of the American Medical Association*, CO is the number one cause of poisoning deaths in the United States.

CO is produced when a fossil fuel, such as gas, oil, or wood, burns in a gas or oil furnace, water heater, fireplace, or similar appliance. If these appliances aren't properly vented (for example, when there's a clogged chimney), CO may seep into living spaces and other populated areas of a building. The symptoms of CO poisoning include headache, fatigue, shortness of breath, nausea, and vertigo. Because CO is an invisible gas, most people who are poisoned with low concentrations of this gas don't seek help for these symptoms because they mistakenly think they're just not feeling well.

Because landlords are charged with maintaining their building systems, including heating, they are often held responsible when a heating system ventilation problem causes CO buildup. When a tenant is injured or killed due to CO exposure, the consequences to you will be dire—thousands of dollars in damages, on top of living with the knowledge that someone has been hurt or killed. Fortunately, you can reduce this risk by vigilant maintenance (and proper early warning equipment), as explained below.

Prevention: Maintain all heating systems and appliances

The way to prevent CO poisoning is simple: Maintain and promptly repair every heating system and appliance. Proper ventilation will waft this would-be killer to the great outdoors, where it will do no harm.

Your heating system may need repair even if tenants haven't complained about the heat and your building seems quite warm. Properties in areas with long, cold winters put a sizable strain on their heating equipment, and over time the ventilation systems can become clogged by soot, rust, or even birds' nests.

Your heating company probably offers plans for regular maintenance of your system, including tune-ups, in return for a modest annual fee. Signing up for regular service not only helps prolong the life of your furnace and other heating equipment, but even more importantly, it should help remove the risk of developing a CO problem at your property.

Detection: Install detectors and make sure they work

CO detectors are like smoke alarms—they sound a shrill alert when they detect CO. They aren't expensive (they typically cost between $50 and $75) and can literally be a lifesaver by alerting tenants to a CO problem before it has a chance to cause any serious harm. Not surprisingly, many municipalities in the country now require CO detectors. Even if not required by law, it's a good idea to have detectors in place throughout your building.

The Consumer Product Safety Commission recommends placing detectors outside bedrooms and making sure that furniture and draperies don't cover up the alarm. It is also a good idea to place them near fuel-burning appliances that emit CO. However, avoid placing detectors directly above or beside such appliances, within 15 feet of heating or cooking appliances, or in or near humid areas such as bathrooms.

Finally, make sure you and your tenants follow the manufacturer's instructions for proper use of your CO detectors, and that you inspect them annually to make sure they're working properly.

It Won't Happen to You ...

What happened. In 2000, a Chicago tenant and her two daughters died of carbon monoxide poisoning from a 1950s heater behind their bedroom wall in their apartment building. When city inspectors discovered that the landlords' seven properties had a whopping 387 building code violations, including 52 violations at the property where the tenants died, the landlords agreed to an extraordinary settlement. For the first time in Chicago Housing Court history, the landlords agreed to sell all seven of their properties, give the proceeds to the victims' family, and never again own or manage rental property in Chicago.

How you can avoid it. This is an extreme example of what can happen when landlords ignore laws and ordinances that are designed to ensure tenants' safety. But don't imagine that a single violation will entitle you to a pass—especially if a tenant is hurt, she can use the fact that you didn't follow the law as powerful evidence against you in court.

4 Environmental Hazards: My To-Do List

In Step Four, you learned about environmental hazards, which come in a handful of nasty varieties and can be responsible for serious health problems, not to mention property damage. You also read about what you can do to control environmental hazards and even prevent them from creating problems. Use the checklist below to help you accomplish these goals.

☐ **Lead paint dust:** Learn what my state law requires.

☐ **Lead paint dust:** Warn tenants and applicants about lead and disclose lead information about my property.

☐ **Lead paint dust:** Inform tenants about lead before renovations.

☐ **Lead paint dust:** Monitor lead-based surfaces for signs of deterioration.

☐ **Lead paint dust:** Buy a high-efficiency particulate air ("HEPA") vacuum for my property.

☐ **Lead paint dust:** Use qualified contractors who know how to deal with lead.

☐ **Lead paint dust:** Encourage my tenants to communicate with me about accumulations.

☐ **Lead paint dust:** Keep disclosure form receipts and other records to prove compliance.

☐ **Asbestos:** Check property for asbestos-containing materials.

☐ **Asbestos:** Keep an eye out for disturbed asbestos.

☐ **Asbestos:** Protect tenants, block off access, and hire an asbestos professional to address deteriorated asbestos issues.

☐ **Radon:** Get my property tested by a professional.

☐ **Radon:** Take action to disperse high levels out of my building.

☐ **Mold:** Fix leaks promptly and focus on preventing reoccurrence.

☐ **Mold:** Get tenants to help by reporting all leaks and floods.

☐ **Mold:** Remove all mold before it can grow into an even bigger problem.

☐ **Carbon monoxide:** Maintain and repair heating system and appliances.

☐ **Carbon monoxide:** Install detectors in key places and make sure they work.

Prepare for and Handle Disasters and Emergencies

Being a landlord can be tough under normal, everyday circumstances. But how about during an emergency? Have you spent much time thinking about what you would do if there were a fire, flood, bomb, or other disaster at your property? Do you have a plan for evacuating tenants and employees to safety, and how would you account for everyone? Is your property equipped with basic first-aid items? Are your important documents and computer files safe?

These are just some of the many questions landlords need to consider, no matter how carefully they've followed the accident-avoidance recommendations outlined in previous chapters. It's impossible to anticipate—let alone prevent—every misfortune. But taking time to prepare for disasters and plan for emergencies will enable you to handle these situations confidently and effectively, if and when they arise.

Step Five tackles the ugly threat of emergencies and disasters head-on. You'll learn how to take action by discovering ways to lower the risk that certain disasters or emergencies will occur, and to prepare for the possibility that an unpreventable misfortune strikes.

What Do You Have to Lose?

Unlike with most other chapters in this book, you don't need to read in detail about how much you have to lose from a disaster or other large-scale emergency at your property. Fires, floods, earthquakes, bombs, or any other widespread assault or service deprivation can result in serious injury or loss of life, property damage, and business interruption. Plus, if tenants believe that you acted carelessly during and after such a disaster or emergency, and thereby made it worse, you could face lawsuits for compounding their losses—the last thing you need while you're trying to steer your business toward recovery.

Disasters and emergencies can strike in many forms. Here's a sampling of just some of the emergency situations you may face when you own rental housing, especially a multifamily apartment building:

- A nearby plant accidentally releases toxic chemicals, poisoning the air.
- Severe storms overwhelm city drains, flooding your building and making it impossible to enter or leave.
- Fires engulf the neighborhood, threatening to spread to your building soon.
- A citywide blackout persists for days, making it impossible for you to access key computer files in your office.
- A tenant or visitor suffers a heart attack on your property.
- Your manager opens a package from a disgruntled former tenant, which explodes or contains a powder or other mysterious substance.
- The manager receives a threatening phone call, warning of a bomb on your property.

There's no denying that the likelihood of these events happening at your property is comparatively small, and you may feel that your efforts and money will be better spent making sure your property is free of the more common hazards that bedevil landlords and frequently result in accidents (such as burnt-out lighting). But, given the seriousness of the harm a disaster or other emergency can cause, it would be a mistake to let the lower statistical chance of an emergency dictate your priorities. As you'll see in "Take Action!," the steps you can take to prepare for an emergency aren't too difficult or costly, and will prove well worth your effort should they ever come into play.

Is This You?

Because disasters and other major emergencies are relatively unlikely, chances are you're not doing everything you can to make sure that you and your staff are totally prepared to handle them. And you might not be taking the proactive steps and vigilant measures you need to stave off disasters effectively. See if you recognize yourself in any of the following portraits.

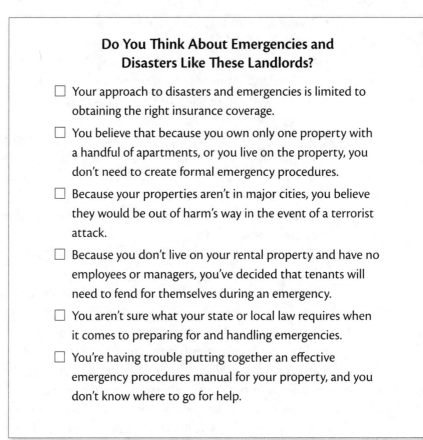

Do You Think About Emergencies and Disasters Like These Landlords?

☐ Your approach to disasters and emergencies is limited to obtaining the right insurance coverage.

☐ You believe that because you own only one property with a handful of apartments, or you live on the property, you don't need to create formal emergency procedures.

☐ Because your properties aren't in major cities, you believe they would be out of harm's way in the event of a terrorist attack.

☐ Because you don't live on your rental property and have no employees or managers, you've decided that tenants will need to fend for themselves during an emergency.

☐ You aren't sure what your state or local law requires when it comes to preparing for and handling emergencies.

☐ You're having trouble putting together an effective emergency procedures manual for your property, and you don't know where to go for help.

If you recognized yourself in the descriptions above, don't fret. Read on to learn what you can do to prepare for and handle emergencies that occur at your property.

Take Action!

The following strategies are divided into three groups: those that will help you lower the chances that a disaster will strike at your property; those that will prepare you to deal with disasters, should they strike; and those that you can use to minimize the consequences and return your business to normalcy after a disaster has arrived.

Lower the risk a disaster—or its consequences—will occur

While you can't prevent every misfortune, you can be on the lookout for common disasters and deflect some that may be headed your way. You can also take steps to minimize the consequences of an unavoidable disaster. Let's look at three quick, easy preventive measures you can take that will also ensure peace of mind.

Protect key documents from disasters

No matter what the large-scale physical disaster—fire, flood, explosion, electrical failure and so on—you can at least take solace knowing you'll get help from your property insurance. But insurance proceeds won't replace important documents or reconstruct the contents of computer files relating to your property or business if they are destroyed. Dealing with the loss of important documents and files could be an expensive nightmare:

- Your leases and rental agreements are key documents that you'll depend on to enforce the terms of your tenancies. Without copies, you may be reduced to arguing from memory about who agreed to what, and when.
- Your copies of lead paint hazard disclosure notices will prove to any questioner, including the EPA, that you've complied with this federal rule.
- Replacing mortgages and other financing documents with certified copies could be an administrative headache, and the cost could add up.
- If your property's survey is destroyed and you can't locate a copy, you might need to get a new survey—for a fee.
- Landlords who participate in federal, state, or local housing programs may need to keep several documents as proof of their compliance with the program. For example, landlords in the federal low-income housing tax credit program must keep documents relating to the first year of the property's compliance period for 21 years—six years after the program's compliance period has actually ended. Without these files, the IRS could

recapture the credits you claimed over 15 years, a loss that could prove devastating.

Given the risk of these and other scary scenarios, taking precautions is key. Here are a few simple ideas for keeping documents and other information safe in the event of a disaster:

- **Keep key documents in a secure, off-site location.** Store original documents related to your property (for example, mortgages, leases, regulatory agreements) and your business (articles of incorporation and bylaws, partnership agreements, vehicle registrations, and sensitive bank account information) away from your rental property, in a secure location such as a safe-deposit box or self-storage facility. If available, opt for a facility that offers a fireproof environment. Keep a full set of copies of these important documents in a secure location, so you can access them. To save space and further minimize the risk that your copies will be damaged or destroyed, consider scanning the documents to store the data on your office and home computers, and on a portable storage device such as a CD-ROM or USB flash drive.

- **Follow record-keeping rules.** If you participate in a housing program, make sure you're aware of any record-keeping rules of that program, and follow them to the letter. It may be worth the expense of copying several documents (for example, entire tenant files) and renting space in which to store them. This will ensure that an office fire or other calamity won't automatically trigger a costly disqualification.

- **Back up computer files.** It's easy to get lazy and not regularly back up computer files. We all know at least one person who lost valuable information thanks to a computer crash, power outage, or other frustrating situation. Commit to making backups part of a weekly or biweekly routine, by uploading files to an off-site server. (Search for "online storage solutions" on the Web to learn of easy, low-cost options that make sense for your business.) Alternatively, put files on a portable USB flash drive that you can conveniently carry with you in your briefcase or purse. If you regularly save your data to a CD-ROM, be sure to store the CD off-site.

> **TIP**
>
> **Imagine losing everything—then save what comes to mind.** You can't copy every piece of paper and every email, but you can copy what you know you'd be lost without. At a minimum, include your property ownership and loan documents, leases and rental agreements, regulatory agreements, tax returns and backup, insurance policies and open claims, and documents relating to your business formation (such as a partnership agreement or articles of incorporation). If you've done a property inventory, by all means include it.

Report suspicious objects and activities

If you've visited New York City since 2003, you've probably noticed the "If You See Something, Say Something" terror awareness campaign. The city's transit authority launched the campaign in response to the demand for increased vigilance following 9/11.

You can apply its simple message to your property. If you or your employees see something suspicious, take careful note. Whether it's suspicious behavior (by a stranger or even by a tenant) or just an unattended bag, pay attention. If you feel there may be danger, call the police. Here are some examples of suspicious behavior you might observe at or near your property:

- When you approach someone about his business on your property, he runs or sneaks away.
- A tenant lets your staff enter his apartment only after an excessive amount of notice.
- When you visit a tenant's apartment for maintenance, it looks barely furnished, as if no one lives there.
- You spot someone holding or creating diagrams or drawings of your building.
- You see someone taking numerous photographs of your property or watching it with binoculars, especially from inside a vehicle or other out-of-the-way location.

- Your employees are getting calls from people with unusual requests for sensitive information about your property, security system, staff, or business.
- A prospect or visitor gives you a driver's license or other official identification that you know or suspect is fraudulent.

Don't Focus Attention on Certain Ethnicities or Nationalities

While it's important to be vigilant and use common sense, it's also important that you not generalize about what kinds of people are likely to pose a threat to your property or tenants. First, remember that criminals come in every size, shape, and color (think of the 9/11 terrorists and the Oklahoma City bombers), and from every corner of the world. Second, if you're quick to question or report someone simply because he appears to come from a certain country, you could be in for a nasty discrimination lawsuit if it turns out he's blameless. Aside from fairness, it's more effective to focus on behavior, not appearance.

Look out for suspicious mail

Remember the anthrax scares in the months following 9/11? If nothing else, it showed that individuals and businesses need to be careful when sorting and opening the mail. In fact, suspicious packages, whether they arrive in the afternoon mail or appear mysteriously abandoned on the stairs, have been a growing problem. The number of suspicious packages reported to the police in New York alone has risen from 814 in 2002 (the first year statistics are available) to a whopping 37,614 in 2006. To help reduce the risk of handling or opening suspicious mail, adopt this two-part strategy:

First, be observant. You and other employees who are responsible for sorting or opening the mail should be familiar with the signs that may indicate a letter or parcel could be dangerous, such as:

- a powdery substance, oily stains, or other unusual markings on the outside of the package

- a peculiar smell
- wires sticking out of the package
- a ticking sound from within the package
- hate symbols (such as a swastika) or offensive slogans, especially handwritten, on the package.

Be aware of additional indications of danger in a letter or parcel you receive. Chances are, if only one or two of these signs exist, your mail isn't dangerous. But when many of them exist, or when these signs appear in conjunction with one or more of the more telling clues listed above, you should be suspicious. Be especially wary if:

- The parcel clearly has too much postage.
- The recipient's name or address is outdated.
- The letter or parcel is unusually bulky or was packaged sloppily.
- The package was wrapped in an excessive amount of packing tape or string.
- The sender's name or address strikes you as odd, or there is no return address at all.
- The letter or parcel is marked "Personal" or "Confidential."

Second, call the professionals. If you have reason to believe that mail you receive is dangerous, call 911. Instruct your employees to bring suspicious letters and parcels to you or a supervisor if possible, before calling 911.

You may be tempted to open or investigate suspicious mail out of curiosity, or you might be worried about reporting what turns out to be a harmless item. Don't take any chances by shaking the object or handling it more than necessary. Bomb squad professionals are trained on how to evaluate suspicious mail—you're not.

When you call 911, follow the instructions you receive and in the meantime, don't leave the letter or parcel lying around for others to encounter. Try to avoid touching your face and other people, and wash your hands thoroughly as soon as you can. Make a list of the names of anyone else you believe may have handled the suspicious mail, even if they are no longer with you after you've called 911.

TIP

For quick reference, display the Post Office poster on what to do when encountering suspicious mail. Place it in a conspicuous place, near the place where mail is sorted or picked up. You can download the free poster from the Post Office website at www.usps.com. Type "suspicious mail poster" into the search box.

Take all bomb threats seriously

It's of course unlikely that an international terrorist will single out your building. But bomb threats can come from other quarters, including common criminals with no political agenda who use a bomb threat to create a diversion, enabling them to enter your building and commit theft or other crimes. Also, calling in a bomb threat is a favorite among pranksters.

Careful landlords take these threats seriously. For example, just a few months after 9/11, the Lawrence Apartments at Princeton University received a written bomb threat. After the superintendent found the threatening note posted to his door, the police evacuated 200 people from the 12-story building. Tenants were allowed to reenter a few hours later, after police determined through bomb-sniffing dogs that there was no danger.

Many landlords have never thought about actually getting bomb threats. But you and your employees need to be prepared in case you do. Without a plan, your employees could panic, which could spread to your tenants. Here are some tips for handling bomb threats that you or a staff member receive by phone:

- **Try not to panic or talk quickly.** Aim to come across as calm and confident. Don't play into the fear the caller is trying to incite.
- **Keep the caller on the phone as long as possible while trying to get as much information as you can.** Ask the caller to repeat the information to ensure its accuracy.
- **Get more detailed information.** Ask the caller to fill in any important blanks in the information, such as the location or detonation time of the alleged bomb.

- **Listen carefully.** Listen for background or environmental noises, such as a train whistle, highway traffic, or an echo. Such details could prove useful to authorities in pinpointing the caller's location.
- **Analyze the caller's voice.** Focus on remembering as much as you can about the caller's voice. Did it sound like the caller was speaking through a filter? Note the sex, age, and quality of the voice and whether the caller had an accent, speech impediment, or other notable characteristic.

Instruct employees to immediately inform you or a supervisor, and if no one is available, to call 911 without delay. Upon learning of a bomb threat, you or the supervisor should immediately phone 911. Keep the employee available to talk to the police, fire department, FBI, or other authorities investigating the threat. If you get a bomb threat in the mail, by hand, or by email, treat it just as seriously and call the authorities to investigate.

It Won't Happen to You ...

What happened. A Florida landlord received bomb threats to his apartment complex, but he didn't warn his tenants or guests or take any other steps to protect them. One day, after an overnight boating trip, a tenant returned to his apartment just as a bomb exploded, which claimed his life. His daughter, who was near the tenant when the bomb went off, suffered physical and emotional harm and sued the landlord for negligence.

How you can avoid it. Take all bomb threats seriously, and don't assume they're the work of a harmless prankster. Contact the police after the first threat and follow their recommendations for taking reasonable precautions, such as warning tenants and their guests to be vigilant, while the police investigate.

Prepare for when the disaster or emergency hits

Despite your careful efforts to minimize emergencies (or their consequences), you might get hit. Prepare now for how to handle the problem, by following these steps. After taking care of the initial tasks, you'll be well positioned to devise an evacuation plan, covered at the end of this section, which is your master plan for keeping tenants and property safe.

Always Have a Current "Rent Roll"

A rent roll lists the names and number of occupants in each apartment. Keep your rent roll current and have a copy handy to give to the police or fire officials. If you are instructed to evacuate, you or emergency personnel can use the rent roll to make sure every known occupant is accounted for. This small, simple step can make the difference in saving lives.

Document the location of utility shut-off valves

If a disaster strikes, you may need to shut off utility valves such as the electricity, gas, and water. Emergency personnel may even ask you to do so. If you don't already know where your valves are located, take the time now to map them out—a simple drawing of your property with electricity, gas, and water shut-off locations will do. Having such a map will also benefit your employees or manager, who may need to act in your absence. If you rent out a single-family home or your building has a few tenants, consider giving the map and explaining the process to your tenants, in case of an emergency. Make sure your map notes whether special tools are needed to turn the valves, and where these tools are located. To prevent vandalism, keep the tools in an accessible but nonobvious location near the valve.

Electricity. In addition to locating the main shut-off on your circuit breaker, identify the coverage of each individual circuit. For example, if circuits 3 and 4 control apartments A and B, make that information clear, in a map or in a written list, so that any employee or emergency person can act on it. For safety reasons, when turning off electricity, don't turn off the main breaker until you've turned off the individual ones.

Gas. Turning off the gas may be more complicated than flipping your circuit breakers. Contact your gas company and make sure you know how to properly turn off the natural gas, as different systems require different procedures. After turning off a natural gas valve, hire a professional to turn it back on. Incorrectly turning the gas back on can lead to explosions and serious injury.

Water. Your drinking water may become tainted following a failure in the water system or extensive flooding. The water company may instruct you to turn off the main water valve. To be sure you can perform this simple mechanical chore, check the valve shut-off handle now and on a regular basis to make sure it works and isn't rusted. If it is rusted or broken, hire a plumber to fix it immediately. Also, make sure it's properly labeled (attach a weather-resistant tag or place a sign in the ground next to it), in addition to being well identified on your shut-off valve map.

Know how to "shelter-in-place"

"Shelter-in-place" is a term that every business owner—especially landlords—should be aware of. This term is actually an instruction that you, your employees, your tenants, and any visitors on your property may be given by authorities in an emergency that involves the release—or suspected release—of hazardous materials. The goal of sheltering-in-place, in which you take refuge in a room with as few windows as possible, is to minimize the harm from any chemical, biological, or radiological contaminant that may have been released into the air. For example, if an 18-wheeler collides with a tanker on the road in front of your property and the tanker starts to leak gas, or if there is an explosion at a nearby chemical plant, you may need to shelter-in-place. Sheltering-in-place usually lasts no more than a few hours. After this time, authorities usually give you the all-clear or order you to evacuate.

The Department of Homeland Security recommends that businesses be prepared to follow shelter-in-place orders, which will most likely be communicated through television, radio, and the Internet, by having a plan. Here's what you should consider for the shelter-in-place plan you create for your property:

- **Ask visitors to stay.** Ask vendors, prospects, and other visitors who may be in your building to stay and follow your instructions to a safe place. Although you can't force them to stay, you may convince them by explaining that leaving could endanger their health and safety and would be in violation of the order by authorities. Close your office.

- **Gather essential disaster supplies.** Collect nonperishable food items, bottled water, battery-powered radios, first-aid supplies, flashlights, batteries, and materials you may need to seal cracks, such as duct tape, plastic sheeting, and plastic garbage bags.

- **Select an interior room on the lowest floor possible, with the fewest windows or vents.** Good options include large storage closets, utility rooms, pantries, and copy and conference rooms without exterior windows. Select more than one room if needed to avoid overcrowding.

- **Look for a room with a hardwired telephone.** Because cell phone reception could be tricky during an emergency, select a room with a hardwired telephone. This way, you, your employees, and any visitors can successfully reach emergency contacts as well as report any life-threatening situations that may arise.

- **Close and lock openings to the outside.** If you are in a room with windows, exterior doors, and other openings to the outside, make sure they are closed and locked.

- **Close window treatments.** Shut the blinds, curtains, and shades if you are told there is a danger of an explosion occurring near your property.

- **Shut down ventilation systems.** Instruct maintenance staff to turn off all fans, heating, and air-conditioning systems.

- **Seal cracks to prevent contamination.** Use items such as duct tape, plastic sheeting, and plastic garbage bags to seal cracks around doors and vents to prevent contaminated air from entering the room. Put a wet towel at the bottom of the door as an extra precaution against contaminants.

- **Encourage communication with emergency contacts.** If the situation appears stable, let employees and others call home or reach out to their emergency contacts to let them know their location and that they are safe.
- **Account for everyone in the room with you.** Write down employees' names and position, and write down the names of visitors and what their purpose was in visiting your property. Use this list to tell authorities who is in the room with you.
- **Monitor the situation.** Listen to the radio and television, and check the Internet, if possible, to stay current on the situation and learn if everything is safe or if you must evacuate.

Give employees and tenants an emergency contacts card

Effective communication is key during emergencies. Just think of the October 2007 California wildfires, where an estimated 515,000 residents in San Diego County alone evacuated their homes. If authorities order you to evacuate your building or if you decide to let employees leave (for example, to get in touch with their families and friends following a blackout or other neighborhood disaster), your employees should leave knowing how to contact each other and stay up-to-date about the status of an emergency and whether it's okay to return to your property. Similarly, tenants who are ordered to evacuate for a while will want to know when they can return to their apartment, and you'll want to make sure you know that all your tenants are safe.

To ensure effective communication, create two concise versions of an "emergency contacts card" for employees and tenants. Your cards should be small enough to fit into your employees' and tenants' wallets. Give the card to employees on their first day on the job and to your tenants the day they sign their lease, and tell employees and tenants to carry the card with them at all times.

Your employee emergency contacts card should contain the following information:

- **The names of all employees and their phone numbers.** Include the names of all employees, whether they work on-site or off. If you own several properties and have a separate staff assigned to each, it may make sense to have multiple cards and include only the employees who work together on each card.
- **Where employees will report their whereabouts.** If employees must evacuate your building or office, each one may find safety in a different location. Instruct employees to call a certain number or send an email to a certain address to report their whereabouts. The number can be a company hotline or simply a dedicated extension with voicemail that you set up for this purpose. If you run a small operation, it may be easiest just to have your employees call you.
- **How employees can check for updated information.** You'll want to communicate updates on the situation, such as telling employees not to report to work the next day, that it is now safe to return to the property, or that power has been restored. Even if you manage a small staff, it's usually not feasible to call every employee each time you have an update. Instead, leave the update on a voicemail extension at your main number. On your card, instruct employees to call this number to get updated information.

Your tenant emergency contacts card should contain the following information:

- **The names of tenants and their phone numbers (optional).** If you manage a property with a small number of tenants and they all agree, list their names and apartment number along with their cell phone or other emergency contact number.
- **Where tenants will report their whereabouts.** Ask your tenants to call a certain number or send an email to a certain address to report their location following an evacuation. This can be the same number you use for employees, or you may choose a different dedicated extension with voicemail.

- **How tenants can check for updated information.** Tenants, even more so than employees, need to know when it's safe to return home. Communicate updates on a voicemail extension at your main number. (You'll probably find it easiest to use the same number for employees and tenants.) List the number on the card and tell tenants to call it to get updated information.

Encourage Employees to Keep Cell Phones Charged

Cell phones aren't very helpful when the batteries are dead or running low—especially during an emergency. To prevent problems, encourage employees to bring their cell phone chargers to work or get a second charger to keep at work. This way, all your employees should have full juice even as the workday nears its end.

It Won't Happen to You ...

What happened. When the Blackout of 2003 took New York by surprise, it happened after 4 p.m. on a business day. At that late hour of the workday, many New Yorkers were struggling with phones with little power left in their batteries. That problem, combined with the unusually high call volume, meant that few people benefited from having a cell phone during that emergency.

How you can avoid it. It's frustrating to have the right communication tools but no power to use them. You can avoid the specter of employees unable to communicate with you or each other by encouraging them to keep their cell phones charged throughout the day. Also, make sure your employees know the closest working landline phone during a power outage, in case they need to call 911. As discussed in Step Two, a 911 call from a cell phone can get routed to a responder who's many miles away, causing significant delays.

Have first-aid kit available at each property

If you don't already have a first-aid kit available at each property, go out and purchase one. They're not that expensive—a basic kit should cost around $25, and a very large or specialty kit can run between $100 and $200—and they can prove very handy in limiting the extent of a tenant's, employee's, or visitor's injuries. For example, you can use a tourniquet to stop severe bleeding until the paramedics arrive, possibly saving a victim's life.

Along with purchasing first-aid kits, set up basic first-aid and cardiopulmonary resuscitation (CPR) training for you, your manager, and any employees. Contact your local chapter of the American Red Cross to get on-site training for your employees. To find your local chapter, visit www.redcross.org and enter your ZIP code. You can also read descriptions of available Red Cross courses by typing "employee training" in the search box on the Red Cross home page. Getting employees trained will ensure that they know how to use each item contained in your kits.

Get an automated external defibrillator (AED) for your property

An AED (automated external defibrillator) is a device that restores normal heart rhythm to people who go into cardiac arrest. Through electrodes, an AED first analyses a person's heart to detect for abnormalities. If it finds rhythmic abnormalities, the AED charges and the user presses a button to send a shock to "defibrillate" the heart— that is, restore the heart to its normal rhythm.

Just a decade ago, AEDs were not common outside of medical facilities. But today, AEDs have become increasingly popular in schools, airports, community centers, offices, hotels, and in other properties where many people live, work, or visit. The Red Cross estimates that a quarter of those who die from cardiac arrest could have been saved had an AED been used.

Cardiac arrest must be treated within minutes of its first signs, which often means it's too late to wait for paramedics to arrive. Having an AED on-site with employees who are trained in its use isn't required by law, but it could be crucial to saving the lives of your tenants, employees, and visitors. You'll gain a marketing edge, too, because prospects (especially seniors) will be attracted to your property, knowing that you go beyond what the law requires when it comes to keeping your tenants safe. Finally, having life-saving equipment such as an AED and a first-aid kit will help paint a stronger picture of you as a safety-conscious landlord if you ever need to defend yourself against a negligence claim in court.

You can purchase AEDs through medical supply stores or online. Their cost, $1,200–$2,000, won't fit every landlord's budget. But the more people who live, work, and visit your property, the more you should consider the purchase. As an incentive, states are starting to offer tax credits for purchasing an AED. For example, New York offers a tax credit of up to $500 per AED—with no limit on the number of AEDs purchased in any tax year. Visit your state tax agency's website and search for "defibrillator" to find out whether your state offers a similar credit. (For more information about finding your state tax agency's website, see Step Ten.)

After you purchase an AED, be sure you (and any staff) learn how to use it. Using an AED isn't too difficult, but some training is needed to use it effectively. (Also, using it improperly could expose you to the risk of a lawsuit.) Ask your vendor about training, and consider making AED training a requirement for all employees. (The Red Cross also offers AED training; refer to the website mentioned above.)

Follow state and local law on emergency preparedness

Your state or municipality may have laws aimed at making sure property owners are prepared for an emergency. For example, Occupational Safety and Health Act (OSHA) regulations may require you to install fire extinguishers and train employees in their proper use. If your rental property is located in Chicago, you must conduct annual safety drills. And Washington state landlords who own rental properties larger than a single-family house must send tenants a written disclosure form that spells out the specific fire protection devices installed (such as a sprinkler or alarm system) and safety procedures developed for their building (such as an emergency evacuation plan).

For help locating your state and local laws, see the instructions in Step Two on locating particular statutes in your state codes. For more information about OSHA requirements and for some useful tips, read the "Evacuation Plans and Procedures eTool" on the OSHA website (www.osha.gov). Type the title into the search box on the home page.

Create an effective evacuation plan for your property

If you follow the suggestions above, you'll be in a good position to develop an evacuation plan that your staff can implement and your tenants can follow in the event of a fire or other emergency. Evacuation plans may vary considerably, depending on the size and layout of a property, so make sure the plan you adopt is tailored to the realities of your property. Your plan may also need to incorporate any emergency-related requirements you've determined your business must meet under the law (see "Follow state and local law on emergency preparedness," above).

For example, in a multifamily property, you'll need a current rent roll (see "Always Have a Current 'Rent Roll,'" above). You'll want to post floor plans showing evacuation routes out of your building by each elevator or stairwell entrance, and identify each floor inside your stairwell and your elevators. You should also appoint employees to assume certain duties during evacuations. For instance, designate a male and female employee to check the men's and women's bathrooms when the alarm sounds or you otherwise learn you must evacuate. You can also put a few employees in charge of accounting for tenants and guests with special needs (see "Take Note of Tenants With Special Needs," below).

Take Note of Tenants With Special Needs

Tenants who are mobility- or vision-impaired may have trouble leaving the building on their own during an evacuation. Those who are hearing-impaired or suffer from dementia might not even learn about an evacuation until it's too late. To prevent problems and help disabled tenants reach safety, identify which tenants, if any, need assistance during emergencies.

To avoid accusations of fair housing violations, ask tenants to tell you only if anyone in their household or any frequent guest would need special assistance in the event of an emergency or evacuation. Don't ask unnecessary questions about the nature of tenants' or guests' disabilities. Make it clear that you need this information for health and safety reasons only and that you will keep all responses confidential, sharing it only with property staff and emergency personnel.

Compile a list of the tenants and guests who have special needs and include it in your property's written evacuation plan. In the event of an evacuation, employees you designate can either provide assistance to these tenants and guests or alert emergency personnel to them.

Create an emergency procedures manual

To make sure your emergency planning is available to those who may need to use it, put your emergency information into a single emergency procedures manual. The manual should include your evacuation plan, rent roll, map of utility shutoff valves, and emergency contact information. Also, include any written policies you have set for your employees' behavior or actions during an emergency. For example, it's a good idea to emphasize your employees' need to be firm when dealing with tenant requests during and after an emergency. Your policy on this point might look like this:

"If authorities inform us that all or parts of the building are not safe to reenter, don't make exceptions for tenants for any reason (for example, for a tenant who claims she left something valuable behind in her

apartment). If a tenant believes that a person or pet was left behind, alert the authorities on the scene. Under no circumstances should anyone reenter parts of the building that we have been warned are unsafe."

Give the manual to your staff. If your property has no paid staff, consider giving copies to your tenants.

Once you've created an emergency procedures manual, go over the manual—particularly your property's evacuation plan—with all employees, being sure to point out the location of fire extinguishers, fire alarms, stairways, roof accessways, and other exit routes.

Keep the manual as a file on every employee's computer, give a hard copy to employees the day they start working for you, and place a copy in each office and at each property you own, so that it's available in case of an emergency. Realize that people will forget the drill unless you periodically review the manual's contents with your staff or manager. Finally, as you do with other important documents, keep at least one copy of your manual in a safe off-site location.

Review your manual periodically so you can update any phone numbers or other information that have become outdated, and add new procedures to your manual when necessary. Since you should expect to update your manual regularly, you may find it convenient to organize the manual into a loose-leaf binder. Also, for even easier use during an emergency, use tabs with clear headings to separate the sections of your manual.

If you need assistance drafting an effective plan, contact your local fire department and ask for its recommendations. (The department may also offer training on proper response measures.) Depending on the size of your property and your needs, you may also find it worthwhile to hire a risk management consultant for help, if your budget allows.

Get the Facts, Quell the Rumors

During a crisis, solid information is hard to come by and people are anxious to get it. Mix these two ingredients together, and it's no wonder why misinformation and rumors spread fast. Not only do you need accurate information to escape danger, but spreading misinformation can also lead to harm and liability. For example, suppose a landlord relies on unverified misinformation and orders a tenant to remain in her apartment, while authorities actually want all tenants to evacuate. If the tenant suffers harm, she may be able to convince a judge that the landlord's negligence caused it, entitling her to recover damages.

You and your staff can take steps to distinguish solid information from empty rumors and stop the latter type from spreading.

- **Question the reliability of information.** Don't assume that what you're told is correct, no matter how sincere or urgent the informer may sound. Unless you're speaking with someone in authority, such as a firefighter, question the source of the statement. Evaluate the reliability of the source—a string of "I heard it from A, who heard it from B" is less credible and compelling than "I saw it myself."

- **Stop the spread of rumors.** If the information you hear seems unreliable, try to stop it from spreading. By asking direct questions such as "How do you know this?" or "How do you know this information is correct?" you'll put potential rumors to the test and uncover any flimsiness. If you discover the original source of possible misinformation, consider confronting the source to get to the bottom of the rumor (time and circumstances permitting).

Most importantly, however, resist the urge to believe questionable information yourself. If you are skeptical as information drips in during an emergency, you can help weed out the misinformation from the good information.

> ### Locate Your State Homeland Security Office
>
> Your state office for homeland security and/or emergency management can be a useful source of additional emergency and disaster information pertaining to your business. For example, you may find suggestions for drafting an effective emergency procedures manual for your building, get tips on preparing for disasters common to your area of the country, read current news, and learn about grants and other forms of postdisaster assistance that may be available to your business.
>
> You can access the Department of Homeland Security's and the Federal Emergency Management Agency's state-by-state directories here:
> - www.dhs.gov/xgovt/grants
> - www.fema.gov/about/contact/statedr.shtm
>
> These directories also provide you with contact information for your state offices, if you need further information or help.

Respond appropriately after the emergency

Despite your preventive steps, careful risk-avoidance practices, and readiness for an emergency, you may find yourself dealing with the aftermath of a disaster. Besides making sure everyone is safe and your property is as secure as possible, you'll want to take prompt steps to get your business back in shape with minimal fallout. Here are some ways to prepare for that situation—should it ever occur.

Work with your insurance agent or broker

Getting yourself and others to safety comes first during any emergency. But when an emergency situation is under control, bring your insurer into the picture. Working together helps ensure your claim won't automatically be denied, and that you'll get paid what you're due. The longer you delay, the greater the chances that your insurer will claim your adjuster can't make an accurate assessment of the damage and use your delay as the basis for denying the claim. Taking the following basic steps will put you in an optimal position when it's time to meet the adjuster.

Lessen the damage if you can

If you take the time to read the fine print in your insurance policy, you'll find a clause that requires you to "mitigate damages" in the event of an emergency or disaster. This means that you must take reasonably prompt steps to lessen the damages your property will suffer, sometimes even during the disaster or emergency itself. For example, if you see that a skylight is leaking but don't take commonsense steps, such as positioning buckets to catch the water as it drips or hire a roofing company to make a temporary fix, you may find yourself arguing with your insurance company when trying to make a claim for the ruined hardwood floor under the leaking water. You aren't expected to take superhuman steps to mitigate damages or put yourself in harm's way, but you are expected to do what you reasonably can to prevent further loss. An insurance company can deny a claim (or pay less than you've asked for) if it feels that you didn't do your part to prevent matters from getting any worse than they needed to.

If disaster strikes at your property, take reasonable steps to lessen your property's damage and to keep tenants safe from additional harm. For example, if an earthquake shatters several windows at your property, clean up the glass to avoid injury. Then, as a temporary fix, board up the windows (to protect against storms, vandalism, and theft) until you can arrange to have new windows installed.

Notify your insurance broker or agent

Call your agent or broker as soon as you reasonably can, either right after the incident or during a lull, if it's ongoing. You may not have too much to convey, but even making a quick first call to report the incident and promise to be in touch is key.

Your insurance company wants to be in the loop early so it can advise you on how to proceed. (If nothing else, your agent is likely to talk with you about what steps you've taken—and what steps you can take—to minimize the damages.) Depending on the agent's sophistication, you might also get some advice on how to tread carefully in the future so you don't invite more claims. For example, your agent may advise you to refrain from talking to the press (so that unguarded observations don't form the basis of any legal claims against you). Finally, an experienced agent can offer suggestions for recovery that you can implement right away, and can point out parts of your policy (such as coverage for business interruption) that you may not have remembered but will find reassuring.

Gather critical information

Put together an inventory of damaged items, and include as much information as you can about their value. For example, include receipts and proofs of purchase or other information that shows the date of purchase and the price you paid, and write down manufacturer names and product serial numbers of computers and other equipment. Also, take photos and videos of damaged property to complement your documentation. Compiling all this information soon after a disaster will help your insurance adjuster make a correct assessment of your property's damage and get your claim processed more quickly.

Check policy for coverage

Review your policy to see whether it covers the damage your property suffered from the disaster or other emergency. Also, check whether your claim exceeds the amount of your deductible (or if you've already hit your deductible from a claim you made earlier in the year). For more information about insurance, see Step One.

Call your lawyer

If your business has been significantly affected by a disaster or other emergency and you have an ongoing relationship with a lawyer or law firm, let the lawyer or firm know. Your lawyer can confirm that you're doing the right things or give helpful suggestions for making your disaster recovery efforts more efficient and less prone to risk. If you don't have a regular lawyer on retainer, you may want to contact one if problems arise that may require legal action, such as if your insurer denies your claims. For tips on finding the right lawyer for your business, see Step Nine.

Emergency Preparedness: My To-Do List

In Step Five, you thought about various emergencies and disasters that could befall your property and tenants, and took steps to not only prevent them, but to be ready should they occur. Use this checklist to guide you as you prepare for an emergency.

☐ **Protecting documents:** Make copies of important documents to keep off-site and/or online.

☐ **Suspicious packages:** Check mail carefully before opening, and report all suspicious objects to the police.

☐ **Bomb threats:** Take each one seriously, even though it might be a hoax.

☐ **Utility shut-off valves:** Find and map each water, gas, and electricity valve, and include the location of necessary tools.

☐ **Sheltering-in-place:** Know what to do in case I'm given the order.

☐ **Emergency preparedness:** Give tenants and employees an emergency contacts card.

☐ **Emergency preparedness:** Make sure my property complies with applicable federal, state, and local laws.

☐ **Emergency preparedness:** Gather emergency supplies and periodically check to see that they're fresh and usable.

☐ **Emergency preparedness:** Educate tenants about our plan and resources in the event of a disaster or emergency.

☐ **First-aid:** Purchase first-aid kits and possibly AEDs for each building.

☐ **First-aid:** Train employees in first-aid and CPR and in using equipment such as an AED.

☐ **Evacuations:** Create an evacuation plan and include it in our emergency procedures manual.

☐ **Evacuations:** Find out which tenants and guests would need special assistance.

☐ **Postdisaster recovery:** Be familiar with the steps to take to protect my business should a disaster befall my property.

Lower the Risk of Crime
at Your Property

You probably don't need convincing that making your property as crime-free as possible is a worthwhile goal. The last thing landlords want is to see their tenants hurt, their homes broken into, and personal property damaged or stolen. But if you're like many landlords, your first thought may be, "What am I, the police?" Indeed, until recently, landlords weren't charged with taking steps to protect their tenants from crime, and if tenants were hurt or burglarized, their only recourse was to hope the police nabbed the culprit (and that their renters' and health insurance policies would cover their losses and injuries).

Not so any more. Since the first case holding a landlord liable for his tenant's injuries at the hands of a criminal (Massachusetts, 1970), landlords have been increasingly expected to pay attention and take steps to make their properties safe.

Though landlords are increasingly held responsible for the results of crime on their properties, no law makes them *automatically* liable, and you needn't maintain a crime-proof property. But, to be safe, you do need to:

- comply with state and local laws concerning security measures on rental properties
- screen your applicants and employees carefully (covered in detail in Step Nine)
- advertise your security situation honestly, answer prospects' questions candidly, and make good on what you promise, and
- respond reasonably with appropriate, added security measures when circumstances change, such as when a crime occurs on your property or crime rates rise in your neighborhood.

These "to dos" might seem daunting, but they're actually easier and less expensive to implement than many landlords think. Read on to learn more about the consequences of not paying careful attention to this issue and the steps that will result in reasonably safe properties and good nights' sleep for all.

What Do You Have to Lose?

In addition to the direct harm that crime inflicts on its victims, your bottom line will suffer, too. When criminal activity occurs at your property, tenants will feel less safe, making it more likely they'll want to move out. Prospects who learn that your property has doubled as a crime scene will probably think twice before signing a lease or even applying for an apartment. The result is vacant units and a stalled rent steam.

Landlords who don't properly address security issues may be in violation of state or local laws requiring landlords to install and maintain basic security measures, such as adequate lighting and sturdy door and window locks. Some laws come with a punch—if the owner fails to implement these protections, tenants can break the lease without responsibility for future rent, or take care of business themselves (such as installing proper locks) and deduct the cost from the rent. You never want to lose a tenant midlease because you haven't followed the law, nor do you want to be in a position where tenants are working on your property—and you're paying for it.

As if the reasons just described aren't enough to convince you to do your reasonable best to prevent crime, think about this: If you don't follow local and state laws to provide security, and take extra steps when you know that the situation at your property warrants them, you could end up being at least partially liable for a prospect's, tenant's, or guest's injuries or property loss if a crime occurs. The amount a judge may order you to pay for the results of a criminal's act can easily hit the six or seven digits. Plus, as explained more below, the more crimes that occur at your property, the more likely your insurance premium will rise to cover the increased risk.

With so much at stake, you can't afford to skip this chapter. The last thing you want is for a judge to tell you that you've been lax about security, or for you to discover that you've taken your property's excellent safety record for granted. Step Six will show you how to lower the chances that a crime will take place at your property, and make it less likely that you'll be held liable in the unfortunate event that a crime does occur.

Is This You?

Chances are that the majority of the people reading this book have not had a problem with crime at their rental properties. Those who have conscientiously maintained their property's physical appearance and integrity may be reaping the benefits of not only low accident rates (good lighting equals fewer slip-and-falls), but also fewer crime incidents (good lighting deters criminal intrusions). But even these owners shouldn't be complacent. Ironically, "nice" properties are often the target of choice among burglars who think, rightly enough, that the owners have lowered their guard, assuming that only run-down properties will get hit. It could just be a matter of time until a criminal enters your property and takes advantage of a security hole you didn't realize you had.

Take a look at the portraits of several rental property owners, below. You may recognize yourself in one or more of them.

Take Action!

Perhaps you've been addressing a crime problem for a while at one of your properties, but you're not sure whether you're taking the right steps. Or perhaps you're sitting tight, relying on your property's good track record as an indicator that you don't need to worry about preventing crime. You don't have to build a moat around your property or hire an army to protect your tenants. But you do have to follow the law and take reasonable steps to protect your tenants from foreseeable harm at the hands of criminals.

Below, you'll read about practical and relatively inexpensive ways to address the question of security at any rental property. If you take action now, you can keep tenants safe and lower the risk that a court will hold you liable if a crime occurs at your property despite your best efforts.

Do You Think About Crime Like These Landlords?

☐ You don't know whether your state or local law requires rental property owners to install and maintain security features, such as door and window locks.

☐ Because you've never had a crime occur on your property, you haven't given the issue much thought.

☐ You assume that since you aren't responsible for a criminal's decision to commit a crime on your property, you can't be held liable for the crime.

☐ You want to increase security at your property but you're not sure where to turn for help, or you believe getting professional help would prove too costly.

☐ You have a one-security-plan-fits-all approach for every property you own.

☐ You don't communicate regularly with your tenants about safety or enlist their help in keeping your property secure.

☐ You run credit reports for all applicants, and assume that criminal histories will show up there.

☐ Your neighborhood has experienced some crime, but since your property hasn't been hit, you don't think it's necessary to increase your security measures.

Learn and implement your local or state requirements for rental property security

The first step toward running a safe rental property is following specific security requirements that your state or local legislators may have adopted. For example, Texas law requires residential landlords to equip apartments with a latch (exterior windows); a doorknob lock or keyed deadbolt, and a keyless bolting device and peephole (exterior doors); and a sliding door pin lock, and a sliding door handle latch or security bar (exterior sliding doors). In Berkeley, California, the municipal code gets even more specific. Berkeley landlords must make sure that the deadbolts they install have hardened inserts aimed at repelling a criminal's attempt to cut the lock with a tool.

To find out whether your state or municipality requires you to follow security provisions, check the laws (see the chart in the appendix for help). Before making efforts (and spending money) to comply with a law, read it carefully to make sure it applies to your building. For instance, the Berkeley law mentioned above applies to apartment buildings that have at least two floors or at least five apartments. Upon careful reading, you may realize that other laws apply only to hotels or other commercial buildings.

Learn what's going on in the 'hood

After learning about and following any state or local laws that require security measures or features, your next step will be to find out what's going on, crime-wise, in your neighborhood. This will allow you to fine-tune your efforts, and it will prevent a "one-security-plan-fits-all" approach to tackling crime risks if you own more than one property. Assess the crime situation at each property and in each neighborhood, and implement security measures that make sense given the reality of each situation.

If you own properties in very different neighborhoods, your security needs and concerns may very well be different. It may be worthwhile to invest more money for increased security at one property. Or, you may be able to save money if you determine that extra-tight security would not be necessary to protect tenants at another property. It's also important to look at what your neighbors are doing. For example, if you learn that your neighborhood has a very low crime rate and other rental properties in your area don't spend a fortune on security measures, you probably don't need to, either.

Find out about crime in your neighborhood and at your property by contacting your local police precinct. The police can give you statistics on different types of crime in your neighborhood and tell you about trends. Also, ask your precinct for a listing of 911 calls and other reports of criminal activity on your property, and request incident reports, where available. As you review this data, try to learn the answers to basic questions, such as:

- Have crimes either occurred or been attempted in the past 12 months? What about the past 24 months?
- What kinds of crimes have occurred?
- Why did any attempted crimes fail?
- If there haven't been any crimes in a while, what factors have been responsible for this positive trend?

After you've gathered answers to these questions, put them aside for now. Your job isn't done just yet—the reasonable and informed security measures that make sense for your property must also be informed by what you discover when you "case the joint," as explained just below.

It Won't Happen to You ...

What happened. A tenant was robbed and killed while getting his mail late one night at his complex's mailbox in metro Atlanta. The tenant's family sued the complex, claiming it provided inadequate security, given that there had been several prior robberies in the common areas in the past two years, including two robberies in the past 63 days. The owners settled with the family for $1,325,000.

How you can avoid it. It's tough to argue that part of your common area is safe when a look at the area's recent history proves otherwise. If even one crime occurs at your property, you must investigate and take steps to increase security. Not only will taking this action stave off future crimes, but your anticrime efforts will help shield you against a liability claim if another crime does occur and its victim decides to sue you.

Inspect your property for vulnerabilities

In Step Two, you read about how important it is to walk through your property and check for potential safety hazards, such as weak balconies, loose handrails, burned-out lighting, and torn carpets. Inspecting your property in this way often proves to be an effective tool for spotting potential crime issues. (For example, poor lighting invites both accidents and crimes.) Similarly, landscaping that features tall bushes, low-hanging trees, and other good hiding places make a criminal's job that much easier.

Walk through your property as if you were a criminal looking for vulnerable spots. Pay particular attention to these elements:

- **Lighting.** Take a walk at dusk and in the evening, looking for burned-out or dimmed exterior lights or areas that can benefit from greater illumination, such as the front gate, parking lot, and interior corridors.

It Won't Happen to You ...

What happened. A visitor at a Texas apartment complex was stabbed during a night carjacking in the parking lot, suffering serious internal injuries, and post-traumatic stress disorder. The visitor sued the landlord and manager, claiming they didn't live up to their duty to keep tenants, visitors, and others safe from crime. The landlord and manager should have taken certain steps, the visitor claimed, such as maintaining adequate lighting in the parking lot and adding certain security devices. The landlord and manager settled with the visitor for a confidential amount.

How you can avoid it. Keeping people safe at a rental property doesn't require much money, but it does require action. If you've noticed that your parking lot or other common area is dimly lit, don't hesitate to brighten it up with stronger lighting. While you're at it, consider adding cameras and other security features to bolster your efforts. Tenants and their guests will feel safe, and criminals will get the message that your property is protected.

- **Landscaping.** Examine the bushes and trees on your property, especially near entrances. Do they lower visibility or provide easy hiding places for would-be assailants? As a rule of thumb, it's best to keep bushes trimmed to no more than three feet from the ground.

- **Existing security equipment.** Check that all your technology is functional. For example, make sure automatic gates that require security codes are actually requiring the codes, and check that all surveillance cameras are operational.

- **Existing security personnel.** Many properties employ night guards, doormen, or other security services. Are you getting what you need? If not, change the type of service you provide or use a different company. For example, if everyone likes your doorman but he doesn't take a firm stance when it comes to enforcing your security policies, don't hesitate to replace him with someone who's more committed to helping you keep your property safe.

- **Vulnerable places that need added protections.** As you inspect your property, look out for areas that are prone to becoming crime scenes. If you find any such areas, promptly remove whatever it is that could make the area attractive to criminals. For example, say there's an outdoor staircase leading down to your basement in a small inlet between two parts of your building. You might think it's secure because the doors to your basement are locked. But the inlet, especially with its sunken stairwell, can be a criminal's ideal out-of-sight place to nab an unsuspecting victim. To remove this risk, consider installing a security gate to block entry to the inlet itself, along with a warning sign to keep out. This way, the entire area—and not just the door to your basement—will be inaccessible to anyone except those employees and contractors you authorize.

During your inspection, pay attention to both the exterior aspects (doors, garages, parking lots) and the interior aspects (individual apartments) of your property. Even though your building's entrances and surrounding areas may be secure, you must still make sure your apartments' doors and windows are secure, too.

It Won't Happen to You ...

What happened. After a burglar broke into an apartment at a Maryland complex through a sliding glass door and killed a tenant, the tenant's wife sued the landlord and property manager, claiming they provided inadequate security. The landlord and manager tried to get the court to dismiss the case, by arguing that the burglary occurred inside the tenant's apartment (and not in a common area). The court disagreed and ruled that just because the assault took place inside an apartment doesn't mean that the landlord couldn't have been negligent.

How you can avoid it. There's no escaping the risk of liability, whether it's from a crime that occurs in your common areas or inside a tenant's apartment. Fortunately, you can lower this risk by inspecting your property top-to-bottom, taking tenant repair requests seriously, and fixing any holes in your property's security, such as broken sliding doors. This way, no one can argue that you've provided inadequate security—and win.

It's always helpful to conduct your own inspections of your property for crime hazards. (After all, no one is more familiar with your property than you.) But thorough landlords don't stop there. Consider also talking to your insurer about getting a safety assessment and recommendations for loss control, hiring a security consultant, or contacting your local police precinct to arrange for an officer to conduct a formal security inspection, as explained below.

Make sure apartment burglar alarms work

If you have individual burglar alarms installed in your apartments, or if you decide to add this amenity for tenants, don't let the alarms become a liability trap for you. Ward off your risks from the get-go by doing three things before each new tenant moves into an apartment that's equipped with an alarm:

First, inspect and test each alarm to make sure it works. If an alarm doesn't work properly, get it repaired before your new tenants occupy the apartment or as soon as possible after move-in.

Second, show tenants how to activate and use the alarm, even if they express doubt that they'll use it.

Third, have your new tenants sign and date an alarm acknowledgment that says the tenants understand and agree that:

- there is an alarm in the apartment that is currently inactivated
- they may activate the alarm, if they choose
- they understand how to activate and operate the alarm, and
- they will promptly notify you if they notice a problem with the activation or proper function of the alarm.

> **TIP**
>
> **Tell your insurer about any burglar alarms you've installed in your rentals.** Your extra efforts at increasing security may earn you a discount on your premium. At the least, your insurer will appreciate the fact you're taking proactive efforts to minimize risk (and reduce the likelihood of insurance claims) at your property.

Don't list apartment numbers on intercom panel

If you have an intercom system for visitors at your entryways, list your tenants' names on the panel—and not their apartment numbers. If your intercom system requires visitors to dial a code, assign a random code to each apartment instead of the apartment number itself. Taking this privacy step costs nothing, and it will help prevent strangers from learning a tenant's apartment number simply by reading your intercom panel. Most importantly, criminals who wish to rob or attack a certain tenant won't be able to find out which apartment their intended victim occupies.

Create written policies for keys and locks and don't budge

Not all criminals rely on sophisticated equipment or techniques to gain access to property and commit a crime. Some simply take advantage of holes in a property's security, most notably a property's lax key and lock policies.

Many apartment complexes either don't have strict rules when it comes to keys and locks or have written rules that staff members don't consistently follow. Below are the essential key and lock policies that careful landlords follow.

- **Limit access to master keys.** Allow only selected employees to have access to master keys, and impress upon them the need to guard these keys closely. Never allow an employee to give a master key (or any tenant's key) to a contractor, vendor, guest, or anyone else, even for a short while. If you decide to let someone into an apartment, have your employees accompany them.

- **Change locks with each move-in.** Change the locks every time a new tenant moves in, even though you require tenants to return their keys when vacating their apartment. Even if your state or city doesn't require you to change locks, it makes good business sense to do so. Don't run the risk that a former tenant who secretly made a copy of his key will use it to enter the apartment later to commit a crime, or sell it to a criminal to do the same.

If you and your staff haven't already been following these two rules, it's not too late to start. Document each time you change a lock, whether before each new move-in or at a tenant's request (see "Keep a Log of Lock Changes," below).

It Won't Happen to You ...

What happened. A female tenant at an Iowa apartment complex was raped by a stranger who used keys to gain access. The tenant sued the complex's manager for inadequate security. An appeals court ruled that a jury must decide whether the manager should be held liable for the tenant's harm. The court noted that there had been at least one attempted assault at the property by a groundskeeper who used an apartment key. The court also found that the complex didn't control access to the master keys and didn't change the locks of each apartment before each new move-in.

How you can avoid it. Keeping strict control over keys and locks results in more than good organization. By limiting who has access to your apartments, you'll make the difference between running a safe property and opening the door to serious crimes and hefty judgments against you.

- **Code your keys and keep them secret.** Don't organize keys by tenant names, apartment numbers, or any other easily identifiable information. Although this makes the most sense from an efficiency standpoint, such organization makes it easy for criminals to determine which key will get them into targeted apartments. Instead, code your keys in a way that only you can figure out, and keep the explanation of your codes in a safe, locked place (other than the safe, locked place where you should be keeping your keys, of course).

- **Honor tenants' requests for new locks promptly.** If you're like many landlords, you don't let tenants change locks on their own—too often, tenants won't give you copies, and you won't be able to enter. But there's a flip side to this method of key control— when tenants ask you to change their locks, fulfill their request promptly. You may charge tenants for the expense of changing their locks. Doing so will help encourage tenants to practice good key control of their own, so you won't have to change locks for tenants who repeatedly misplace their keys.

It Won't Happen to You ...

What happened. A South Dakota property had a policy of barring tenants from changing their own locks and requiring a fee for the landlord to change the locks. So, when a tenant discovered that her key was missing, she told two property employees and allegedly asked for a new lock. The landlord didn't change the lock, and an assailant used a key to enter the tenant's apartment and kill her. The tenant's estate sued the landlord and property manager.

How you can avoid it. It's okay to restrict tenants from taking certain steps to increase security on their own, such as changing their apartment door's locks. But if tenants follow your rules and promptly request an important security measure, you must follow through. In this case, if the landlord had changed the locks, as requested, the assailant wouldn't have been able to enter the tenant's apartment with her lost key.

Keep a Log of Lock Changes

Document your efforts to change apartment locks before each move-in and in response to each tenant's request. It's simple to do—just create a log like the one below and make sure your employees are committed to recording new entries promptly after each new lock change.

Date	Unit #	Reason	Request Date	Fee Paid?	Employee
1/17/08	3G	Move-out	N/A	N/A	JAL
1/22/08	4B	Lost keys	1/21/08	Yes	CJB
1/29/08	1C	Move-out	N/A	N/A	HRS

Follow professional recommendations offered to prevent crime at your property

If your insurer, attorney, a police officer, or a risk management consultant you hire suggest measures to help lower the risk of crime at your property, seriously consider following the advice. Most of the time, when professionals offer advice after inspecting property and reviewing its history, they know what they're talking about, and their suggestions will very likely reduce your risk of crime.

Missing out on crime reduction isn't all that may follow if you ignore recommendations. If you receive professional advice but don't follow it, and your inaction contributes to a criminal's success with a subsequent crime (for instance, a burglar gets past the slow-closing garage gate that your consultant told you was worthless as a barrier to intruders), defending yourself against liability will be nothing short of an uphill battle. The lawyer for the injured person will no doubt discover that you ignored a professional's specific recommendation to beef up your security. Once a judge or jury learns this information, the trial may effectively be over. Don't let this happen to you.

It Won't Happen to You ...

What happened. A criminal kicked down the front door of a Georgia apartment and raped the tenant inside. In the 23-day period before the attack, there had been eight similar break-ins at the same complex. Two years earlier, the complex's security consultant had recommended that striker plates be installed on apartment front doors with three-inch screws—advice the landlord ignored. The landlord and manager paid later when they settled with the tenant for $550,000.

How you can avoid it. This landlord failed to listen to the professionals he hired. Don't make the same mistake—choose your consultants wisely and follow through. If you don't understand why a consultant is making a certain recommendation, ask for an explanation. Also, if you think a recommendation will require you to spend money you can't afford, ask about less costly alternatives.

Failing to implement recommended security measures can affect your insurance, too. Your insurance policy's premium may be based in part on the fact you've committed yourself to following certain loss control recommendations at your property. If you stop following these recommendations, or if you let your property's crime rate rise, your insurer will likely up your premium to reflect the increased risk.

Make sure your liability insurance provides enough coverage to compensate you if you suffer a loss from crime. If you don't know how much liability coverage you're paying for, or if you haven't looked at your policy in years, it's time to dust it off and review it carefully. Talk to your broker to determine how much coverage you need, considering the crime level in your neighborhood and any history of criminal activity at your property. (For more information about choosing the right types and levels of insurance for your property, see Step One.)

Use your good sense when hiring or speaking with security consultants. Many of them are excellent and can give you ideas for keeping your property safe. But if you think a consultant you hire isn't qualified, is being pushy, or if you just don't agree, hire someone else. Don't let discouragement with one professional interfere with your goal of keeping your risks at bay. If money is tight and following certain recommendations would be too costly, ask any professional you consult about less expensive alternatives that may still prove effective.

To find a good security consultant, ask around for recommendations. You can also search for a qualified consultant on the Web, or by using the International Association of Professional Security Consultants' (IAPSC) free Skills Match Program. To search, visit www.iapsc.org and click "Find a Security Consultant" in the left-hand navigation. Then, click "Find Your Consultant Now" to access the search form, and focus your search as desired (for instance, you can limit the results to consultants who specialize in residential rental properties). When interviewing a consultant (even one who comes with a glowing recommendation from a friend or colleague), the IAPSC recommends asking questions such as the following before hiring:

- What is your experience in the rental property industry?
- How many consulting jobs have you performed in this area?

- How many of these were for properties like mine?
- How recent were these engagements?
- What references may I contact?
- Would you have the time and resources to complete the job in a timely manner?

Be honest when prospects ask about crime at your property

If your property has an excellent track record for avoiding crime, that's certainly a strong marketing point that can help you draw good tenants. But suppose your property's crime rate has been less than stellar, or an exception to your perfect crime record occurs a week before an excellent prospect visits your property and inquires about recent crime. You don't want to trumpet bad news—but you don't want to be dishonest, either. What should you do?

Answer prospects' questions truthfully, but don't let the conversation end with the bad news. If you must reveal or confirm something negative that has happened at your property, continue by outlining what your property is currently doing to increase security and stave off crime. If you can, mention the "neighborhood watch" program sponsored by the local police. Some prospects won't be reassured—they'll leave and search for an unblemished property. But don't let that possibility push you toward hiding the truth. If you don't reveal the facts, and this person becomes the victim of a criminal incident, the chances of your being found liable go way up.

When responding to questions about prior criminal incidents, try to paint a convincing picture of an owner who learns from history, takes crime seriously, and works hard to keep tenants safe. Prospects may feel that in fact they'll be safer living at a property such as yours (instead of one that's never had a problem) because you've learned from your experience and have taken steps to minimize the chances that a crime will occur again. In your zeal to convince prospects that you're serious, however, don't go so far as to leave them with the impression that you're guaranteeing your property will stay crime-free. No landlord can make good on such a promise.

It Won't Happen to You ...

What happened. After living in her Virginia apartment complex for a few months, a tenant was attacked and raped by an assailant who entered her apartment through a window with faulty locks. The tenant had just been accepted into law school, but her chronic post-traumatic stress disorder and a mild brain injury prevented her from excelling, costing her an estimated future income loss of more than $1 million. The tenant sued her landlord and property manager, claiming they provided inadequate security because of the faulty locks. She also claimed the landlord and manager committed fraud by not telling her about the property's recent criminal activity, even after she had asked several times before signing the lease. The landlord and manager settled for $1.5 million.

How you can avoid it. Be honest when prospects ask you about your property's history. If you paint a picture that's too rosy, a judge or jury may conclude that because you promised a safe place but didn't deliver, you should pay. Regularly inspect door and window locks, and tell tenants to promptly report any security problems they notice.

Carefully screen applicants

As important as it is to be honest about the realities of your property and the neighborhood, it's equally important to do your best to weed out applicants whose history suggests they may become a problem. The challenge for any landlord is to identify such applicants through proper screening and eliminate them without violating fair housing or other laws.

Many landlords categorically reject applicants who have *any* criminal convictions. Such a policy may not be so wise, however. First, under fair housing laws, you cannot automatically exclude applicants who have convictions for past drug use (although you can exclude current drug users and applicants convicted for the manufacture or sale of illegal drugs). Second, as a practical matter you may determine that it's better to limit your rejections to those applicants who have committed relatively recent violent crimes or thefts. Often, the type and nature of an applicant's conviction, along with other factors such as how long ago the incident occurred and the applicant's past landlord references, may convince you that renting to an applicant with a criminal history wouldn't pose a threat to your tenants or property.

If you decide to adopt a policy on renting to applicants with a criminal history, consider discussing it with your lawyer, who should be able to help you formulate a sensible policy that won't expose you to risk under your state's or municipality's fair housing laws. Once you decide on a policy, be sure to apply it equally to all applicants to avoid discrimination charges.

If you discover a tenant has a criminal history after he's already signed the lease, this fact alone normally isn't enough to justify an eviction. However, if your rental application asks whether applicants have ever been convicted of a crime and the tenant lied on his application, this could be grounds for terminating the lease (assuming that your lease provides that false and material information can lead to eviction). If your tenant has a month to month rental agreement, you may be able to terminate by following the notice requirements in your state. Consult your attorney immediately if you find yourself in this situation.

For more information about screening tenants, see Step Seven. Also, refer to Step Nine for help with hiring the right employees. For a comprehensive understanding of criminal background checks (and their limits), see *Every Landlord's Guide to Finding Great Tenants,* by Janet Portman (Nolo).

Don't let your apartments become meth labs

Since the 1990s, a growing number of tenants across the country have turned their apartments into laboratories for manufacturing the drug methamphetamine, creating serious problems for landlords. Methamphetamine is a stimulant that physicians sometimes prescribe in pill form for conditions such as attention-deficit disorders, narcolepsy, and obesity. But it can be easily manufactured using ephedrine or pseudoephedrine, the active ingredients in many popular over-the-counter cold medications. Meth makers turn these medications into a powder that users snort, smoke, inject, or swallow.

According to the 2005 National Survey on Drug Use and Health published by the U.S. Department of Health and Human Services, an estimated 10.4 million Americans aged 12 or older admit to having used methamphetamine for nonmedical reasons. Legislation by states and the federal government, most notably, the USA PATRIOT Improvement and Reauthorization Act of 2005, aims to limit the sale of ephedrine or pseudoephedrine and stop the spread of so-called "meth labs" throughout the country. So far, this legislation has proved effective, according to the "National Drug Threat Assessment 2007," a report issued by the National Drug Intelligence Center.

Although recent trends appear encouraging, meth labs are still quite prevalent (particularly in the Midwestern, Southwestern, and Western part of the country), and the liability risk to landlords is too great to ignore.

Meth labs are costly problems for landlords

Apartments that have been used as meth labs aren't safe to be occupied by new tenants until they have been cleaned. A simple cleaning and paint job will rarely do, and in cases of serious contamination, even drywall and wiring must be removed and replaced. Because of the significant health risks, you'll need to hire contractors that have special Hazmat training, and you should expect to pay a bundle for it. Meth lab cleanup costs can run you $5,000–$15,000 per apartment, depending on the apartment's size and the extent of the contamination.

On top of the cleanup costs, you'll face a loss of rent revenue for the apartment while it remains unsuitable for occupancy, not to mention the risk that people won't want to rent the apartment (or will even avoid your property) if they learn that it recently was a meth lab. (Don't count on being able to clean up and stay mum—a growing number of states, including California, Colorado, and Michigan, require landlords to disclose the past presence of a meth lab on their property.)

Landlords who don't properly clean up former meth labs at their property risk that new tenants—especially children—will get sick and sue for millions of dollars. It's no wonder, then, that states have been starting to enact laws that require landlords to clean up apartments before allowing new tenants to occupy them. For example, Indiana requires landlords to have a qualified inspector clean up hazardous substances from interior surfaces caused by the manufacture of methamphetamine and other controlled substances before rerenting the apartments to new tenants.

Prevent meth labs

With so much at stake, the best way to avoid a "meth mess" is to make sure tenants don't use their apartments—your property—for this illegal purpose in the first place. If tenants do convert your apartments into meth labs, you'll want to find out as soon as possible to stop the contamination and minimize harm. Here are some proactive steps you can take:

- Run thorough criminal background checks on applicants and, when talking to prior landlords, ask about any drug problems the landlord had with the prospect.
- Look for suspicious behavior from tenants, which includes keeping their windows darkened or blocked by curtains; having frequent visitors at all hours of the day or night; acting impatient, nervous, or guilty when employees enter their apartment for repairs or any reason; and leaving their apartments frequently to smoke. (Smoking can easily ignite the chemical fumes created by the meth production process.)
- Educate your maintenance staff about meth labs and tell your employees what to look for when they visit apartments to make repairs. (The U.S. Drug Enforcement Administration has a useful list of warning signs at www.dea.gov/concern/clandestine_indicators.html.)
- Tell your employees that if they believe an apartment is being used as a meth lab, they shouldn't perform any repairs or touch any items or surfaces. Instead, they should leave the apartment

immediately to avoid health problems. Employees should promptly report their observations to you so that you may call local law enforcement, if necessary.

Avoid promising to implement a security measure by a certain date

You'll probably recognize this scenario: You just found a great tenant, who has a few final questions about security before signing the lease. To help sweeten the deal, you promise the tenant you'll address her security concerns by a certain date.

This may sound like a great idea at the time, but the truth is it's risky business. At the very least, if you haven't done the work when the tenant moves in, that may be grounds for her to cancel the lease, without responsibility for rent. And if the tenant signs the lease relying on your promise and then becomes the victim of a crime after you didn't deliver, your chances of liability go up. Even if you fully intend to address the tenant's concerns by a certain date, think twice before making definitive promises during negotiations or agreeing to timetables or deadlines in your lease.

By changing your words slightly, you can show your commitment to security and still avoid backing yourself into a liability corner by making promises you can't be certain you'll keep. See "Security Measures: How to Say It—And Not Say It," below, for a few examples of what you might be tempted to say versus what you should say.

Security Measures: How to Say It—And Not Say It

Be careful how you describe your plans to implement security measures at your property. An unwise promise, not fulfilled or over-promised, could result in liability if an incident occurs.

What you might be tempted to say	What you should say
The alarm system will be upgraded by the first of the month.	We're working on getting the alarm system upgraded—hopefully by early next month.
It won't take more than a month to implement our new security measures.	It probably won't take more than a month or so to implement our new security measures.
If there's a problem with any of your windows, locks, or doors, let us know and we'll get it fixed the same day.	If there's a problem with any of your windows, locks, doors, let us know so we can address the problem promptly.
No one has a safer property than ours.	We do our best to help keep you safe.
You can rest easy here—no one gets past our security measures.	We take your safety seriously, and are always interested in refining and improving our security measures.

Prioritize crime-related repair requests

If you've read Step Three, you know how important it is to act immediately when dealing with emergencies like broken pipes. Equally important are requests for repairs that, until addressed, expose your property to a serious risk of crime.

For example, suppose the locking mechanism on a tenant's ground-floor window breaks. If you learn about this problem but don't respond promptly and a criminal gains entry through this window, the tenant can claim your delay left open the window—literally and figuratively—for crime.

> **TIP**
>
> **Don't forget to track your progress when handling crime-related and other repair requests.** Use the Tenant Repair Request Log shown in Step Two to document your efforts. You may need this log to prove that your response time was reasonable.

Get tenants' cooperation in fighting crime

When you think of who would be the best resource for keeping tenants safe, you might think of the police, a risk-management consultant, or your attorney. But you'd be missing one excellent ally—your tenants themselves. After all, it's in their best interest to help you make your property a safe place. When tenants see you're committed to security, they'll usually be more than happy to cooperate with you.

Here are ways that smart landlords get their tenants to cooperate with them in lowering the risk of crime at their property.

- **Hold regular safety meetings.** You want tenants to learn how they can make their home safe and secure. To educate them, conduct safety meetings on a regular basis, such as a few times a year Invite police officers (who may offer to initiate a neighborhood watch program), risk-management consultants, and safety experts to make presentations about crime safety tips. Have at least one or two employees attend the meetings to run them and answer questions. Hopefully, your tenants will leave feeling empowered and confident in your commitment to maintain a secure property.

- **Encourage proactive tenants.** Encourage your tenants to support your efforts by taking action. In Step Six, you read about New York City's "If You See Something, Say Something" anti-terrorism slogan. This strategy works with more common crimes, too. At safety meetings, encourage tenants to report suspicious criminal activity either to you or, in case of an emergency, to the police. This is a good way for you to learn, for example, of increased late-night traffic from visitors (which may be a sign of drug activity).

- **Inform your tenants.** Don't assume that your tenants are aware of all your security measures. For example, your long-term tenants in particular are probably unaware of your current efforts at screening applicants for a criminal history. All your tenants will be happier and rest easier once they hear you outline the ways you've been working to ward off crime and keep the property safe.

- **Solicit tenants' ideas.** Invite tenants to tell you their ideas about how to fix security issues they spot. Do it the old-fashioned way by having a suggestion box in your office or other common area, or slip a survey under each tenant's door. You can also set up an email address for tenant communications that's easy to remember, such as suggestions@yourproperty.com.

- **Suggest safety measures.** Sometimes a small behavioral change on the part of your tenants can help increase security. Often, your tenants won't be aware of these tips. For example, it's not a good idea to open a locking door for someone the tenant doesn't know (or even hold it open after entering), no matter how nice or innocent the stranger may appear. If every tenant hears this suggestion, no one should be offended when another tenant (whom they don't know) doesn't open a locked door or hold the door open for a stranger.

It Won't Happen to You ...

What happened. An armed robber pistol-whipped and shot a tenant in the common area of his Georgia apartment complex. His injury required two costly surgeries, on top of lost wages and time at work. The tenant also lost his ability to run and play with his children as he used to do. The tenant claimed the apartment complex was liable for not making the property safe. Police reports showed that seven burglaries, one armed robbery, and several other crimes had occurred at the property in the past year. But the tenant claimed that the complex didn't heed the police records, didn't spend money to increase security, and didn't pay attention to security measures tenants requested in surveys. The tenant settled with the complex for $400,000.

How you can avoid it. Learn about crime at your property by checking police records, and if you discover you have a crime problem, promptly increase security. Although you may have been planning to use the money for something else, spending some money to remove a crime problem at your property will always prove to be the cheaper—and safer—alternative in the long run.

Take firm action against violent tenants

If a tenant complains to you that another tenant has been harassing her, or an employee witnesses a tenant committing a violent or illegal act on your property, take such matters very seriously. Because every case is different, you may decide it's best to consult your attorney about a plan of action, which could range from sending a warning notice and then confronting the tenant about his alleged harassment (often a good idea for verbal altercations), to pursuing eviction proceedings and calling the police (highly recommended if things get physical or a tenant threatens violence).

Unfortunately, if you don't take appropriate action to address a problem with a violent tenant, the problem may escalate. A victim can use your failure to act responsibly as a reason why you should be held at least partially liable for the victim's loss.

It Won't Happen to You ...

What happened. Two female tenants at a California apartment complex were attacked by a neighboring male resident, who bound and sexually assaulted them. The assailant had a history of harassing behavior at the property, such as knocking on tenants' windows and doors in the middle of the night, for which he received only a verbal warning. The attacker got into the apartment through a sliding glass door, whose missing handle lock the landlord knew about. The landlord had insisted that the pin lock at the base of the door was adequate for security.

The tenants sued the landlord for inadequate security, claiming that he should have taken steps to protect them from the assailant, such as by reporting his past harassing actions to the police. The women also argued that the landlord should have replaced the missing handle lock. A jury agreed and awarded the tenants $1.13 million.

How you can avoid it. If you know you have a violent tenant on your property, you must take prompt and serious action, starting with reporting the tenant's behavior to the police and terminating the tenancy. You can't expect these situations to quietly go away; on the contrary, they usually just get worse, as it did in this case.

6 Crime Prevention: My To-Do List

Your tasks in Step Six are a mixed bag, from checking up on legal requirements pertaining to safety (do you need to comply with door and window security laws?) to walking around your property and trying to put yourself in the mindset of a would-be intruder. These actions don't take much effort—but you'll reap a real benefit if you accomplish them.

☐ **The law:** Determine whether state or local laws require security measures at my rental property.

☐ **The situation in the neighborhood:** Talk to neighboring landlords and police officers, and consult other sources to learn the level of crime at my property and in my neighborhood.

☐ **Lighting:** Increase lighting in interior or exterior parts of my property, where inadequate.

☐ **Landscaping:** Remove or alter landscaping that invites criminals to hide or sneak up on potential victims.

☐ **Security first:** Prioritize tenants' security-related repair requests.

☐ **Alarms:** Make sure burglar alarms work and tenants know how to use them, if they choose to.

☐ **Intercom listings:** Remove apartment numbers next to tenants' names on the intercom panel at my buildings' entryways.

☐ **Key policies and control:** Adopt written key and lock policies that my staff must strictly enforce.

☐ **Security device maintenance:** Check for malfunctions of security devices (such as surveillance cameras or automatic gates), and promptly get them repaired.

☐ **Insurance:** Check whether my insurance liability policy provides adequate coverage for loss from crime.

☐ **Vigilance:** Commit to taking firm action against tenants who commit a crime or violent act on my property.

☐ **On-site reviews:** Take regular walks through my property to check for potential crime hazards, and take appropriate follow-up action.

☐ **Professional help:** Consider hiring a professional to inspect my property for potential crime hazards.

☐ **Professional recommendations:** Follow advice from my insurer, risk management consultant, attorney, or other professional on steps aimed at preventing crime.

☐ **Candor with prospects:** Instruct employees to be honest when prospects ask about the incidence of criminal activity at the property.

☐ **No over-promises:** Avoid making oral or written promises or guarantees to prospects and tenants about specific plans to increase my property's security.

Avoid Fair Housing Complaints When Choosing Tenants

E ven landlords who are lucky enough to have perfect tenants occupying all their apartments can't expect these tenants to renew their leases forever. Sooner or later, most tenants are going to move—for a job, significant other, change of scenery, or to purchase a home of their own. When that happens, you'll need to be ready to attract the best candidates, using effective marketing and careful screening. But like many tasks landlords face, these come with hidden landmines you need to be aware of and avoid. Getting the right tenants with minimal expense and risk—and without turning eager prospects into angry plaintiffs—is what Step Seven is designed to help you accomplish.

In Step Seven, you'll read about the liability traps that have taken down countless landlords, and you'll learn effective strategies for sidestepping these traps. If you control your risks in this way, you'll free yourself up to focus on effective marketing campaigns and growing a successful business.

What Do You Have to Lose?

If an interaction with a prospect goes awry, you may lose a potentially good tenant. Worse, just as courteous, professional dealings with would-be tenants will encourage them to spread the word about your business, mishandling prospects will lead them to advise their friends to look elsewhere for good rental housing.

As if continued vacancies and bad press weren't enough, prospects who believe you violated their civil rights may take legal action against you. Even if you win, having to defend yourself means diverting money, time, and energy that you would rather apply to happier or more productive endeavors for your business and property.

Prospects don't have to work too hard or come up with much money to cause you serious legal trouble or tarnish your reputation. To file a complaint with the U.S. Department of Housing and Urban Development (HUD), the primary federal agency in charge of enforcing fair housing laws, prospects (or tenants) need only complete a brief online form or call a toll-free number. If HUD investigates the claim and chooses not to pursue it, prospects still have two more years to decide if they want to sue the landlord on their own. (For a concise outline of the process, see http://www.hud.gov/offices/fheo/complaint-process.cfm.)

If HUD pursues a prospect's claim against you and an administrative law judge rules in the prospect's favor, the judge may order you to pay up to $11,000 (for first offenders) per violation as a civil penalty, plus damages to the victims, attorneys' fees, and more. If you lose in federal court, you risk getting slapped with punitive fees, as well. Prospects and tenants whose claims are unsuccessful risk at most only having to pay their attorneys.

It Won't Happen to You ...

What happened. In 1996, the owners of a 160-apartment complex in a white, middle-class neighborhood in Miami agreed to settle for a record $1 million for turning away prospects because they were black or had children. Under the settlement with the Department of Justice, the landlords agreed to pay $750,000 to the victorious prospects, $90,000 to fair housing organizations, $60,000 toward advertising the settlement, and $100,000 as a civil penalty.

How you can avoid it. Know the fair housing laws and apply them consistently. These Miami landlords were hardly backwoods, small-time operators—yet they managed to get into trouble for violating fair housing basics. You can do better.

Is This You?

Many landlords don't realize that the process of simply renting out their properties can expose them to serious liability. They can't imagine that people who haven't even signed a lease are legally protected. Landlords who also live on the property often think that since they're choosing the people who will be their neighbors, they should be able to use their own selection criteria. While it is true that the federal fair housing laws don't apply to owner-occupied properties of four or fewer apartments, many states and some cities have their own fair housing laws that do apply to small, owner-occupied properties. In sum, if you think prospects don't pose much of a risk, you may very well change your mind by the time you're done reading this chapter. See if you recognize yourself in one or more of the following portraits.

Do You Think About Choosing Tenants Like These Landlords?

☐ For years, you've trusted your "gut" when selecting tenants, and you've never been disappointed—or sued.

☐ Since you live on the rental property yourself, you assume you have greater leeway in choosing tenants than if you lived off-site.

☐ You reject applicants for having any prior drug-related convictions.

☐ When you encounter a minority applicant, you bend over backwards to find that person qualified in order to avoid trouble

☐ You don't rent to physically disabled applicants because your property isn't "set up" for them.

☐ Your application fees are a profit center—they're higher than your actual expenses, but you figure that it's okay because everyone does it.

☐ You turn away prospects because they have Section 8 vouchers, (which very-low-income households use to help pay the rent for apartments at privately owned properties), but you never thought that it might actually be illegal to do so.

☐ You don't tell unsuccessful applicants why they were rejected because you're afraid it will just cause controversy.

Take Action!

Fortunately, learning how to handle prospects in a fair and legal way isn't a monumental task. If you stick to consistent, neutral business policies (such as charging reasonable application fees), and keep a few legal principles front and center (such as not inquiring into the specifics of a disabled applicant's condition), you'll be on safe ground. For a comprehensive approach to tenant screening, selection, and rejection, see *Every Landlord's Guide to Finding Great Tenants*, by Janet Portman (Nolo).

Learn the basics of fair housing laws

Most of the risks associated with renting out your property can be avoided if you understand the basics of fair housing laws—the anti-discrimination rules you must follow when dealing with prospects and tenants. Whole books have been devoted to this subject, and lawyers in particular spend hours debating the fine points and gray areas. Fortunately, you don't have to sign up for a university seminar to learn what you need to know. It all boils down to this one, simple rule: Make decisions and treat prospects and tenants based on solid business reasons—not stereotypes or your personal preferences. Let's see what this means in practice.

Understand who gets special protection under the law

Because certain groups of people have historically suffered discrimination at the hands of landlords (and employers), Congress has given them special protection—they're known as "protected classes." Members of these classes can't be treated differently than other people simply because they're in the class. Under federal law, these classes include race, color, religion, national origin, sex, familial status (including pregnancy), and disability. Included in this list are people who have convictions for illegal drug use, because prior drug addiction (legal or not) is considered a disability. People who are currently using illegal drugs, or who have drug distribution or manufacturing convictions are not protected, however.

It Won't Happen to You ...

What happened. In 2002, a federal jury returned a verdict for $451,208 against a Mississippi landlord for sexually harassing female prospects and tenants. Most of the victims were low-income, single women with limited housing choices. Among other actions, the landlord asked the prospects for sexual favors in exchange for tenancy, threatening to retaliate against prospects who refused his advances.

How you can avoid it. When many people think of sexual harassment, this behavior in the workplace comes to mind. But understand that sexual harassment in the rental housing context is just as illegal—and its consequences can be just as dire. Be especially vigilant if you have staff, and make sure they get proper fair housing training (including sexual harassment, which is covered in Step Nine). If you don't pay for their training, you'll probably pay for their misdeeds.

Several states (and even some cities and counties) have added more protected classes to the list, such as marital status, sexual orientation, source of income, and even arbitrary discrimination. In a word, landlords who treat certain prospects or tenants differently than others based on their membership in a protected class have broken the law. For example, rejecting a female Muslim applicant simply because she's Muslim or a woman is illegal, but rejecting her because she has poor credit and insufficient income to afford the rent is perfectly valid.

Unfair Housing

Fair housing laws protect tenants in every phase of their rental experience. As a landlord, you can't discriminate—act on the basis of a person's membership in a protected class. This means you can't do any of the following for a discriminatory reason:

- Refuse to negotiate with a prospect
- Set screening policies that exclude prospects
- Use different lease provisions for different tenants
- Use any quota system to achieve a desired result
- Limit the use of facilities or services
- Knowingly give inaccurate information about vacancies
- Steer prospects to certain apartments or parts of your building
- Advertise or market your property with preferences
- Make exceptions to lease clauses or house rules
- Deny reasonable accommodation and modification requests from people with disabilities.

Focus on prospects' tenant-worthiness, not their personal characteristics

Some landlords think they'll be on safe ground if they just learn about the protected classes that apply to their property and avoid discriminating against prospects and tenants who belong to these classes. There are two problems with this limited approach.

First, because there are so many protected classes, prospects and tenants are likely to belong to one—or, at least, try to argue that they do. For example, though it may not be illegal to reject applicants because they have a beard, a bearded applicant whom you reject may claim that your decision was actually based on his national origin or religion. Although you may prevail in the long run, is it worth inviting all this trouble?

Second, even if a prospect or tenant belongs to a protected class, it may not be obvious to you. (Think of a prospect with a nonobvious disability or a religiously observant tenant who doesn't wear any visible traditional garb in public.)

Strictly limiting your compliance efforts to avoiding offending people who belong to protected classes is both impractical and risky. Instead, make sure each policy you adopt and action you take is grounded on a valid business reason that any reasonable landlord in your position would make.

Create a tenant selection plan

Landlords have the right to accept only those applicants who are likely to be good tenants and pay their rent on time. Making these basic qualifications for acceptance part of a selection plan will keep you focused on the right questions and answers and give you the added benefit of evidence, should you ever need it, that your business practices were legal. You'll also save yourself some time—announcing your requirements in advance will result in some prospects choosing not to apply, when they realize they can't measure up.

Your tenant selection plan doesn't need to be long. Unlike a lease or other legal document, it certainly doesn't need to be written in legalese or include any special language. Aim to make your plan as user-friendly as you can, keeping in mind that your goal is to clearly communicate your screening policies to prospects and make them feel comfortable applying for an apartment at your property. Here are the most common components of a tenant selection plan:

- **Nondiscrimination statement.** It's important to lead off by telling tenants you comply with the Fair Housing Act and all applicable state and local discrimination laws. Applicants who read this up front will understand they're dealing with a savvy landlord who's committed to playing fair.

- **Income-to-rent ratio.** The industry's rule of thumb is to require income to be at least three times the rent. You may want to vary this, depending on the nature of your property.

- **Fiscal stability.** You want to rent to tenants who don't have a blemished record of delinquent payments and accounts, bankruptcies, and other financial red flags.
- **Occupancy policy.** Give the maximum number of tenants per apartment. See discussion on occupancy requirements, below, for more information.
- **Reference checks.** Identify whom you will contact as part of your screening. For instance, say you'll contact current and prior landlords and employers.
- **Rental history.** You want tenants who pay the full rent on time. So, it makes sense to check applicants' rental history for clues.
- **Criminal background.** State your policy on checking applicants' criminal history. For instance, say that you check for convictions and won't rent to applicants who have a history of violence or, in your opinion, would pose a threat to tenants and property. Putting this policy in writing has an added benefit: Would-be applicants who have a criminal history may decide to apply elsewhere after reading your policy.

Don't create occupancy requirements based on personal views of family living

Fair housing laws take special aim at landlords who treat families differently than other groups of tenants. Many landlords strongly believe, for example, that children of different sexes need their own bedrooms, or that a child past a certain age shouldn't share his parents' bedroom. But applying these personal beliefs as policies for a rental business is risky because they could result in illegally denying a rental to a family because they have children

This is not to say that you have to allow every family into any rental they apply for. You're entitled to apply and enforce occupancy standards (specifying how many people may live in each rental) that are based on the law and follow good, common sense. In practice, this means you'll need to:

- **Follow occupancy standards for your state and municipality.** The federal government, through HUD, says that landlords should allow two persons per bedroom as a general rule. Some states are more lenient—California, for example, specifies two persons per bedroom plus one more. To learn whether your state or municipality have a more generous standard than the federal rule, check your law. See Step Two for information about how you can do this conveniently from your desktop.

- **Use some flexibility when dealing with tenants who have a newborn.** A newborn baby can easily share a bedroom big enough for the parents (and, in fact, the American Academy of Pediatrics strongly recommends it), whereas putting a teenager into that room would clearly violate the two-per-bedroom rule of thumb.

- **Know and apply housing code restrictions.** In addition to knowing the applicable occupancy standard, learn what your local codes say about minimum square footage for rentals. For example, in Herndon, Virginia, a single-occupant apartment must have at least 70 square feet of floor area. For two or more occupants, there must be at least 50 square feet of floor area per person. These rules might make it impossible to designate certain small rooms as bedrooms.

- **Vary the occupancy standard with care.** Landlords may deviate from the applicable occupancy standard if they can show a valid business reason to do so. For example, you might limit the number of persons in a rental based on its limited septic capacity. Be advised, however, that judges closely scrutinize these deviations when tenants challenge them. You'll need some solid backup, such as engineering reports or an expert's statement, to get your variation past a judge.

It Won't Happen to You ...

What happened. An Idaho landlord had a policy that barred parents from letting children of the opposite sex share a bedroom, regardless of age. When a family with a two-year-old boy and a one-year-old girl asked to apply for a two-bedroom apartment, the management refused. The family pursued a discrimination claim through the Department of Justice. In 2002, the landlord and management agreed to change their policy, pay the family $6,250 in damages, and take other measures to ensure compliance with all discrimination laws.

How you can avoid it. Never make rental decisions based on your view of how a family should set sleeping arrangements. Your only legitimate question is whether the apartment is physically large enough to house the intended number of occupants.

Give your tenant selection plan to all prospects

Some landlords treat their tenant selection plan as an internal document for employees. It's better to also give your plan to prospects, so they know what you're looking for in a tenant. Include it with your rental application, so prospects who are serious about living at your property will know your selection criteria up front. By removing the potential for unpleasant surprises, you'll lower the chances that a prospect will get angry or confused. An angry or confused prospect is likely to accuse you of treating her unfairly and may believe you're making up the reasons for your rejections as you go along.

Respond promptly to all apartment inquiries

When prospects call or email to inquire about vacancies but don't get a quick response, you risk losing that would-be tenant. But an even greater risk is that you might leave the prospect wondering why you're not communicating. Perhaps it was his accent in the voicemail? Or was it the awkward grammar combined with the hard-to-spell surname in the email that implied a foreign nationality? Prospects who feel ignored may believe you're engaging in either "linguistic profiling," a fancy term for making decisions based on what you surmise from a person's speech or writing, such as his grammar, accent, or spelling; or "name profiling," which refers to making decisions based simply on the prospect's name. For example, suppose you don't respond to Juan Alvarado, Mordechai Rothstein, and Jennifer Wright. They all conclude that you're discriminating—Juan based on his national origin, Mordechai because of his religion, and Jennifer because of her sex.

You never want to give a disappointed applicant the feeling that such discriminatory reasons underlie your valid decisions. The key to avoiding this situation is to adopt a policy to respond to all phone calls and emails promptly.

It Won't Happen to You ...

What happened. A local fair housing agency spent three years gathering evidence to show that the landlords of a Pennsylvania apartment complex discriminated by treating black prospects differently than white prospects—based on how they sounded over the phone. For example, the landlords told a white phone prospect about an available apartment (and encouraged the prospect to apply), shortly after telling a black prospect that there were, in fact, no vacancies. In 2002, the landlords settled with HUD for $10,000.

How you can avoid it. Take phone inquiries seriously and don't make judgments about phone prospects based on what you think their voice might tell you about their race, national original, or other protected class.

> **TIP**
>
> **If you accept email inquiries, make sure your staff treats emails with the same level of seriousness as phone calls.** Add language in your ad or on your website saying that you invite email inquiries and will handle them promptly. Give a time frame but don't lock yourself in—"usually within 24 hours" or "usually by the end of the next business day" are good options.

Avoid liability traps with application fees

Do you charge applicants fees to cover a credit check and other expenses related to processing their applications? If you do, you should know that there are two ways in which such fees can come back to bite landlords. Make sure the situations below don't happen to you.

Charge what the law allows and what you actually spent

As tempting as it may be, don't think of your application fees as a profitable side business. Your state or municipality may impose a cap on what you can charge applicants to check their credit history or process their application, which should include the cost to pull a report and some compensation for your time. For example, Maryland requires landlords who charge more than $25 to return any amount over the $25 that was not actually used to process an application to prospects within 15 days of move-in; California sets an outer limit also. If you exceed the cap, you risk getting cited for violating the law. Even if your state and local law don't impose a cap, you still risk getting sued for consumer fraud if your fees are excessive and unrelated to your application processing expenses. If you're not sure whether your state or local law imposes a cap, check the law online (see Step Two for help).

Explain the fee's purpose

Make sure your rental application clearly states the purpose of your application fee. It should say that the fee is intended to cover your expenses in processing the prospect's application. Most importantly, it should make clear that paying the fee doesn't guarantee a prospect an apartment or improve a prospect's chances of getting one. It should also say that by accepting an application fee from a prospect, you're not claiming that the prospect is eligible (or even likely to be eligible) to rent an apartment at your property.

Treat all prospects like testers

HUD, fair housing agencies, and housing advocacy organizations often employ "testers" to check whether a property is complying with federal, state, and local discrimination laws. These testers visit properties posing as prospects interested in renting an apartment. Usually, agencies will pair together two testers, one of whom has a characteristic that's often the basis of discrimination (for example, the tester uses a walker, has dark skin, or speaks with a foreign accent). Each member of the pair will be assigned the same financial profile, so that they appear equally qualified to rent an apartment. If testing reveals that a landlord is offering different terms and conditions to a tester because of the tester's race, religion, sex, or other protected characteristic, the agency will likely file a complaint with HUD. If HUD is doing the testing as part of its investigation of a real prospect's complaint, the results could help bolster the government's case against the landlord.

There's a good chance you'll have testers visit your property, and in fact you may already have. If a tester concludes that you're discriminating, you're more likely to face a discrimination claim than if a nontester had suffered the same experience. Remember, it's the tester's job to find discriminating landlords, and when they find one, they won't hesitate to pounce; ordinary people who are discriminated against may decide not to pursue the matter (and in some cases, may not be as familiar with the law to know they've just been discriminated against).

Play it safe by adopting an attitude of treating every prospect as if he or she is a tester. If your employees understand that any prospect they meet, talk with, or even email could be a tester, they'll focus more on consistently doing and saying the right things, and you'll no doubt see an improvement in your staff's compliance efforts.

It Won't Happen to You ...

What happened. In 2004, the owners of 29 Georgia apartment complexes agreed to settle accusations, which were confirmed through the Department of Justice's testing program, that they allowed white prospects to inspect apartments while telling black prospects that no apartments were available. The landlords were ordered to pay $170,000 to the shunned prospects, plus a $10,000 civil penalty.

How you can avoid it. This appears to be a case of blatant discrimination. But it's a good wake-up call for all landlords to review their policies and practices to make sure they're not discriminatory. You never know if that nice couple who just looked at some of your available apartments were actually undercover testers!

Don't have inappropriate conversations with prospects

You probably don't baldly ask an applicant questions about her religion or age, whether she's pregnant, or what country her family comes from. But many landlords get tripped up because they don't realize that more subtle conversations can also violate the law. Here are the two key points you must know when it comes to spotting inappropriate conversation topics with prospects.

Avoid describing your property in protected-class terms

Be very careful not to describe your property in ways that prospects could reasonably interpret as a signal that they're not welcome there. Even if you're truthfully describing a feature or situation and have no intent to discriminate, using protected-class descriptions could land you in legal hot water. For example, statements such as "There aren't many Hispanic people living here" or "Not many families with children apply for apartments here" may be accurate, but a Hispanic prospect or a family could reasonably feel discouraged by such remarks, and use them against you as the basis of a discrimination complaint.

Your house rules can also run you afoul of the law (even without ill intention), such as if your rules prohibit children (but not adults) from acting rowdy in hallways and other common areas. Finally, your advertising and marketing materials must be crafted with the same precautions in mind. For example, avoid using phrases such as "perfect for empty nesters," "adult community," "near church," or "not handicap-accessible."

Don't get lulled into discriminatory exchanges

A charge of discrimination could also come from the most unexpected quarter—the prospect who invites you to innocently partake in a conversation that turns out to have discriminatory overtones. For example, suppose a prospect of a particular ethnicity asks to see apartments near others that house tenants of the same ethnicity; or a family asks about being near other tenants with children. Should you lead the prospects to the available apartments that correspond to their request? In general, it's safest to step away from these minefields, and show prospects all available apartments.

This advice might sound legalistic, but it makes sense. Suppose these prospects apply for an apartment and you reject them for perfectly valid business reasons. If they cast about for some reason to blame you, it may come down to a case of your word against theirs when they claim that when you showed them only certain apartments, you were illegally steering them toward specific areas of the property. ("Steering" is industry lingo for encouraging, guiding, or directing prospects to certain apartments—or even parts of buildings—for discriminatory reasons.)

It Won't Happen to You ...

What happened. Several tenants accused Louisiana landlords of racial discrimination at their 140-apartment complex. They claimed that the landlords steered black prospects to one side of the building, and they pointed to the fact that the side was occupied entirely by black tenants, a white woman with biracial children, and a white woman who lived with a black man. That part of the building was inferior because its tenants couldn't adjust the air-conditioning or heating in their apartments without first calling management. Also, when the swimming pool that served the "black side" of the complex closed for two seasons, the landlords refused to let the affected tenants use the pool on the "white side" of the complex. The landlords settled the case for $325,000.

How you can avoid it. These landlords practiced steering to a point where it amounted to wide-scale segregation. But remember that guiding prospects to certain apartments or parts of your building for a discriminatory reason even once is unlawful. To avoid the risk of steering, tell prospects about all vacancies for the size they request, and let them tell you about any special requirements or preferences they might have.

It Won't Happen to You ...

What happened. Pennsylvania landlords required families with children to rent apartments on the first floor of their 91-apartment complex. To accomplish this, the landlords gave different information about apartment availability to prospects depending on whether they planned to have children living with them. After the Department of Justice investigated, the landlords settled for $31,000.

How you can avoid it. Remember that all steering is illegal, regardless of your motive. Even if you think families with children would be happier or safer living on the first floor, you must present them with all options and let them make the call.

> ### Take Your Cue From Your Applicants—Don't Assume You Know What's Best
>
> Landlords who take fair housing laws seriously may understandably be tempted to anticipate the needs of someone who is (or appears to be) disabled, and to suggest accommodations that the prospect hasn't yet asked for—and possibly never will. For example, when showing available apartments to a person who walks with a cane, you might assume that an apartment close to the front entrance would be best, and you might offer that apartment instead of showing all available apartments. Though your motivations may be pure, your actions are illegal. You're not in a position to decide what's best for anyone else, however sensible your conclusions may appear. Instead, tell prospects what apartments you have available, and let prospects tell you which apartments they'd like to see.

Make reasonable accommodations for prospects' disabilities

Federal law requires you to consider all prospects' requests for accommodations to your rules, policies, and procedures. If would-be tenants can show (usually through a physician or other qualified third party's statement) that they are physically or emotionally disabled and need a requested accommodation for the disability, you must grant the request—but only if it's reasonable. Common examples of reasonable accommodation requests include:

- a visually impaired prospect's request to let his guide dog occupy the apartment, despite your "no pets" rule
- a mobility-impaired prospect's request to let her use her motorized wheelchair in your clubhouse, despite your rule banning motorized vehicles from common areas, and

- an emotionally disabled prospect's request to have an employee pick up or drop off forms that tenants would normally deliver or pick up at your rental or maintenance office, if the prospect's disability makes her afraid to leave her apartment or the building.

You must decide whether an accommodation request is reasonable based on each prospect's particular circumstances and your property. Generally, a request is unreasonable if granting it would impose an undue financial and administrative burden on your property, fundamentally alter the nature of your business, or require you to violate the law. Keep in mind that you must use the same evaluation process when tenants who are already renting from you ask for accommodations, too.

It Won't Happen to You ...

What happened. A female tenant at a Montana property had a valid disability that caused her to have "a great fear of adult males in a residential setting." To accommodate this tenant's disability, the landlord created a policy of not renting to single males. A male prospect who was rejected under this policy complained to a local fair housing organization, which resulted in the Justice Department taking the landlord to federal court. In 2003, the landlord agreed to change her discriminatory policy, pay $18,000 in damages, and get fair housing training.

How you can avoid it. The policy this landlord put in place was not only unreasonable, it was a blatant example of illegal discrimination on the basis of sex. A better course of action would have been to talk to the tenant's physician or other appropriate professional to come up with legal, reasonable alternatives. If neither the tenant nor her physician or other third party can present a reasonable option, then you needn't make any accommodation in this situation.

It Won't Happen to You ...

What happened. Third-floor tenants at a Texas apartment complex, whose disabilities made the long walk to the elevator quite difficult, asked to transfer to an available ground-floor apartment, which was near the front entrance. When management refused, the tenants complained to HUD. In 2006, the landlords and managers settled with the Department of Justice, agreeing to grant the tenants' transfer request as a reasonable accommodation, pay $125,000 in damages and fees, and take other steps to ensure future compliance with fair housing laws.

How you can avoid it. Take all accommodation and modification requests seriously—not just from prospects, but from tenants, too. Grant requests when they're reasonable (like the request in this case).

Don't ask about the severity of prospects' disabilities

Many landlords who meet prospects with disabilities ask them questions about the nature or extent of their disabilities. Sometimes it's out of curiosity, but often it's because these landlords believe they need to know more so they can provide the housing that's needed. Practically speaking, however, you don't need to know the details. (All you're entitled to is corroboration from a doctor or other skilled professional that the person is disabled and needs a specific accommodation.) Asking prospects to explain their disabilities only puts you at risk of getting sued.

The temptation to inquire about the details often comes up when you're faced with competition among disabled prospects for accessible apartments. Though it might seem sensible to weigh the prospects' disabilities and give the apartment to the prospect who appears to be the most disabled, this would be a mistake. The law doesn't require you to investigate prospects' disabilities and pass judgment on who is more deserving of an accessible apartment based on the extent of the prospect's disability. In any event, making medical determinations based on lay observations is likely to be inaccurate. Instead, create a waiting list of qualified prospects and, as accessible apartments become available, take prospects off the waiting list on a first-come, first-served basis.

Don't penalize tenants for using wheelchairs

If you impose special conditions on tenants who use wheelchairs, it's time to rethink those policies. Because tenants who use wheelchairs need them for a disability, making them pay extra to use a wheelchair is a clear-cut case of illegal discrimination. Here are the most common ways in which this situation may arise:

- **Additional security deposit.** Some landlords argue that tenants who use wheelchairs should pay a higher security deposit than other tenants because of extra anticipated wear and tear from their wheelchairs. But charging tenants more for housing just because they use wheelchairs amounts to discrimination. That said, if a tenant causes substantial damage to her apartment with a wheelchair, you can expect her to pay to fix the damage—just as you would go after any tenant (disabled or not) who damages her apartment through other means.

- **Motorized vehicles.** Many landlords understandably ban motorized vehicles from their common areas because of the potential for injury and property damage. If you have such a ban, you must allow disabled tenants to use motorized wheelchairs as a reasonable accommodation. You must also follow through by not requiring them to pay extra for this accommodation or carry liability insurance. Keep in mind that your policy is aimed at preventing injuries that can result when tenants race mopeds and such through your hallways or clubhouse. Tenants who own motorized wheelchairs use them to compensate for a disability—not for sport.

It Won't Happen to You ...

What happened. A Minnesota landlord recently had to defend itself in front of a HUD administrative law judge after a tenant complained that the landlord's requirement that she buy a personal liability insurance policy because of her motorized wheelchair violated fair housing law. The judge ruled that the landlord didn't have a valid business reason for requiring the tenant to buy the insurance and ordered the landlord to pay the tenant $7,500 in damages and $36,301 in attorneys' fees, in addition to $8,000 in penalties.

How you can avoid it. Don't require wheelchair-using tenants to carry insurance, no matter how sensible this idea may seem to you. Unlike the situation with renters' insurance (which you may be legally entitled to require, depending on your state law), requiring a disabled person to carry liability insurance is a clear violation of federal law.

Don't be afraid to reject applicants for valid reasons

No landlord wants her wallet emptied and her reputation tarnished by an ugly discrimination claim—especially when the landlord acted legally. But don't let a fear of getting sued influence your screening decisions or convince you to accept an applicant that good business sense tells you to turn away. Though you may not reject applicants because of their membership in a protected class, not every member of a protected class is entitled to live at your property—they must first meet your reasonable "good tenant" criteria, which you've developed in your tenant selection plan, as described above.

Apply your screening criteria consistently to all applicants, and keep careful records outlining the reasons for each rejection. If you do this, you'll build a defense to any potential discrimination charge by being able to show that you always treat applicants the same and reject them only for valid reasons.

Ironically, landlords who accept applicants based on fear are actually still discriminating by illegally giving preferences to certain applicants based on their race, religion, or other characteristic. Think of the landlord who enforces screening policies strictly against all applicants but bends the rules for prospects of minority races because he fears such prospects may file a fair housing complaint against him. By bending the rules, this landlord not only risks renting to tenants who won't be able to pay the rent on time, but he may get sued by white applicants who fared just as well during the screening process but got rejected.

Reject Uncooperative or Untruthful Applicants

You don't have to rent to an applicant who doesn't cooperate with your screening process (by refusing to pay a reasonable credit check fee, for example). With these folks, you won't have what you need to make a proper, informed decision on their application. Nor must you do business with those whose rental applications contain incomplete or untruthful information. These applicants may be hiding something important about their background that would prompt you to reject their application. And regardless of what a prospect may be hiding, you don't want to legally commit to a tenant who has shown himself to be elusive or a cheat.

Don't be too quick to assume that an inaccurate answer that a prospect gave you is a lie—it could be an honest or careless mistake. Raise the issue and give applicants a chance to explain.

Give the reason for each applicant's rejection

Don't leave applicants guessing as to why you rejected their application. As much as you may want to shy away from delivering unpleasant news ("Your references didn't measure up," or "Your rent-to-income ratio doesn't meet my standard"), doing so leaves applicants wondering why they didn't get the nod. Some will conclude that you had illegal reasons ("She rejected me because of my kids"), and accuse you of discrimination. Being honest won't prevent that outcome, but it may discourage it.

Send unsuccessful applicants a letter that spells out the reason for the rejection. Federal law requires you to do this when you reject applicants (or accept them with conditions) based on their credit history or other information you get from a consumer report. This is known as an "adverse action notice" and must include the following information:

- the nature of the adverse action (such as a denial, higher security deposit, or a month-to-month arrangement instead of a lease)
- the name, address, and telephone number of the agency that provided the consumer report. (If the agency issues reports nationwide, you must include a toll-free number.)
- a statement that the agency did not decide to take the adverse action and therefore can't answer specific questions about it
- a statement that applicants have the right to obtain a copy of their consumer report from the agency, by making a request within 60 days, and
- information for applicants on their right to dispute the accurateness or completeness of the consumer report.

If you're rejecting an applicant based only on information that you came across on your own or via one of your employees, then you don't have to send an adverse action notice. But it's still wise to tell applicants why they were rejected. Taking this step will lower the chances that an applicant will get angry and retaliate by suggesting a discriminatory reason for her rejection.

Whether or not you let applicants know why you rejected them, always note the reason for an applicant's rejection in the prospect's file. This way, you'll help protect yourself against a complaint from that person, and you'll help establish a long-standing record of a nondiscriminatory rejection policy for your property.

Know whether you can turn away prospects for having Section 8 vouchers

Many landlords shudder when prospects call their offices with the question, "Do you take Section 8?" For these landlords, such a call conjures up fears of taking on unacceptable administrative and financial hassles while renting to stereotypically shady prospects who have trouble paying the rent.

Whatever your opinion of the Section 8 voucher program (which, since 1999, has been officially referred to by HUD as the "housing choice voucher program"), you might not have a choice when it comes to deciding whether to welcome prospects with Section 8 vouchers or turn them away. Many states and municipalities that ban discrimination based on Section 8 do so indirectly, as part of a broader ban. For example, Minnesota and Vermont ban discrimination based on "public assistance status," and Utah and Oregon ban discrimination based on "source of income."

To find out whether Section 8 voucher holders are protected in your state and municipality, contact your local fair housing agency. If you learn that no ban covers your property, then you are free to decide whether you want to accept prospects with Section 8 vouchers.

If you must comply with a ban on Section 8 discrimination, note that it doesn't mean you must accept *every* applicant with a Section 8 voucher. A ban means only that you can't reject applicants simply because of the fact that they have Section 8 vouchers. If applicants don't meet your screening criteria, you can confidently reject them regardless of whether they have Section 8 vouchers.

Destroy—don't discard—sensitive applicant information

For years, conscientious landlords routinely threw unneeded applications and credit reports in the trash—what better way to get rid of these documents? But as of June 1, 2005, simply throwing away information from an applicant's consumer report (which may include an applicant's credit history, employment background check, or rental history, among other information) is a violation of federal law. Under the FTC's "Disposal Rule," owners of all types of businesses (and even individuals) must destroy such information, rather than just discard it. This thwarts identity thieves who go "Dumpster diving" for sensitive information such as an applicant's Social Security number, driver's license number, and bank account number, all of which typically appear on a consumer report.

When you get rid of consumer reports or even information that's based on these reports, you must take "reasonable measures" to ensure that the information can't be read or reconstructed—that's what the FTC means by "destroy." Shredding is the most common and easiest way of complying with the rule when it comes to physical documents, and sturdy office shredders typically cost no more than $100–$300.

The Disposal Rule also applies to situations in which you want to discard consumer report information that's stored electronically (for example, when you upgrade your computers and dispose of the old ones). In such situations, simply deleting files does not guarantee that identity thieves can't reconstruct the information. To truly remove such data, the FTC suggests running a computer utility that "wipes" (permanently removes) all data on a hard drive or storage device before you dispose of it.

The Disposal Rule doesn't require you to get rid of any screening information that you wish to keep in order to bolster any defense you might have against later claims of discrimination. You may also keep information that your attorney advises you to retain. The rule addresses only what you must do when you decide to discard such information.

> **TIP**
>
> **Learn what you can do to prevent identify theft at your property.** To find out how you can also minimize your liability, visit the FTC's Identity Theft site at www.ftc.gov/idtheft.

Keep updated log showing apartment availability

Many landlords keep a log showing which apartments are available at their properties. But not all landlords keep their log updated to reflect every new rental, eviction, serious maintenance issue, or other change that affects an apartment's availability status.

It's essential to update your log promptly. If you don't, you'll invite liability. Testers or prospects who chat with other prospects with the same housing needs might jump to conclusions that you didn't show them a certain apartment for a discriminatory reason. The reason might be that the apartment just became available, but you or an employee didn't know it.

On top of the risk of discrimination complaints, keeping an availability log that you don't update is likely to hurt your bottom line. You might turn away good prospects based on the mistaken belief that you have no available apartments of the size they need.

7 Choosing Tenants: My To-Do List

Setting yourself on a safe road to choosing tenants involves practical steps (such as developing a tenant selection plan) and a clear understanding of the supreme fair housing rule (base every decision only on sound business reasons that any reasonable landlord in your position would apply). Here are some specifics:

☐ **Rental criteria:** Develop a written list of the reasons to reject applicants, and give a copy of this list to prospects who apply for apartments.

☐ **Occupancy:** Create occupancy requirements that make sense and comply with the law.

☐ **Follow-through:** Respond promptly and professionally to all serious apartment inquiries from prospects.

☐ **Section 8:** Find out whether I can legally turn away prospects because they have Section 8 vouchers.

☐ **Application fees:** Charge reasonable amounts to cover expenses.

☐ **Advertising:** Describe my apartments—not the type of people I want to rent them.

☐ **Document retention:** Destroy consumer reports and related information once I no longer need them.

☐ **Rejections:** Use an adverse action letter to communicate rejections based on credit or other consumer reports, and tell all applicants the reason for their rejection.

☐ **Availability:** Keep up-to-date apartment availability logs.

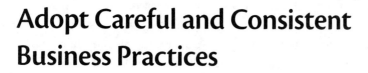

Adopt Careful and Consistent Business Practices

The advice so far in this book has urged you to look carefully at several specific areas of your rental business, such as your insurance, your property's physical condition, and the way you handle prospects. In each area, you probably identified vulnerabilities and found action steps that will lower your risk of problems. This chapter concerns various ways in which you do business (such as your approach to consistently applying your house rules), rather than issues related to specific areas of your business. You'll learn about risks that are associated with common (but ill-advised) ways of doing business—and you'll find helpful suggestions on how to turn a risky approach into a safe one.

What Do You Have to Lose?

Many landlords create risks just by the way they go about their business. The most worrisome risk is a high tenant turnover rate. When tenants believe that their landlord is unfair, inconsistent, clueless, or uncaring, they're more likely to consider leaving when their lease is up. (Worse, if a landlord's actions are egregious, tenants may gain a legal opportunity to break their lease without further responsibility for their rent.) While some turnover may be acceptable, too much turnover can put a serious dent in your bottom line. Professionals estimate that landlords shell out the equivalent of at least two months' rent for each instance of turnover at a rental property.

As if losing good tenants and having to scramble to fill vacancies isn't unpleasant enough, your business will suffer in other ways. Poorly managing the use of your facilities can trigger a fair housing lawsuit; sloppy handling of sensitive tenant information can facilitate identity theft (for which you could be held liable); and a lukewarm policy on renters' insurance could mean that your own policy will have to step up when a tenant's carelessness injures someone on your property. These consequences are annoying at least, and expensive at worst.

Is This You?

Want to adopt the best business practices? Don't repeat the mistakes of those landlords who learned valuable lessons the hard way (and, when applicable, take cues from your own mistakes before they turn into regrettable blunders). See if you recognize yourself in one or more of the following descriptions of landlords whose approaches to various business issues landed them in legal and financial hot water.

Do You Do Business Like These Landlords?

☐ Instead of using a written lease or rental agreement, you rely on oral understandings and a firm handshake.

☐ You sometimes have trouble getting tenants to cooperate with you on important matters relating to their tenancy and your business.

☐ You don't have clear procedures for handling tenant repair requests or complaints.

☐ You and your employees don't always enforce your rules against all your tenants.

☐ You're very involved in your tenants' lives and problems, to the point that you consider them your close friends.

☐ When you want a tenant to leave but haven't started the eviction process, you take certain "self-help" measures, such as shutting off utilities or changing the locks, to encourage the tenant to leave.

☐ You don't have rules on how tenants and guests should use your property—for example, you let tenants keep pets in their apartment but you don't require them to abide by a set of pet rules.

☐ You let tenants and guests use your pool, fitness center, and other facilities without imposing limitations aimed at protecting their health and safety.

☐ Tenants have formed—or are thinking of forming—a tenants' association, and you make your disapproval known.

!

were to read and follow only one Step in this book, the current ly be the best choice. The problems described in this Step relate to your style of running your business, and they know no geographic, economic, physical, or social boundaries. Whether you own a single-family home in an upscale neighborhood in the middle of a busy city, or a midsize apartment complex in a modest rural setting, you should have consistent, fair, law-abiding approaches to your tenants and every issue that arises in the course of running your business. The action steps that follow will minimize your risks while guiding you toward successful approaches and methods your business can follow.

Use a written rental agreement or lease

Many landlords rely on oral understandings instead of using a written lease or rental agreement. If you're lucky—that is, everybody's memory is clear and consistent—you may be able to get away with a conversation and a handshake to settle the key terms of the tenancy. But far too often, memories fade and what you thought was a clear understanding will be construed differently by your tenants. Don't hesitate to write down the essential aspects of the rental situation—it's not unfriendly but simply good business practice.

Some landlords shy away from written leases because they don't want to go to a lawyer to have them drawn up, or don't trust generic stationery store forms that are too often dripping with legalese. Fair enough. But there's an alternative, and it's right inside the back cover of this book. Nolo's *LeaseWriter Plus* is a software program that allows you to create a valid lease or rental agreement for a property in any state. Best of all, like this book, it's written in plain English. By using a form that you know is compliant with your state law, you'll make essential aspects of each tenancy clear, including:

- the rent, how it should be paid, and when it's due
- the amount of the security deposit and how you'll use it
- the length of the tenancy, if it's a lease

- late fees, if you choose them
- who pays for utilities
- your pet policy
- who pays for attorneys' fees if there's a lawsuit concerning the lease, and more.

Importantly, a written lease or rental agreement also gives you the opportunity to educate your tenants on their responsibilities. *LeaseWriter*'s rental documents cover essential issues, such as your limits on occupancy and use of the property (for instance, no unauthorized occupants or commercial use), your policy against subletting or assigning without your prior consent, tenants' maintenance responsibilities (including your ban on excessive noise and other disturbances), your right of access, your policy on extended absences, and who is authorized to receive legal papers on your behalf. There's a place for you to include state- or locally required disclosures, and to add more provisions if you wish. Importantly, a concluding clause tells tenants that their failure to abide by these provisions will be grounds for terminating their tenancy. With this information front and center, you won't have to argue whether the tenant was aware of the rules in case you need to terminate a tenancy because a tenant ignored those rules.

Secure your tenants' cooperation

If you've been in the rental business for even a modest amount of time, you know that your tenants' willing cooperation is essential to your ability to run a smooth and profitable business. From something as minor as getting into their rental to perform needed repairs, to showing their apartment to prospective occupants, your tenants hold the key to an efficient and hassle-free business. And should you need their active participation in order to provide evidence to a government agency—such as showing that your tenant population is of a certain age, thus establishing your right to continue to offer senior housing—this cooperation isn't just convenient, it's essential.

Convincing tenants to work with you, not against you, involves equal applications of a savvy management style and a carefully drafted lease or rental agreement. Begin now to cement that cooperation—it's too risky to assume that tenants will be accessible and helpful when you need them to be. Some tenants may be hard to track down or just not eager to help you. Worse, some might try to use your need for their cooperation as leverage for getting favorable treatment or special benefits. Here are the action steps that will set the stage for smooth sailing when you need it.

- **In every tenant interaction, emphasize the benefits to the tenant, not your own needs.** You'll get more cooperation if you can show tenants how *they* will benefit by cooperating with your plan or request. For example, though entering their homes for a yearly inspection can be viewed as an intrusion, emphasize that you're doing so in order to make sure the rental is safe and sound—something most tenants will appreciate. Similarly, asking to show their apartment to prospects is always intrusive, but you can sweeten the occasion by offering a reduction in rent for that month or some other perk. (If doing so enables you to rerent the apartment more quickly, then it's money well spent.)

- **Determine whether you'll need tenants' cooperation *after* the lease is signed.** For example, do you have a loan that requires you to rent to a certain number of low-income tenants? Do you participate in affordable housing programs (such as HUD's project-based Section 8 or Section 236 programs, or the IRS's low-income housing tax credit program) that require you to rent to tenants earning below certain income levels? Have you made any promises to state housing agencies to rent to special population groups (such as large families or people with mental illness), are you trying to qualify your property as senior housing, or do you have another reason why you'll need to prove that you rent to certain types of tenants? In these situations, you'll need your tenants' cooperation after you've all signed the lease. For instance, if the regulatory agreement, occupancy handbook, or compliance manual you have in connection with an affordable housing program mentions "recertification," you'll need your tenants' ongoing cooperation to show continued eligibility.

- **Require tenants' cooperation in your lease or rental agreement.** Once you've determined that you'll need specific information from your tenants during their tenancy, make sure your rental documents contain two key clauses (check with the program's administrators to make sure your language comports with their rules and regulations):
  - **Identify why you need tenants' cooperation and how frequently.** For example, say that you need to recertify their income at least annually to ensure continued compliance with the federal low-income housing tax credit program.
  - **Spell out the type of cooperation you need.** For example, explain that you'll need to hold interviews with tenants and obtain documentation to verify all current information concerning income, assets, and related information. Or, to qualify for the "55 and older" exemption to the ban on familial status discrimination, say that you need tenants to complete surveys and affidavits, and provide copies of driver's licenses, birth certificates, passports, and other official identification documentation to verify their age.

When specifying the type of cooperation you need from tenants, be sure to include "catch-all" language that will enable you to ask for information from tenants other than what you actually spelled out. For example, your clause should specify what you need, "as well as any other cooperation or assistance that Landlord determines is reasonably required."

It Won't Happen to You ...

What happened. An Oregon landlord lived in a space in his mobile home park and rented the remaining 14 spaces to tenants. After prospects claimed the landlord turned people away because they had children or because they were under 55, HUD investigated. Although the landlord had told prospects he owned an "adult" property and explained that this meant that tenants were over the age of 55 and no children were allowed, a judge found that the landlord didn't comply with HUD rules showing that his property qualified for the familial status exemption. In 2001, the judge ordered the landlord to pay $8,745 in penalties and damages and take other steps to ensure compliance with fair housing laws.

How you can avoid it. When you need to qualify your property for senior housing, get tenants to agree in their lease to help you verify the current age of their apartment's occupants.

Retain your professional relationship with tenants

As important as it is to cultivate your tenants' cooperation and good will, you also need to make sure that you remain on a professional footing with all of them. In practical terms, this means recognizing that once you become friends, you've changed the nature of your relationship in ways that may make for difficulties later. For example, suppose your tenant cannot pay the rent, and appeals to your friendship when asking you to give him one, two, or more months' grace. You'll have a tough time saying no if you have truly become this tenant's friend.

The extent to which you become friendly with your tenants (or rent to a friend) is, of course, up to you. But if you go down that path, be prepared for some tough calls ahead if the tenant asks for special favors or causes problems. When renting to a friend (or becoming close with a tenant), decide whether you're prepared to lose the friend (when you enforce your rights) or compromise your business decisions (thus preserving the friendship). Although the idea may seem awkward, you might find it helpful to acknowledge this issue by having a short talk with any tenant friends you have. This way, the tenant will know that, while you may be committed to her as a friend, she can't expect any special favors from you as a landlord.

Enforce lease requirements and house rules consistently

Your lease or rental agreement should include key terms such as the amount of rent, rental term, pet policy, and so on. Many landlords supplement their leases and rental agreements with "house rules," which typically concern more mundane or specific matters such as the use of common facilities, parking, and noise. House rules are more flexible than rental documents (you can change them without having to amend tenants' leases or rental agreements, and sometimes you can make changes without notice). Carefully drafted rental documents, plus comprehensive house rules, give your tenants information on what you expect and what you allow, and also give you important support should you need to terminate the tenancy of someone who violates them.

With all the rules you have on the books at your property, ask yourself whether you're enforcing them consistently with all your tenants. If the answer is no, take a moment to figure out why. If you haven't enforced the rule very much, if at all, because you don't think it's needed, consider removing it altogether from your lease or house rules. For example, say that several years ago, you changed your no-pets policy and decided to allow tenants to keep pets in their apartments. You still had concerns, so you created several rules governing the types of pets your tenants may keep. Now, because you no longer care about some of these rules (for example, a weight limitation) and have no intention of enforcing them, you should remove them. If, however, you decide that a rule is important, make a renewed commitment to enforce it consistently with all your tenants.

Consistently applying the rules is more than just a matter of fairness. Sporadically enforcing a rule is risky and can lead to two unfortunate outcomes:

- **You'll lose the right to enforce the rule.** If you don't enforce a rule against a tenant and later decide to employ it, the tenant may refuse to comply, arguing that you can't enforce the rule because your past failure to do so means you've waived your right to insist upon it now. Worse, if other tenants learn of your alleged waiver, they may also refuse to comply with the rule.
- **You'll face a discrimination claim.** If you enforce rules inconsistently among your tenants, some tenants might claim you're acting this way to discriminate. Even if you have no discriminatory intent and act only out of laziness, you may have trouble defending yourself against such a claim.

Unfortunately, it's very easy to fall into the trap of irregularly applying some of your rules. Suppose you have a rule that your swimming pool closes at 8 p.m. A few white tenants are still in the pool one day when you go to lock it up at 8 p.m., and they ask if they can stay for a while. Since you have chores to do in the area anyway, you say okay and return at 8:30 p.m. to lock up. A week later, a black tenant still in the pool at 8 p.m. asks if he can stay for a few minutes longer. You have an appointment to show an apartment in a few minutes, and so you explain that the pool closes at 8 p.m. and that you must lock up. A few days later, the black tenant learns that you had bent the rule for white tenants, and he complains to the local fair housing agency. Although you didn't intend to discriminate, you're nevertheless on the defensive.

Establish reasonable rules covering your facilities' use

In apartment complexes, facilities such as a swimming pool, playground, or fitness center are excellent marketing tools. You no doubt play them up in your ads and property tours, and often they spell the difference between a closed deal and a continued vacancy. But unless your tenants and their guests use these facilities safely and in keeping with your rules, they can also be a source of worry and liability for you. For example, roughhousing in the pool area can lead to slips and falls; misuse of playground equipment by older children can damage the equipment, making it unsafe; and unsupervised children in a fitness center—well, you can imagine what might happen there.

To stave off problems, create rules for each facility, and include them as part of the house rules that you give tenants. Your lease or rental agreement should include a clause telling tenants that serious and repeated violations of these rules (by tenants or guests) will be grounds for termination. Take steps to bring these rules front and center—chances are, your tenants read the rules when they received their copy of the lease and tossed them in a drawer, where they've laid ever since. Even if the rules are short and simple, post them at the facility. Users will see them just as they're about to use the facility, and will be reminded that their enjoyment of the pool, playground, gym, or meeting room depends on their cooperation.

The substance of the rules themselves depends on the facility or equipment being used—obviously, pool rules will differ from playground rules. There are, however, some universal practices that should figure into any set of rules. Here they are.

Limit use to tenants and authorized guests

You probably want to let tenants' guests, as well as tenants, enjoy your facilities. That's fine, but you should limit use to "authorized guests," which are people who are using your facilities with a tenant's express permission. You may, therefore, wish to require guests to use facilities only when accompanied by a tenant, or you might issue guest passes that guests must obtain from consenting tenants.

If you don't limit who may use your facilities, you'll end up with too many people using your facilities who may not care what shape they leave them in. And remember—guests haven't seen your house rules and may blithely ignore any rules that you've posted (after all, what do they have to lose if they ignore them?). An authorized guest, on the other hand, is the responsibility of your tenant, and if an authorized guest seriously and repeatedly breaks the rules, you'll have grounds to take action against the tenant. Knowing this, your tenants have some incentive to monitor their true guests' activities. Without such monitoring, you'll risk liability from people whose unchecked behavior may lead to damage and injuries.

Where appropriate, set users' minimum age or require supervision

Common sense tells you that children under a certain age shouldn't use facilities or equipment such as your swimming pool, sauna, or weight equipment. Likewise, it's reasonable to insist that children under a certain age use a playground or other facility only with adult supervision. Without such restrictions, children are likely to get hurt, and their parents or guardians might sue you for not taking steps to safeguard them. You needn't worry about violating fair housing laws by creating rules that single out children, as long as your rules are based on legitimate health or safety concerns.

To determine the proper age restriction for different facilities, start with your common sense, but don't stop there. Look for external confirmations of your conclusions—for example, learn what age restrictions other landlords and properties use (you're looking for an industry standard), and follow any age restrictions recommended in the instruction books accompanying playground and other equipment. You can also contact the U.S. Consumer Product Safety Commission (CPSC)'s toll-free hotline, 800-638-2772, or your local chapter of the National Safety Council by visiting www.nsc.org/chaptop.htm.

Retain the right to bar certain tenants and guests from facilities

Tenants who misuse your facilities despite your rules are likely to break equipment, cause injuries to other tenants and guests, and injure themselves. Sometimes, warnings aren't enough to ensure a tenant behaves properly in your facilities and uses them safely. Give yourself the right in your lease or house rules to bar unruly tenants or their guests from future use of facilities. To give your rule some teeth, add that repeated and serious misuse of your property will result in a tenancy termination. Also, give yourself the right to close any facility at any time and for any reason.

Don't use tenants' Social Security numbers as their account numbers

As many as eight to ten million adults in the United States fall each year to identity theft, according to Javelin Strategy & Resea. Identity thieves are more likely to succeed in their crime if they know an intended victim's Social Security number (SSN). Although it's currently not against the law to assign tenants their SSN as their account number, doing so is unnecessary and puts tenants' private information at risk. Their account number may appear in your computer files, rent checks, correspondence, and other forms that many employees and others may be able to access. All it takes is for one tenant who falls victim to identity theft to sue you, claiming your negligence caused her SSN to become known and used for illegal purposes.

Although using a tenant's SSN as an account number may not be illegal, an increasing number of states are enacting laws that restrict the way in which you may use others' SSNs. For example, California, Illinois, and Maryland don't allow you to print a tenant's SSN on any mailings (unless required by law). If you're mailing a letter or package to a tenant in Virginia, you must make sure that a tenant's SSN isn't visible on the mailer. In Michigan, you must hide at least five digits so that no more than four sequential digits of a tenant's SSN show.

Urge tenants to get renters' insurance

Two-thirds of tenants don't have renters' insurance, according to a recent survey by the Independent Insurance Agents & Brokers of America (IIABA). Many of these tenants assume that their landlords' insurance for the building will reimburse them in the event their belongings are damaged in a fire or other disaster, or stolen in a burglary. They also think they'll be covered if someone is injured in their apartment and blames them in a lawsuit.

As you no doubt know, however, your property insurance protects only *your* property; and your liability policy covers you when injured people claim that *your* negligence caused their injuries. Renters' insurance protects your tenants' property (even when it's off the rental property), and covers them if their negligence causes injuries. But why should you care whether your tenants are covered? After all, if they can't replace that stolen bike, or come up with the money to settle a guest's claim that their carelessness caused the guest's injury, it's their problem, not yours, right? In a sense, yes, but there are solid ways in which renters' insurance also benefits landlords:

- **Insurance proceeds protect the rent money.** If your tenant has to shell out a lot of money to replace stolen or destroyed belongings, or to settle a personal injury claim, that could render him unable to pay the rent. Far better to have tenants who have a cushion they can fall on (the policy limits of their insurance policies), keeping them financially sound and able to pay the rent.

- **Renters' insurance shields your own policies.** Sometimes it's not clear whose carelessness caused an injury. For example, was it the tenant's fault that a guest slipped on a loose bit of carpet, or your fault in not replacing it sooner? In situations like this, the lawyer for the injured person will typically sue both the landlord and the tenant—and let the evidence fall where it may. A judge or jury may decide you're both at fault—but don't count on having to pay only "your share." The injured person might be able to collect it all from whatever side has the money. If the tenant has no insurance, and no assets to draw on, you (under your insurance policy) may end up paying all of it. Far better to have two insurance companies divvy-up the hit than for yours to pay everything. The more claims you need to pay out under your own insurance policy, the more likely your insurer will raise your premiums.

Fortunately, renters' insurance isn't expensive (it usually costs no more than $10–$20 per month). Because of its obvious benefits to you, should you *require* tenants to carry insurance? As tempting as it may be, perhaps not. First, your state or local law may bar you from requiring tenants to get renters' insurance. (Ask your insurance agent or broker if you're not sure.) Also, if your property gets federal funding, imposing a renters' insurance requirement might mean you'll need to either lower the rent or forfeit the funding. Finally, as a

practical matter, requiring renters' insurance is difficult to enforce—
how will you ensure that tenants pay their premiums and renew their
policy on time? If you take time to show tenants how insurance is in
their best interests and how little it costs, there's a good chance they'll
take your advice.

If you allow pets, use a pet agreement

Plenty of landlords allow tenants to keep pets. Some owners are
pet lovers themselves; others think it's good marketing, because
such a policy will broaden the pool of potential tenants (and reduce
turnover rates, since pet-friendly rentals are harder to find than no-pet
properties). If you let tenants keep pets, consider the risk-lowering
step of putting your pet rules in writing, to ensure that your pet-
friendly policies won't add to your risk of disgruntled tenants, property
damage, or lawsuits.

> **TIP**
>
> **Announce your pet policy.** If you don't allow tenants to keep pets in
> their apartments, then of course you don't need a pet agreement. But make sure
> you include a statement of your "no pets" policy in your lease, so that tenants
> are aware of your rule.

Include your agreement as part of your lease. This way, tenants
who have pets will understand they must comply with special rules
throughout their tenancy, and that their continued tenancy depends
on honoring these rules. New tenants who don't have pets may
decide to get a pet later, so it's important to have all tenants sign the
pet agreement—even if they don't have a pet (or even contemplate
having one) when they sign. Here are common provisions found in pet
agreements that you should consider including in yours.

Identify the pets you'll allow

You may wish to restrict the types of pets you'll allow at your property
to common domesticated animals such as dogs, cats, birds, fish, guinea
pigs, rabbits, hamsters, gerbils, and small reptiles. You may also want

to limit the number of such pets, especially the number of cats and dogs.

Some landlords ban certain dog breeds that many people believe have a propensity toward violence, such as pit bulls and Rottweilers. Although the question of whether certain breeds are truly dangerous and should be banned is a topic of continuing controversy, you are legally entitled to ban certain breeds from your property, if you choose to do so. (Fair housing laws apply to human beings, not to dogs.) Be sure to check with your insurer—some companies won't issue liability policies if certain so-called "dangerous breeds" are kept on the property. Instead of—or in addition to—banning certain breeds, you may consider limiting the weight of dogs to below a certain number of pounds, such as 20 or 60 pounds.

Besides noting which kinds of pets you'll allow, make it clear that you welcome only tenants' pets. You don't want other people's pets visiting your tenants' rentals for any length of time. Also, consider whether you will allow guests to bring their pets with them while visiting tenants in their apartments.

Pets must meet with your approval

Don't lead tenants to assume that because you run a pet-friendly property, anything goes. Require tenants to get your approval for any pet they wish to keep in their apartment. (You may wish to forgo this approval requirement for certain types of pets that you allow but believe shouldn't cause problems or trigger complaints, such as goldfish.) Ask applicants and tenants questions about their pets, such as how long they've had the pet or where they're getting the pet from, if the pet has caused any property damage or other problems, and who would look after the pet when the tenant is away. (For more helpful questions, refer to the San Francisco SPCA's "Checklist for Landlords" at www.sfspca.org.). Finally, state that your approval is conditioned upon the tenants' continued compliance with the terms of your pet agreement. Say that you have the right to ask the tenant to remove the pet from your property or terminate the tenancy in the event of serious or repeated violations of the agreement.

Insist on proper identification, licenses, and vaccinations

Make sure tenants understand that all dogs and cats must wear identification collars or tags, which include proof of current vaccinations. Learn what your local ordinances require concerning regular cat and dog vaccinations and licenses, and insist that tenants give you current proof that they've complied (such as a copy of their municipal license receipt or the vet's bill).

Make tenants responsible for their pets

Tenants should agree to keep their pets under control at all times, so that they don't disturb other tenants and their guests. Require tenants to clean up after their pets, both inside their apartment and in all common areas and other parts of your property. Tenants should also agree not to leave pets outdoors or unsupervised in their apartment for an unreasonably long period of time, and to keep pets in appropriate, contained areas within their apartment. For example, small reptiles such as lizards should be kept in terrariums and birds should be kept in cages.

Make it easy to change your pet rules

From time to time, you may want to change your pet policy. For example, you may decide to allow only dogs, but no more cats. In order to implement such a change, state in your rules that you have the right to amend your pet rules by giving tenants reasonable notice (typically 30 days). Keep in mind that when changing your pet rules, you might create a situation where a number of tenants are suddenly in noncompliance with your new rule and can't easily fix the violation. For example, if you change your rules to add a weight limitation to pets, tenants whose pets exceed the new limit would have to get rid of their pets immediately to comply, which is certain to trigger considerable resistance and damage your tenant relations efforts. So, consider including a "grandfather clause" that will exempt existing pets from having to comply with new rules. Any new pets these same tenants wish to keep, however, would be subject to your new rules (just as is the case with your other tenants).

Should You Charge a Pet Fee?

Many landlords routinely impose a "pet fee," in addition to the normal security deposit, reasoning that pets typically cause added wear and tear to an apartment. Think carefully before implementing such a policy, for these reasons:

- **Is it legal?** In some states, such as California, landlords may not charge more than a specified sum as a deposit. If you charge more than one type of deposit, the total of your deposits, regardless of their name, can't exceed this sum. So, if the total of your deposits has already hit the maximum, you can't impose a pet deposit (or any other additional deposit).

- **Is it a good idea?** Setting aside a certain sum as a deposit to cover pet damage isn't always practical. Suppose a pet is well behaved but the tenant who owns the pet is a slob. You'll want every penny of the deposit to cover the tenant's damage, but if you've marked a sum for pet damage only, you may have a hard time applying that money toward cleaning up the tenant's mess. As you can see, it makes sense to impose a nonspecific deposit and use it as needed.

- **Is it reasonable?** If you decide to impose a specified pet deposit, keep it reasonable, such as $200 to $300 per year. Otherwise, if your tenant challenges it, you risk that a judge won't enforce it.

Finally, be sure to remember not to impose a pet deposit or fee for a tenant who keeps a service or companion animal. Such animals aren't pets—they're animals that some tenants need to accommodate a disability.

Play by the rules when terminating tenancies and evicting tenants

When dealing with tenants who cause serious problems, you may be tempted to pressure them to leave, by shutting off the hot water or electricity, removing privileges such as a parking space, arbitrarily hiking the rent, or just making life as miserable for the tenant as you think he or she has done for you. Instead of following the rules for terminating and evicting, some landlords will hope that short cuts, such as changing the locks and removing the tenant's belongings, will save them the time and trouble of following proper procedures. But even if you believe you can get away with such actions, behaving this way will only lead to more trouble. These measures, known as "self-help evictions" (because your intent is to get the tenant off the property without the normal court involvement) almost always run afoul of state law. You're asking for an expensive lawsuit if you go down this road.

When dealing with a problem tenant, keep your emotions in check and take the high (and legal) road. If you're unsure on how to proceed, consult your attorney to determine the best legal course of action. Look at it this way: The cost of a consultation is probably less than the damages you're risking if you hand your tenant a ready-made self-help eviction lawsuit.

It Won't Happen to You ...

What happened. An Ohio landlord changed the locks just before the end of the month, assuming that the tenants vacated early because they had shut off the utilities and removed most of their belongings. Deprived of the use of their apartment for a few days, the tenants sued and were awarded $96.77. But that wasn't the end of it—the judge ordered the landlord to pay $1,000 in punitive damages and $1,462 in attorneys' fees.

How you can avoid it. When tenants must give up their apartment at the end of the month, locking them out even a few days before their time is up can be considered a "self-help eviction," as this landlord learned the hard way. Rather than saving himself some time, this landlord found himself having to pay his tenants' lawyer (and his own), plus a penalty for violating state law.

Embrace—don't fight—tenants' associations

Many landlords dread the prospect of tenants joining together to form a tenants' association or union. They fear that tenants will convene for regular gripe sessions, exchange unreasonable complaints about the building, and generally cause trouble. Sure, this can happen, but remember that it doesn't need to. If you learn that your tenants are forming a tenants' association, or if they already have, turn it to your advantage. Use the structure (and the energy) to foster good tenant relations and minimize the chances that you'll be drawn into contentious arguments. Here's what you should do when it comes to handling a tenants' association at your property:

- **Take a good, hard look at your property and business practices.** Why have your tenants decided to form an association? Is it because you are less than conscientious, or make it difficult for individuals to get your attention? Candidly assess the situation, and promptly make changes, if needed.

- **Support, don't thwart.** Making it difficult for tenants to join together isn't a smart business move (they'll simply find a way around your road blocks), and it may be illegal (many states consider this a form of illegal retaliation). Don't threaten or even indirectly discourage the association, and make your meeting rooms available. Also, check your local laws for special rules regarding tenants' associations. For example, in New York City, landlords must waive any clubhouse or other meeting facility use fee for tenants' association meetings.

- **If you can't beat 'em, join 'em.** Offer to attend association meetings, or send an employee as your representative. This way, you'll know first-hand what's going on, without having to wonder or worry. By attending meetings in a spirit of cooperation, you can respond to tenants' complaints promptly before a problem worsens or tenants' moods sour. Hopefully, tenants will appreciate your offer to participate, recognizing that everyone wins if everyone works together.

Business Practices: My To-Do List

A careful and consistent landlord is a successful landlord who sleeps easily at night. Here's a list of what you can do to establish good business practices that keep your risks at bay.

- [ ] **Lease:** Use a written lease or rental agreement with tenants.
- [ ] **Tenant's cooperation:** Require tenants to cooperate with me as needed throughout their tenancy.
- [ ] **Maintaining distance:** Tread carefully when renting to a friend or befriending a tenant.
- [ ] **Consistency:** Enforce lease clauses and house rules consistently or take them off the books.
- [ ] **House rules:** Create rules governing the use of all facilities and post them in appropriate places.
- [ ] **Tenant responsibility:** Make tenants responsible for their guests' use of my facilities.
- [ ] **Child-specific policies:** Limit children's use of facilities—but only as needed to protect their health and safety.
- [ ] **Identity protection:** Safeguard tenants' Social Security numbers and don't use them as account numbers.
- [ ] **Renters' insurance:** Explain the benefits and economy of renters' insurance to all tenants before lease signing.
- [ ] **Pets:** Ban pets or let tenants keep them as long as they abide by my rules.
- [ ] **No self-help evictions:** Follow the law when trying to end tenancies early—don't be tempted to shortcut the rules.
- [ ] **Tenant activism:** Let tenants start or join a tenants' association, and get involved, if possible.

Avoiding Problems
When Hiring Help

L andlords wear many hats as they go about advertising, showing, and maintaining their rental properties. But two of their hats—the employer's cap and the client's cap—deserve special attention. Here's what those caps represent:

- If you have some (or even several) employees working for you, you're an employer.
- If you pay people to take care of certain tasks relating to your business, you're that person's client (and the helper is known as an "independent contractor," or "IC"). For instance, you may pay a property management company to manage your buildings, or an accountant to handle your taxes.

However you do it, you know that hiring help is essential to keeping your business both operational and profitable. Others can do work that you can't do yourself (such as replacing your roof), or accomplish tasks you've been doing but would like to offload, giving you more time to focus on other aspects of your business.

Hiring help brings the promise of efficiency, savings, peace of mind, and profitability to your business—but it also brings risk. Employers in particular must know and follow many federal, state, and local laws; and those working with independent contractors need to be familiar with a few basic contract principles. Most importantly, every landlord who hires help needs to understand the difference between an employee and an independent contractor (no matter what you call your helper, the law is the final word on whether that person is an employee or contractor). But don't let these challenges deter you from using employees or contractors. By the time you're done with this Step, you'll have the basic information to deal confidently with both.

What Do You Have to Lose?

If you don't take steps to manage your risks when hiring and working with employees and independent contractors, you may find yourself doomed to deal with revolving employees and contractors. Job applicants and employees who believe you're treating them unfairly will likely quit, leading you to have to find, hire, and train new helpers, while your business has to manage without this help. Worse, some unhappy workers may bring a claim against you before an administrative agency or in court. If you're sued, you'll need to hire more help—in the form of a lawyer—to protect your business and its good name. Trouble may also come from the government—a mundane mistake such as failing to display required posters for employees could result in fines, which are nothing compared with the headache and expense of a wage or working hours violation.

Independent contractors can also create problems for you. Contractors who don't do what you've hired them to do, or do it poorly, may cost you time, money, and headaches as you try to enforce your agreements and get them to correct their work. If you misclassify a worker—designating someone as a contractor, when in the eyes of the law, this person should be treated as your employee—the fallout can be serious, including claims for back wages, taxes, and even penalties. And although it's rare, it's possible that an independent contractor could successfully mount a charge of discrimination against a landlord-client.

As if it weren't enough to risk problems from employees and contractors themselves, the way these people interact with your tenants can pose a risk, too. If you choose your workers carelessly, be they employees or contractors, and these workers harm your tenants, you could be held at least partially liable. For example, if you hired an employee without performing a background check and the employee (who turns out to have a long history as a thief) steals valuables from a tenant's apartment, the tenant may sue you for negligent hiring.

Is This You?

Nearly every landlord needs help to run a successful business. You may already hire employees such as a resident manager, doorman, or office manager. Even if you have a small business that can run without employees, you might still hire help for specific situations, such as an accountant to prepare your tax returns, a lawyer to help you evict an unruly tenant, or a plumber to replace corroded pipes.

Each time you hire someone to help you with your business, you open the door to risk. Look at the portraits below, and see if you recognize yourself in any of them.

Do You Think About Hiring Help Like These Landlords?

☐ You don't know which key federal employment laws, plus state and local laws, apply to your business.

☐ You don't know how to classify workers as employees or independent contractors, or why it matters.

☐ You don't carefully train employees or monitor their job performance.

☐ You hire service contractors without checking into their reputation, and you rarely use a contract that describes the job.

☐ Your employee policies aren't in writing, or you don't enforce your written policies consistently.

☐ You don't have a firm policy on sexual harassment that, among other things, tells employees and tenants how to make a complaint.

☐ You don't have workers' compensation insurance, and you're not sure if you're required to.

☐ You hire some job applicants with little or no screening, and you don't document the reasons why you fire employees.

☐ When a job applicant has a disability that you believe would interfere with doing his job effectively, you reject the applicant without considering whether reasonable accommodations are in order.

☐ You have a resident manager living in an apartment but don't know whether you'll have the right to terminate her lease if she quits or you wish to replace her.

☐ You keep using the same lawyer when legal issues arise even though you're not happy with her services or fees.

Take Action!

When it comes to hiring help to grow your business, you must be able to proceed with confidence. The strategies described in this Step will help you no matter how large or small a workforce you manage, and no matter what type of help you decide is best for your business. Before hiring any type of help, you need to know what your legal obligations are and how you can protect yourself if things go wrong. Here are the action steps that will get you the help you need—without the headaches.

IC or employee? Choose carefully

When you hire help for your business, it will come in the form of either an employee or an independent contractor (IC). An employee is someone who works for you, following your directions and using your tools and materials. An independent contractor has its own business, usually works for several clients besides you, and normally brings its own tools, materials, and work plan to the job. Often, the same job can be done by an employee (a resident manager) or someone who has his or her own business (such as a janitorial or landscaping outfit). Other jobs cannot practically be handled by an IC—for example, unless you run a sizable rental business, you're not likely to have on staff your own accountant or lawyer, let alone your own roofer.

The difference between an employee and an IC has ramifications beyond practical considerations such as who supplies the tools, materials, and directions. Your decision to hire an employee versus contract with an IC affects your tax obligations. For example, you must withhold payroll taxes from employees, but have ICs complete IRS Form 1099-MISC. (See Step Ten for more information.) Sometimes it's not so easy to know whether the person you're dealing with is legally your employee or an IC. For instance, you might pay an independent contractor to perform a landscaping project, but when the project is done you might have more work for the contractor to do. Before you know it, the contractor, who happens to have no other clients at the time, is working regular hours each week for you making sure your lawn, shrubbery, and trees are well maintained. As you can see, this arrangement is sounding more like an employer-employee relationship than client-IC.

For many reasons, it's simpler and cheaper for landlords to have jobs done by ICs instead of employees, but don't let that temptation lead you down the risky path of deliberate misclassification. For example, in a bid to save time and money, you might decide to call your resident manager an IC, when in fact government agencies would classify this person as an employee. But if you misclassify a worker—even innocently—the IRS and your state tax agency will soon be on your case. Not only will you risk owing penalties and interest, but there's also the risk that the IRS or your state tax agency will find other unrelated mistakes as long as they've got your business under their microscope.

Deciding whether to hire an employee or an IC will also affect how you run your business and whether it turns a profit. Each business owner must decide which type is best based on the business's needs, and most rental property owners hire both types of workers at one time or another.

Why hire an employee?

Many landlords choose to have one or more employees, sometimes living on the property. Here are the top reasons why hiring employees can make sense for you.

- **You have more control.** An employee works for you and is expected to conform to your business's unique way of doing things. You can tell an employee what you want done—and exactly how you want it done. An IC has more independence.
- **The work is consistent.** Employees remain at your disposal day after day—they don't leave after the job is done. Once you're satisfied with their work, you can expect that it will continue in the same vein, time after time. If you and your employees get along, you can maintain a consistent approach to each task for months, if not years. Because ICs typically work for many

clients, they're likely to have their own way of doing things and be less likely to pay particular attention to the details on how you want the job done.

- **You reap the benefits of loyalty.** Good employees who feel they're being treated well are likely to become loyal to you and share your desire to see your business become, or remain, profitable. ICs work for themselves and normally aren't in a position to develop or display such loyalty.

- **You own what your employees produce.** You own the fruits of your employees' labor, just as if you performed their tasks yourself. For example, if you ask an employee to take photographs of your property to include in marketing materials, you own the copyright to those photos. If you hired someone outside your business to photograph your property, the IC would own the rights to the photos (short of a written agreement to the contrary).

Why hire an IC?

After reading the above, you might think hiring an employee is the way to go. Read on to find out why hiring an IC may be the ideal choice for you in certain situations.

- **An IC doesn't require handholding.** An IC is an independent professional, just like you. When you hire an IC, you trust the IC to take care of the job in his or her customary way. Although you may give input, you don't need to provide training or guidance to an IC. For example, if you a hire a company to waterproof your building's basement, you only have to communicate your needs and any special requirements. The IC will accomplish the task by drawing on his or her own expertise and prior experience.

- **An IC has specialized skills.** Landlords often need help with short-term projects that go beyond their knowledge or abilities. Whatever you need done, you can find an IC who's specialized enough to do it, from designing a logo for your company to wiring your new clubhouse for a high-speed Internet connection. It doesn't make sense from a business standpoint to ask employees to handle specialized short-term projects that arise infrequently. (Even bright, clever employees have a learning curve.)

- **It's easy to say goodbye to an IC.** When you hire an IC, it's for a limited amount of time, usually until the day a project is completed to your satisfaction. For example, if you hire an IC to spackle and repaint the interior walls of your fitness center, your professional relationship with the IC ends when the task is complete. When employees finish a task, you need to find more work for them. If things are slow or there's just not much work to be done, you must still pay them for their time—or pursue the unpleasant option of firing them, which you must do in accordance with discrimination and other laws.

- **An IC doesn't need to be managed.** ICs are independent, which means you'll have fewer hassles when dealing with them. Employees, on the other hand, must be managed (no matter how mature or competent they are). You'll deal with ongoing workplace issues and concerns ("I deserve a raise," "You should have promoted me," "I disagree with that policy," "I thought I would be working more regular hours," "Can you give me more challenging work?" "Can I work from home on Fridays?" "Our computers are outdated").

- **ICs trigger fewer legal responsibilities.** On top of managing your employees, you must comply with employment laws that cover overtime, minimum wage, meal and rest breaks, and many other issues, plus create your own policies and procedures and enforce them consistently. Though you must honor the terms of your contract with your IC, it's usually a far simpler relationship, legally, than the one you have with your employees.

There's a lot to know when dealing with employees and ICs alike, but you can get a good head start with help from Nolo. Employers should check out *The Employer's Legal Handbook,* by Fred Steingold; and landlords who utilize the services of ICs will benefit from *Working With Independent Contractors,* by Stephen Fishman.

Avoid discrimination against job applicants and employees

The federal, state, and many local governments prohibit most employers from discriminating against applicants and employees. As a rental property owner, you have a head start on understanding what these laws require, because you're already complying with fair housing laws when dealing with prospects and tenants. Although fair employment laws protect employees from discrimination, you'll see that the basic principles are the same as the principles behind fair housing laws. The sections below give you an outline of the antidiscrimination rules that all smart landlords should follow.

Do Discrimination Laws Protect Independent Contractors?

In most situations, the powerhouse federal and state laws that ban discrimination against employees don't apply to your dealings with ICs. Of course, legal rules aside, just as you would never want to discriminate against employees, you would not want to do so against ICs either. Discriminatory practices start hurting your business and its reputation long before you'll ever see a courtroom.

Aside from the practical disadvantages of ignoring antidiscrimination laws when dealing with ICs, you'd be taking a chance if you assumed that you could safely discriminate against an IC, for these reasons:

- One very significant federal law, the Civil Rights Act of 1991, forbids racial discrimination when making a contract. This law applies to you whenever you contract with an IC for services.
- Your state, under its rules, may determine that your IC is legally your employee. Once that reclassification is made, your discriminatory words or actions could trigger a lawsuit by your recently reclassified employee.
- Federal appellate courts in your state may use creative legal reasoning to conclude that an IC deserves discrimination protection.

Rather than take a chance that inadvertently misclassifying your IC leaves you open to a discrimination lawsuit, or that a judge will craft a way to apply the law to your IC, it makes sense to operate under the assumption that the laws that apply to employees hold sway when dealing with ICs, too.

Don't discriminate on the basis of race, color, religion, sex, or national origin

If you have at least 15 employees, Title VII of the federal Civil Rights Act of 1964 bars you from discriminating against them based on race, color, religion, sex, and national origin. This means you can't let these characteristics influence you when making any employment decisions, especially those concerning hiring, promotions, dismissals, raises, benefits, assignments, and leaves of absence.

The discrimination ban on "sex" also makes it illegal to treat employees or applicants differently because of pregnancy, childbirth, or related medical conditions. So, you can't fire a pregnant woman because you believe she shouldn't work. However, if a woman's pregnancy makes her unable to work, you can treat her differently by accommodating her condition—so long as you extend to other employees who become unable to work for other reasons the same willingness to accommodate their situations.

If you have fewer than 15 employees, your state law will probably still cover your business. For example, New York's employment discrimination laws apply to employers with at least four employees and Idaho's apply to employees with at least five employees, while Minnesota's laws apply to employers with any number of employees. All employers, regardless of how many people they employ, can't discriminate on the basis of race, according to the Civil Rights Act of 1991.

It Won't Happen to You ...

What happened. A woman who served as the Regional Property Manager for four Phoenix apartment complexes complained to the EEOC that her employer fired her because she was pregnant. Although she had received a merit raise and performance bonuses for achieving occupancy and move-in goals, her manager gave her a verbal performance warning within a week of learning that she was pregnant. The manager also wrote a memo to company executives criticizing the woman's performance and outlining a plan to terminate her employment within 30 days. The employer settled with the EEOC, agreeing to pay the woman $135,000 and take other steps to avoid illegal sex-based discrimination in the future.

How you can avoid it. Remember that sex-based discrimination also protects female employees who become pregnant. It's one thing if a pregnant employee is unable to work or can't be accommodated. But if, as here, you decide to fire an employee simply because she's pregnant, you should expect a call from the EEOC before long.

Don't discriminate on the basis of age

A federal law called the Age Discrimination in Employment Act (ADEA) bars discrimination against employees and job applicants who are 40 years old or older. This means you can't choose a 25-year-old over a 55-year-old as a doorman because you want a "younger look" for your building. You can always reject applicants for valid business reasons, regardless of their age, and you're not required to afford older applicants or employees preferred treatment. So, if a 55-year-old isn't as qualified for the job as the 25-year-old, you can reject him.

The ADEA applies to businesses with at least 20 employees. If your business is smaller, a similar state law probably covers it. But that law may protect a different age group. For example, in Minnesota, workers who are under 70 years old are protected against age-based discrimination.

Don't discriminate on the basis of disability

Title I of the Americans with Disabilities Act (ADA) protects job applicants and employees from discrimination based on disability. As a business owner, you can't reject job applicants simply because they're disabled. You also must provide reasonable accommodations to employees with disabilities in all aspects of their employment. Title I of the ADA applies to businesses with at least 15 employees. If you have fewer employees on the payroll, your state law may apply and probably affords similar protections to disabled job applicants and employees.

"Reasonable accommodations" come in many forms. For example, you may need to change the layout of a workstation or modify equipment as needed to accommodate an employee's disability. You may also need to restructure jobs themselves. To do this, you might need to shift responsibility for minor tasks to other employees (and possibly replace it with other minor tasks that the employee can accomplish), or change when or how you expect a task to be performed.

You don't need to make accommodations if doing so will create an undue hardship, financial or otherwise. The Equal Employment Opportunity Commission (EEOC), the agency charged with enforcing federal employment discrimination laws, has determined that the following accommodations aren't considered reasonable (and therefore, you needn't grant them):

- **Eliminating a primary job responsibility.** You needn't make an accomodation that would fundamentally change the nature of the job.
- **Lowering production standards that are applied to all employees.** You may, however, have to provide reasonable accommodations to enable an employee with a disability to meet your standards.
- **Providing personal use items.** You needn't give employees wheelchairs, canes, walkers, hearing aids, prosthetics, eyeglasses, hearing aids, or other medical or assistive devices (even though an employee may need them to do her job).

- **Excusing a violation of a uniformly applied conduct rule.** You don't have to tolerate employee misconduct, such as violence, threats, theft, or property destruction, even if such behavior allegedly stems from an employee's disability. When disciplining an employee, take the same measures you would regardless of whether the employee has a disability.

Carefully ask about reasonable accommodations

As you know from Step Seven, to avoid fair housing trouble you must always let prospects and tenants request any accommodations they believe they need to accommodate a disability. In the employment context, things are a little different. In certain situations during the hiring process, you may ask applicants about accommodations. Here's when:

- **Before you offer the job.** If you know that a job applicant has a disability (either because it's obvious or she told you about it), and you have reason to believe that applicant will need an accommodation to do her job, you may ask the applicant what type of accommodation she'll need.
- **After you've made an offer.** When making an offer to applicants for a particular type of job (for example, leasing staff), you may ask whether the applicants will need reasonable accommodations to perform the job. Or, you can ask this question of only those applicants who you know have a disability and might benefit from an accommodation.

For more information about the ADA, visit the EEOC's disability discrimination website at www.eeoc.gov/types/ada.html. Three publications at this website are particularly useful to landlords: "The ADA: A Primer for Small Business," "Your Responsibilities as an Employer," and "Small Employers and Reasonable Accommodation."

Don't discriminate on the basis of sexual orientation, creed, and other characteristics

Many states and municipalities protect employees and job applicants against discrimination based on characteristics besides the nationally recognized characteristics mentioned so far. For example, several states—such as California, Nevada, New York, Vermont, and Wisconsin——and hundreds of municipalities ban discrimination based on sexual orientation (and, in many cases, gender identity). Other common protections include political affiliation or creed, parental or marital status, weight, and height. Some states have more specific protections, such as "Vietnam-era veterans status" (Idaho) and choice of married or maiden surname (Minnesota).

Check your state and local law to learn which characteristics they protect and whether your business is covered (see Step Two for help in finding your state and local laws). State human rights commissions often provide a helpful summary of their discrimination laws on their websites. If you're not sure of your commission's address, search for the name of your state plus "human rights commission" on the Web.

Military Leave

If an employee has to leave for military service, you may need to keep her job waiting for her when she returns. The Uniformed Services Employment and Reemployment Rights Act of 1994 (USERRA) is a federal law that protects servicemembers and veterans from workplace discrimination. USERRA requires all employers, regardless of the number of people employed, to put employees back to work in their civilian jobs after military service with the seniority, status, and pay rate they would have achieved had they remained continuously in your employ. USERRA also makes it illegal to discriminate against servicemembers in hiring, promotion, and retention.

For more information about this law and which employees qualify for protection, read the article on USERRA on the Nolo website (at www.nolo.com, type USERRA in the search box), see *The Essential Guide to Federal Employment Laws,* by Lisa Guerin and Amy DelPo (Nolo), or visit the Department of Labor's USERRA website at www.dol.gov/elaws/userra.htm.

Take strong stance on sexual harassment

The most troublesome, expensive, and headline-grabbing form of sex discrimination is sexual harassment. The EEOC and local Fair Employment Practices Agencies (FEPAs) across the country receive roughly 12,000–15,000 complaints a year, leading to some $50 million in annual settlements and other administrative resolutions. Far too many of those complaints, unfortunately, were from tenants complaining about harassment from their landlords or property managers or other employees.

Sexual harassment is a complicated concept. It breaks down into the following parts. Sexual harassment includes unwelcome sexual advances, such as kissing, hugging, and fondling. It may also consist of requests for sexual favors, and other verbal or physical conduct of a sexual nature, including repeated requests for a date despite a person's stern refusals, telling sexual jokes, or spreading rumors about a person's sex life. Sexual harassment affects a person's employment, by making it impossible, for example, to be properly respected for her contribution to the business; or unreasonably interferes with one's work performance, by having to put up with lewd jokes or offensive material in the office. Harassment occurs when it creates a hostile work environment (a hostile work environment is one where harassment, or the threat of harassment, interferes with your doing your job to the best of your ability). Here are additional points to keep in mind about sexual harassment:

- The harasser's conduct must be unwelcome (and not just sexual in nature). This means, for instance, that employees who willingly hug each other after one learns that the other suffered a loss or got a promotion aren't creating a problem. But a male employee who decides to hug a female employee whenever he feels like doing so, whether she likes it or not, is harassing her.
- The harasser and the victim each can be male or female, and the harasser and the victim can be of the same sex.
- The harasser can be anyone at your property, regardless of title or position.

- The victims needn't be just the people who were directly harassed—anyone affected by the offensive conduct has a legal right to complain.
- Sexual harassment can occur even if the victim wasn't fired or suffered other economic harm.

Smart landlords can adopt policies that will help prevent sexual harassment at their property and minimize the risk of a lawsuit. At a minimum, these policies include the following.

Adopt a zero-tolerance policy. Create a written policy on sexual harassment so that employees understand both that it's illegal and that you don't tolerate it. Place your policy in your employee handbook, if you have one, or in a simple statement of policy that you ask all employees to read and sign. Let employees and tenants know how to complain if they believe an employee has harassed them (for example, to contact you or an employee you designate). Investigate all claims thoroughly and discipline any offenders accordingly (from a stern verbal warning to a firing). If an alleged victim of sexual harassment sues you, your written policy and strict enforcement efforts will help with your defense.

Keep off-color materials *off* your property. While it's a good idea to encourage employees to make their workspace their own and express themselves by tailoring the decor to their liking, you should ban all sexual and hate-related photos, posters, objects, and other items from display on your property. For example, don't allow employees to use photos of scantily clad women as their computer screensavers— these could be seen by a prospect during an interview, or by other employees. Such displays give a bad impression about the type of business you run, and the experience can come back to bite you if a prospect later claims that an employee harassed her.

Similarly, don't allow tenants to post off-color posters, notices, and other items in common areas such as on tenant bulletin boards, entryways, doors, in community rooms, or in any areas of your property outside the tenant's own apartment. If you don't take this action, you risk giving other tenants the impression that you at least tolerate (if not endorse) this type of behavior.

Screen applicants thoroughly

You no doubt test job applicants to see if they're up for the job, by reviewing their resumes, discussing their backgrounds in interviews, talking with references, and perhaps quizzing them on their skills. Don't stop there. To help avoid hiring well-qualified criminals, consider running criminal background checks on job applicants you're interested in hiring, and don't hire any applicant whose record reveals a history of violence or theft.

If you ignore this step and hire someone with a dangerous criminal background, you'll risk that this person will steal property from you or a tenant, or harm employees or tenants. The victims of this employee's misdeeds may decide to sue you for their harm, claiming that you were careless when you hired someone who had the potential to cause the harm that ensued.

Getting relevant and accurate criminal history for a job applicant is not, unfortunately, a simple task. First, the law varies from state to state on whether, and to what extent, an employer may consider an applicant's criminal history in making hiring decisions. Some states bar employers from asking about arrests, convictions that occurred well in the past, juvenile crimes, or sealed records. Some states allow employers to consider convictions only if the crimes are relevant to the job. And some states allow employers to consider criminal history only for certain positions, such as nurses, child care workers, private detectives, and other jobs requiring licenses. Because of this variation, you should consult with a lawyer or research your state law before digging into an applicant's criminal past.

In addition to legal constraints, as a practical matter it's not easy to get accurate, relevant, and comprehensive information unless you pay for a fairly expensive background search. Despite the rosy promises of online criminal background screening, the instant reports generated by these services are riddled with inaccuracies and even false positives. To obtain a report that isn't prohibitively expensive yet promises an acceptable degree of accuracy, don't go with just any search company. Make sure the company will search using not only the applicant's name but his Social Security number, to ensure that any aliases or spelling variations won't be overlooked. Also, find out (by reading the "FAQ" section of a search company's website or calling the company) which databases the company will search, and compare this to what other companies say they'll search. Finally, many companies offer deals to help you save money with multiple searches (for example, ten applicant searches a year). Although it may be tempting to sign up for these package deals, consider starting by purchasing a single search. If you're satisfied, then commit to a package deal the next time you need to check an applicant's background. If not, give a different search company a try.

You may also want to consider checking applicants' credit histories, especially if they will be handling any financial matters for your business or if you need to be convinced they know how to keep a financial house in order. If you decide not to hire an applicant (or promote an employee) based on information in the credit report, you must provide a copy of the report and let the applicant know of his or her right to challenge the report under the Fair Credit Reporting Act. Some states have more stringent rules limiting the use of credit reports.

Before performing any background or credit check, be sure to get the job applicant's written consent.

 CAUTION

Don't simply discard credit or background reports. Federal law requires all businesses to destroy information from consumer reports before discarding them, such as by shredding the documents first. For more information on handling sensitive applicant information, see Step Seven.

It Won't Happen to You ...

What happened. A maintenance worker at a Georgia apartment complex entered an apartment allegedly to repair the ceiling, but instead assaulted a 17-year-old tenant. The worker was arrested and pled guilty to aggravated assault, and the girl's family sued the landlord for negligent hiring. The family showed that the worker had been arrested 13 times before he was hired, that the landlord should have checked his criminal record to discover this, and that the landlord violated its own policy by not properly checking the worker's background or hiring him despite it. The family settled with the landlord for a confidential amount, and the landlord added its screening policies to an employee manual.

How you can avoid it. Set a clear policy on criminal background checks, apply the policy to all employees, and don't hire any applicant who doesn't meet your screening standards.

Put workplace policies and procedures into an employee handbook

Hopefully, you've already adopted policies and procedures for your workplace and you're applying them consistently to all employees. As is the case with prospects and tenants, making up rules as you go along is likely to invite discrimination claims from employees who think you're treating them differently based on their race, sex, or other legally protected characteristic. Plus, having clear rules is important to ensure you're not violating any employment laws (for example, governing compensatory time off).

If you haven't already done so, put all your workplace policies and procedures into an employee handbook. Your handbook needn't be long but should include the following topics:

- **Introduction and general policies.** Introduce the handbook and explain that its purpose is to outline your business's policies and procedures for employees. Then, use this section to state your general policies, such as: your "employment at will" relationship (allowing you or your employees to terminate your relationship at any time for any lawful reason); your confidentiality policy (requiring employees to keep private or sensitive company-specific information secret); and your conflict of interest policy (requiring employees not to participate in outside activities that go against your business's best interests).

- **Discrimination and harassment.** State your commitment to providing a workplace that's free of unlawful discrimination and harassment. Include a zero-tolerance policy toward sexual harassment that lets employees know what procedure they should follow for making a complaint.

- **Compensation and benefits.** Include topics such as how often you issue paychecks, the basis for bonuses, and performance reviews.

- **Attendance and time off.** State your general work hours and the importance of punctuality, holiday closures, and time-off policies.

- **General policies.** Include your remaining policies in this section, such as a policy limiting work email for business purposes only, a procedure for handling press inquiries, and a reference to your emergency procedures manual (see Step Five). If you find this section includes several policies and procedures on a specific topic, create a new section for them, for better organization.

To make your handbook an effective communication tool, increase the chances employees will comply with your policies, and minimize your risks if they don't, take the following actions:

- **Give a copy of your handbook to all employees on the day they begin work.** This way, you can expect compliance from day one. It's important that employees understand your rules and what you expect before they get settled into their jobs and routines.

- **Have employees sign a statement saying they received the handbook and read the rules.** Taking this step will help you defend yourself if an employee later claims she didn't get a copy of the handbook or didn't read it thoroughly.

- **Enforce the policies consistently.** Having a handbook makes it clear to employees that you have fair policies. But fair policies must be applied fairly, too. Always apply your rules consistently to similarly situated employees.
- **Keep your handbook updated.** Don't forget about your handbook once you've finished creating it. If you learn of any new laws that affect your policies, or if you decide to change a policy on your own (such as the number of vacation days you offer employees), modify the handbook as needed to keep it current.

You don't have to start from scratch to make an employee handbook. Use *Create Your Employee Handbook: A Legal & Practical Guide,* by Lisa Guerin and Amy DelPo (Nolo). The book includes a CD-ROM with suggested policies that you can tailor to your business's needs.

Buy workers' compensation insurance

If you hire employees, your state law probably requires you to purchase workers' compensation insurance. Workers' compensation provides replacement income and pays for medical expenses to employees who get injured on the job or develop a work-related illness. It's a "no-fault" system, which means an injured or sick employee gets compensated without having to prove that the employer was negligent or maintained an unsafe workplace. Although this system appears to favor employees, employers also benefit because a sick or injured employee's recovery is limited to partial payment of replacement income and medical expenses. Employees who become permanently disabled may be entitled to additional funds for retraining or special equipment. Employees covered under workers' compensation can't recover additional money from their employer for pain and suffering or emotional distress.

Workers' compensation requirements vary by state, so check your state workers' compensation office for information about details such as the minimum number of employees (which triggers your duty to purchase coverage) and where to purchase a policy. Many states require employers to buy workers' compensation coverage if they have at least five employees, and employers usually need to purchase a policy through a state fund or private insurance company.

To find your state workers' compensation office, visit the U.S. Department of Labor's Office of Workers' Compensation Programs' website at www.dol.gov/esa/owcp_org.htm and click "state workers' compensation board." Select your state from the list to visit its website.

> **TIP**
> Even if you're not required to buy workers' compensation coverage, you may decide it makes good business sense to do so anyway. Think of a maintenance staff member who falls off the roof while trying to make repairs, or a resident manager who gets sick from exposure to carbon monoxide in your boiler room. Without workers' compensation, you run the risk of getting sued for an amount your business can't afford.

Maintain a safe workplace

As important and helpful as workers' compensation insurance may be, it's no substitute for providing and maintaining a safe workplace for all employees. In addition to your overall goal of not exposing employees to the risk of injury, understand that a safe work environment makes good business sense in that it will affect your bottom line. Like any other insurance, the fewer the number of claims on your workers' compensation policy, the lower the chances that your premiums will go up.

To minimize the risk of injury at your workplace and your liability for lawsuits, be creative and use common sense. Take the suggestions outlined in Step Two, such as inspecting your entire property for hazards and responding promptly to fix dangerous conditions, to make sure your employees stay safe. Hopefully, you won't have any employee get sick or hurt while on the job. But if an employee is harmed, your diligent and consistent efforts to maintain a safe workplace will help ensure that employees' claims properly fall within the workers' compensation system.

Get proper training for employees

Your employees need to get regular training in certain key areas. Fair housing training is perhaps the most important area, for two reasons. First, no matter how well versed you may be in fair housing compliance, your employees must know how to treat prospects and tenants fairly and avoid mistakes that can create liability for you. Second, if a prospect or tenant files a fair housing claim against you, you'll look much better in front of a judge (and be less likely to get hit with heavy damages) if you can show that your staff is already committed to and knowledgeable about fair housing compliance but slipped up.

If your property gets assistance from HUD or participates in a housing program where compliance is complicated, such as the federal low-income housing tax credit program (LIHTC), compliance training is essential for making sure you stay entitled to the low-interest financing, grant, tax credits, or other benefits you're expecting from the government.

Many state housing finance agencies offer fair housing compliance training. They also provide information on how to find training on various housing program rules. To find your agency, visit the National Council of State Housing Agencies' (NCSHA) website at www.ncsha.org. Click "About HFAs" at left and then click the link for "State Housing Finance Agencies (HFAs)."

TIP

Training your staff in first-aid will help prevent serious injury and will minimize your liability. See Step Five for more information about why this training is important and where to get it.

Put required posters on walls

Many federal and state employment laws require employers to attach a poster in a conspicuous place in the workplace to let employees know about their rights under the law. Very often, failing to comply with a poster requirement can trigger a fine. For example, if you're covered under the Family and Medical Leave Act (FMLA) and don't attach the required poster, you can be fined up to $100. If you don't attached the federally required "Job Safety and Health" poster, OSHA may fine you up to $7,000. Some posters, such as the poster for the Uniformed Services Employment and Reemployment Rights Act (USERRA), are required but don't carry monetary penalties for noncompliance. If you don't have an office, you may be able to place the poster in a place where your employees customarily gather and will see it, or you might be able to simply give them the information directly. Check the Department of Labor's website, described below, for more information on how to display the required posters.

The last thing you want is to write a check to the government for not realizing you needed to attach a poster to your wall. If you don't know what posters you need, the Department of Labor's (DOL) website has two useful pages to help you figure that out. First, visit the DOL's "Workplace Poster Page" at www.dol.gov (use the search feature and type "Workplace Poster Page"). This page lists the federally required posters in a handy chart. The posters themselves are just a click away and ready for you to view, print, or order. If you're still not sure which posters you need, try the DOL's Poster Advisor, at www. dol.gov (use the search feature and type "Poster Advisor"). This advisor guides you to the answer by asking you a series of questions about your business.

Finally, don't forget to check with your state to learn whether it has any poster requirements (which may carry additional penalties for violations). Find your state labor department's website by visiting www.dol.gov/esa/contacts/state_of.htm.

Protect yourself when renting apartments to employees

Do you have employees, such as a resident manager, who are also tenants? If so, protect yourself against the situation where they quit or you fire them and you need to give their apartment to their replacement or just want them off your property. To accomplish this, follow a policy of renting to all live-in employees on a month-to-month basis (rather than using your customary fixed-term lease). This way, when an employee leaves his job, he'll have to leave his apartment soon after (with reasonable notice and following your state and local landlord-tenant laws).

If you give employees a break in the rent, consider adding language to your lease that says if the employee holds over, he'll owe you market-rate rent for the period of his unlawful occupancy.

Be careful when firing employees

Not only must you be careful when hiring employees, but you must also be cautious when firing them. First, you'll want to be sure that you're firing the employee for the right reasons. Second, you'll need to be sure to document those reasons, in case the employee later decides to accuse you of operating with illegal motives. The following sections explain these rules.

Which reasons justify firing an employee?

Most of the time, you can fire an employee for any reason, subject to two exceptions—you can't fire an employee with whom you've signed a contract giving the right to stay in the job, and you can't fire someone for an illegal reason.

This first exception is rare. Employment contracts are common among high-level executives and workers with rare and valuable skills. Your resident manager, office staff, and maintenance workers won't fall into that category. You will, however, have to make sure that if your workers also live on your property, you haven't inadvertently given them an employment contract by tying their work to a fixed-term lease, as explained above.

As for the second exception, illegal reasons include discriminatory reasons. You'll generally be okay if you apply the rules you followed when you hired your employees. For example, you can't fire someone because you've just learned that he was born in a country that you don't like, and you can't dismiss someone because you've realized that she follows a particular religion (or no religion). In addition, you can't fire an employee to retaliate when that employee exercises certain legal rights, such as complaining to your state's occupational safety agency about working conditions on your property or filing a workers' compensation claim.

It Won't Happen to You ...

What happened. A Texas landlord hired a housekeeper to clean his two properties and offices. The housekeeper, who had deformed hands when she began the job, complained that cleaning chemicals she was required to use were causing further problems to her hands, despite the fact she wore rubber gloves. Her supervisor, who suggested she quit, believed that other employees were taking unfair advantage of workers' compensation, and allegedly arranged for the housekeeper to be fired before she could file a claim. A court ruled that the housekeeper was illegally fired in retaliation for intending to file a workers' compensation claim, and awarded her $162,500.

How you can avoid it. Don't fire employees or take any other adverse action against them because they filed, or plan to file, a workers' compensation claim. Even if you believe other employees have taken advantage of workers' compensation benefits, you mustn't interfere with an employee's right to file a claim.

Cautious landlords keep one rule in mind when it comes to firing employees: Dismiss employees based only on valid business reasons. Such reasons include theft, violence in the workplace, poor job performance, inability to get along with coworkers or tenants, and insubordination. When your actions are supported by reasons that any sensible businessperson in your position would adopt, you'll be on solid ground if you're challenged.

Document your reasons for firing

Even if you know you have a valid business reason for firing someone —for example, because of an employee's consistently poor job performance—the fired employee might not see it that way. Even employees who are normally levelheaded can feel hurt or become enraged to the point where they want to strike back. Most of the time, they'll claim that you fired them for a discriminatory reason, and they may desire to pursue their claim even against their own attorney's advice. You'll need to be ready to prove that the basis for your decision was anything but.

There are two risks that you need to avoid here. First, there's the risk of a lawsuit claiming you violated the law or otherwise improperly fired an employee. Second, if you worry so much about employee retaliation, there's the risk that you'll become too afraid to fire anyone. Don't forget that you have rights, too. Not only is it your right to fire problematic employees, but unnecessarily hesitating to do so interferes with the growth of your business and ultimately hurts your bottom line. Plus, as explained above, employees who are violent or act out are a liability, and the longer you retain them in your workforce, the more likely people will get hurt and sue you for their injuries.

Protect yourself from these risks by documenting employee misconduct as it happens, including your reasons when you fire an employee. For example, if an employee violates a company policy (such as smoking when performing maintenance work in tenants' apartments), write it down. Cite the policy where it appears in your employee handbook, and explain what happened. For instance, if three tenants complained about smoke after three different maintenance visits, write the dates of the visits, the names of the tenants who complained, and what they said. Also, note any disciplinary action you took (such as giving verbal or written warnings). Giving warnings will show that you acted reasonably by offering an employee a chance to change his behavior.

Enforce all your rules equally with all employees, and make sure your documentation efforts reflect this. Your documentation won't be helpful if it proves that you treated employees differently under similar circumstances. A fired employee who discovers that you treated other employees with greater leniency may argue that you did it for a discriminatory reason. Even if the fired employee misjudged the situation, a jury may still sympathize. Taking this consistent action along with practicing careful documentation habits will help keep your business protected.

Managing and terminating a problem employee can be a challenge, as you may already know well. You'll find helpful guidance in *Dealing With Problem Employees,* by Amy DelPo and Lisa Guerin (Nolo).

Protect yourself before hiring a company to manage your property

Sometimes you need more than just a resident manager to run the show at your property. Many landlords hire property management companies to avoid dealing with prospects and tenants directly and to escape all the hassles involved with hands-on management. Plus, a management company has its own employees, which means you don't have to worry about withholding payroll taxes and other legal requirements.

If you can afford to pay 5%, 6%, or even 10% of your rents as a fee, hiring a good management company, with its knowledge and experience, may be the way to go. Before you sign an agreement with such a company, make sure you are satisfied with the answers to the following questions. If not, you may find yourself stuck with a company that will bring you liability, not profits.

- What is the fee, what does it include, and will there be any extra charges? Does my property's vacancy rate affect the fee? What expenses will need my approval?
- What is the company's experience managing similar rental properties, and can I contact references?
- What kind of customer service does the company provide to tenants? Can tenants call with problems on the weekend?
- How will the company advertise and market the property to prospects, and what will this cost?
- What steps has the company taken to ensure that its employees comply with federal, state, and local fair housing laws?
- How can I terminate our contract, and is there a fee for doing so?
- Does the company send monthly income/expense reports, or quarterly?
- How does the company handle problems with bad tenants, including evictions?

- *(For affordable and other housing program participants)* Is the company qualified to keep the property in compliance with applicable housing programs?

To find a good management company, ask colleagues or contact your local apartment association for recommendations. You can also search for management companies to interview using association directories on the Web. Visit the website of the Institute of Real Estate Management (IREM) at www.irem.org and click "Find a Member." Or visit the National Association of Residential Property Managers' (NARPM) website at www.narpm.org and click "Search Property Managers" at right.

Use written contracts when dealing with ICs

You may find yourself dealing with a range of ICs, from property management companies to the plumber who comes to unclog a drain. The management company will surely present you with a contract for its services, but the plumber probably won't (and it would be impractical to demand one). Between those two extremes, however, are lots of contractors who may offer to work with you on the basis of a conversation and a handshake. Many times, it would be wise to reduce those understandings to writing, in the form of a contract.

Having a contract protects both of you from misunderstandings and failed memories. Sometimes even the act of writing down what you both thought was crystal-clear can expose hidden assumptions (Who's going to supply the scaffold? Was the fee inclusive or exclusive of expenses?) or alert you to the need to talk about an added aspect of the job (How will we handle things if the cabinets don't arrive on time? What quality paints will you be using?). If worse comes to worst and you find yourself taking your contractor to court, you'll be way ahead of the game if you can back up your version of who agreed to what, and when, by referencing a signed contract.

You don't have to write a lengthy tome, and you shouldn't devote time to reinventing the wheel when it comes to creating a suitable contract. Check out Nolo's *Consultant & Independent Contractor Agreements,* by Stephen Fishman, for forms-on-disc that you can adapt to use with your painter, Web designer, or building contractor.

Remove risk of hazards when contractor leaves job early

Sometimes, you may be so dissatisfied with a service contractor that you'll tell him not to continue work on your property. Or a contractor may one day decide to quit in the middle of a job. When a contractor leaves a job early, there's a good chance he's left some hazards behind, too. Even if you hire a new contractor to finish what the first contractor started, inspect the work area immediately and remove or warn of any hazards the contractor may have created. For example, if there are nails jutting out of the wall or floorboards, cover them and cordon off the area with safety tape or traffic cones and a warning sign so that tenants, employees, and guests don't get injured. Once a new contractor takes over, she can manage the day-to-day safety of the work site.

It Won't Happen to You ...

What happened. An Ohio landlord hired a contractor to tear down the retaining walls on both sides of the driveway of the single-family house he rented. After the contractor removed the walls, he quit the job, leaving jagged concrete slabs and uneven surfaces behind. The tenant tried to avoid the construction area when accessing her car in the driveway, but she fell on an uneven slab and broke her foot. She sued the landlord for her injuries, claiming he should be held responsible for letting a dangerous condition exist. The landlord admitted that he knew of the dangerous condition and asked the contractor to put caution tape around the site. But when the contractor quit instead of putting up the tape, the landlord didn't put up the tape or take other steps to warn of or remove the hazard. A judge agreed with the tenant and ordered a trial to determine whether the landlord was negligent.

How you can avoid it. When a contractor you hire walks off a job, the first thing you should do is inspect it to make sure it's safe. If you can't remove any hazards, at least put up warnings or block off areas until you find a new contractor to step in and finish the job.

Require service contractors to get insurance

When hiring service contractors, such as a property management company or landscaping company, require the company to give you a certificate of insurance that proves the company holds a comprehensive general liability insurance policy. If the contractor causes harm or creates other problems and you need to sue, you'll know your recovery won't be limited to the contractor's assets.

Also, have the company name you and your business as "additional insureds" to the policy. (The company's insurer should take care of this request at no cost.) This way, if someone sues you over your management company's alleged misdeed, the company's insurer will defend you and pay any damages. Talk to your insurance agent or broker to ask how much insurance you should require

Find the right lawyer for your business

Sooner or later, you'll need a lawyer to help you keep your business successful—if not keep it afloat. Lawyers can help you in four general types of situations:

- **If you're sued.** You'll probably need to hire a lawyer if you're sued or threatened with a lawsuit. For example, a prospect or job applicant you rejected may accuse you of discrimination, or a tenant who gets injured on your property may claim you should be held liable for her medical bills and lost wages. These kinds of lawsuits generally need the services of a pro. (If you're sued in small claims court over a small matter such as your retention of a security deposit, you can probably handle it yourself.)
- **If you need to sue someone over a significant issue.** You may also need to go on the offensive. Suppose you pay a building contractor a large sum of money in return for what turns out to be low-quality work and shoddy materials. Or consider the problem tenant who stops paying rent or holds over. In both of these situations, you'll probably need a lawyer who can take the necessary legal action to uphold your rights or defend your actions (such as sue for breach of contract or eviction).

- **If you need specific legal advice.** You could read the best self-help books on the shelf and still need the advice of a good lawyer for specific situations. Often, that lawyer's knowledge of local law and how it's applied will help guide your decision, or the lawyer's estimate of what the case or situation is "worth" in your area will make the difference between suing (or settling). For example, a lawyer may give you a reality check on whether you have a meritorious case or whether the time and money spent pursuing your case will be worth it, and a lawyer may help you realize that you're letting your emotions fan the fire of a fight that's just not worth it.

- **If you're making big moves.** Lawyers can help make sure you're following the law and preserving your rights when you're ready and eager to take your business to the next level. For example, a lawyer can represent you in the negotiation and purchase of your building. If you decide to form a partnership or corporation for your business, or change its structure (for example, from an S-corporation to a limited liability company), a lawyer can advise you and take care of the paperwork and filing requirements.

How to find a good lawyer

When it comes to hiring legal help, it's too risky to go with just any lawyer. Here are three tips on how to find the right lawyer for your business.

First, start with recommendations. Recommendations are ideal if they come from other landlords whose judgment you trust. If a friend (who's not a landlord) tells you she used an excellent lawyer for another type of matter, such as a divorce or co-op purchase, find out whether the lawyer has experience representing rental property owners before pursuing this lead further. Ask the friend for the lawyer's or firm's website to try to determine this information before you call. If that lawyer doesn't handle matters such as yours, ask for a referral. Most of the time, good lawyers will refer other equally good lawyers.

Next, try a referral service. The American Bar Association (ABA), the largest voluntary professional association in the world, offers links to state and local bar associations that offer lawyer referral services. An indication appears next to those that meet ABA standards for lawyer referral (which include making sure the lawyers are licensed, are in good standing in their states of admission, and have malpractice insurance). From the ABA's website, www.abanet.org, select "Public Resources" at left and then click "Lawyer Referral Services" to search. You can also try the Lawyer Directory on the Nolo website (www.nolo.com), where lawyers' advertisements give you information on their practice areas and general approach to handling cases and clients. (Nolo confirms only that the advertisers are in good standing with their state's bar.)

Ask Questions Before Choosing a Lawyer

Most lawyers will offer free initial consultations. Approach these lawyers first, so you can "try and buy" without a financial commitment. Before you hire a lawyer, ask about the lawyer's background and about the service the lawyer will provide. Here are questions to ask before hiring:

- What experience do you have representing rental property owners?
- Have you handled this type of matter before?
- How will I be billed (that is, hourly or in a lump sum)?
- How much is your total fee, or what might it depend on?
- Will I be responsible for other expenses (such as document filing, mortgage recording, or court fees)?
- How long do you expect this matter to take (or to be resolved)?
- What additional information and cooperation will you need from me?

Finally, once you've zeroed in on a likely lawyer, you'll want to know if that person has been disciplined (or is being investigated) by the state bar. Contact your state's disciplinary agency to see if lawyers you like check out. For a directory of lawyer disciplinary agencies by state, visit www.abanet.org/cpr/regulation/scpd/disciplinary.html. Only a handful of states, such as California, Florida, Illinois, Michigan, Oregon, and Pennsylvania offer disciplinary action information online. If your state is among the majority that doesn't, call the agency using the contact information provided on the site.

Switch lawyers if you're not satisfied

With such a large number of excellent lawyers in practice across the country, there's no reason you should have to settle for a mediocre one (or worse). When you've completed a matter with a lawyer or law firm, reflect on the experience by asking yourself the questions below. The more "no" answers you get, the more you should consider switching attorneys the next time around. If you're very unhappy with how your lawyer's handling a current matter, you may not want to wait to switch. Although you might think of switching counsel mid-matter as drastic, you may need to do so to avoid further risk to your business. Running through the questions below should help you decide.

- Did the lawyer perform the services I expected?
- Did I pay what I expected for these services?
- Was the payment reasonable?
- Did the lawyer give my matter proper attention?
- Did the lawyer show up late to closings, meetings, or other important appointments with little or no justification?
- Did the lawyer act ethically at all times?
- Did the lawyer keep me in the loop and return calls or emails promptly?
- Did the lawyer explain my options and respect my decisions?
- Was the lawyer qualified to handle my matter?
- If the outcome wasn't favorable, could another lawyer have fared better?

Hiring Help: My To-Do List

In Step Nine, you learned about the risks involved when hiring and firing employees and using ICs, and you also read why it's important to know which type of help you're dealing with. Now, you can follow up by taking action that will help ensure you're hiring help without courting trouble.

☐ **Classifying workers correctly:** Review my employment relationships to determine that I'm properly treating helpers as employees or ICs.

☐ **No discrimination:** Comply with applicable federal discrimination laws and discover which state and local laws apply to my business.

☐ **No harassment:** Create and enforce a zero-tolerance policy against sexual harassment.

☐ **No visual harassment:** Maintain a professional environment—don't let desks, bulletin boards, screensavers, and walls become host to sexual or other offensive materials.

☐ **No disability discrimination:** Grant employees' reasonable accommodation requests and consider asking disabled job applicants about whether they'll need them.

☐ **Proper screening:** Screen employees not just for their qualifications and ability, but for their background, too.

☐ **Employee handbook:** Put all my workplace policies into an employee handbook that employees receive on their first day on the job, update it as my rules change, and enforce the policies consistently.

☐ **Workers' comp:** Check if my state requires workers' compensation insurance, and consider buying it anyway.

☐ **Maintenance:** Maintain a hazard-free workplace.

☐ **Antidiscrimination training:** Get fair housing and other training for staff, as appropriate.

☐ **Posters:** Put all required federal and state employment posters on the office wall.

☐ **Employed tenants:** Rent to employees on a month-to-month basis.

☐ **Firing:** Don't fire employees for a discriminatory reason, and document my reasons for firing an employee.

☐ **Management companies:** Ask the right questions before hiring a property management company.

☐ **Use a contract:** Choose some form of written contract over a handshake when dealing with contractors.

☐ **Contractors' insurance:** Make sure contractors I hire have insurance.

☐ **Good counsel:** Ask questions to find a good lawyer.

☐ **Stay with a good lawyer:** Don't hesitate to switch lawyers if mine disappoints.

Taxes—Stay on Good Terms With Uncle Sam

Y ou've no doubt heard Benjamin Franklin's famous remark, "In this world, nothing is certain but death and taxes." More than two centuries later, his witty observation still rings true, both for individuals and businesses. Not only are taxes a certainty for today's landlords, but landlords who don't understand the tax issues that relate to their business are taking unnecessary risks.

Landlords face two kinds of risks when it comes to their taxes. The first is the worry that the IRS or their state tax agency will audit them and discover mistakes in their returns that will require them to pay taxes they didn't think they owed, plus interest and penalties, at a time when cash is tight. The second is the possibility that misunderstanding tax issues will lead landlords to overpay their taxes, because of an omission or improper treatment of deductions and other items. This second type of risk may not be as scary, but it can prove costly just the same.

Fortunately, you don't need to have an accounting background or even take a tax preparation course in order to be a successful landlord when it comes to paying your taxes and taking advantage of favorable opportunities to save money. But there are still certain things you need to know, even if you rely on an accountant or other type of tax professional to handle your taxes. In Step Ten, you'll learn the basics that will enable you to understand your taxes, manage your risks, and stay on good terms with Uncle Sam.

What Do You Have to Lose?

The mere mention of the word "audit" is likely to send a chill down any landlord's spine. And no wonder—once the IRS gets you in its sights, you'll at best be diverted from the task of running your business. At worst, you'll face the prospect of a long, expensive battle. Here's how an IRS audit can spoil your day:

- **Office and correspondence audits.** If you're a sole proprietor who earns less than $100,000 a year, the IRS may ask you to produce documents and records, either by mailing them in (a correspondence audit) or bringing them with you to meet with an examiner for a few hours at an IRS office (office audit). Complying with either request requires time and energy; paying assessments and penalties only makes it worse.

- **Field audits.** If your business is organized as a sole proprietorship, partnership, limited liability company, or corporation, and has gross receipts of at least $100,000 per year, you're more likely to have the IRS conduct a "field audit." This type of audit takes place at your office (or, if you prefer, at another location), and is much more involved. Taxpayers embroiled in a field audit end up owing, on average, over $17,000 in total assessments.

- **Criminal charges.** Taxpayers who file fraudulent returns have committed a crime. Fraud isn't the result of a careless mistake— it's either a deliberate misstatement of the truth, or a purposeful misuse of a favorable tax rule. In other words, landlords who file fraudulent returns know what they're doing (and are presumably willing to risk the consequences).

Preparing for an audit—even one that you manage to emerge from relatively unscathed—will sap much of your time and energy. In an audit, the burden of proof is on you to convince the IRS that your tax return is legit. This will involve hunting for and producing bank statements, canceled checks, and receipts; your books (or bank statements, checkbook, or ledger or journal); electronic records (credit card statements); appointment books, logs, and diaries; and auto, travel, and entertainment records. What's more is that once you're audited, your chances of being audited again go way up.

Clearly, an audit is something you should strive to avoid at all costs. But it's hardly the end of the matter. At the other end of the tax risk spectrum lies a demon who takes money from businesses and gives it to the government the easy way—by letting businesses blithely hand it over.

Each year, landlords and other business owners overlook valuable deductions or make other mistakes that artificially increase their total tax liability. These blunders may cost a business hundreds—if not thousands—of dollars in a single year. Sadly, many business owners who make these mistakes never discover them and continue their practice of needlessly funneling some of their hard-earned cash to Uncle Sam.

Is This You?

Chances are, this chapter isn't one you'll want to skip. Unless you have a solid tax background and have already minimized the risks you face when it comes to your taxes, you should recognize yourself in at least a couple of the following portraits. Look over the list and check off the descriptions that you find familiar. Then, read on to learn how to keep your tax-related risks under control.

Take Action!

As you read the portraits below, do you find any of them familiar? Even if you do your own taxes and feel confident that you're doing a decent job, there's a good chance you'll see yourself in at least a few of them. Fortunately, the habits reflected in these descriptions aren't hard to reform. By following the action steps outlined below, you'll end up feeling even more confident when preparing your taxes on your own, or better prepared to have a two-way conversation with your tax preparer. And as for Uncle Sam—a relative you must keep in touch with but never want over for a visit—you'll know that you've taken basic steps to keep him at bay, while maximizing the tax breaks he's created for you.

In this final Step, instead of reading "It Won't Happen to You" stories, you'll read "Audit Alerts" that will put you in the shoes of landlords whose mistakes with taxes led to unpleasant audits. At the end of each alert, you'll learn exactly what you can do to make sure you never suffer the fate of these fictitious landlords.

Do You Think About Taxes Like These Landlords?

☐ What you know about taxes you've "learned on the job"—you haven't attended classes, read books or articles, or visited tax-related websites.

☐ Your business records aren't in great shape, and you've had a hard time producing receipts, canceled checks, appointment books, and so on, when you've needed to.

☐ You've been doing your own taxes, without the help or advice of a professional, even though you sometimes have questions or wonder if you're overpaying.

☐ You don't properly withhold taxes from your employees' paychecks.

☐ You hire independent contractors without asking them to complete an IRS Form 1099-MISC.

☐ You've set up your business as a sole proprietorship, partnership, limited liability company (LLC), or corporation without first considering the tax implications.

☐ You haven't devoted much thought to details such as the accounting method you're using, the timing of your tax filings, and the "tax year" you've chosen.

☐ You're so worried about an audit that you consciously forgo claiming deductions, even ones that you think you're entitled to.

☐ When you're done with a tax return, you're quick to file it away without considering whether it could be a valuable tool in assessing how your business is progressing.

☐ You get extensions for filing your returns and you amend your returns without worrying about the consequences of these moves.

☐ You let your fear or anger get the better of you during an audit, causing you to not present organized files or treat auditors courteously and with respect.

Familiarize yourself with IRS and state tax agency websites

If you haven't yet been to the IRS's website, www.irs.gov, take a look now. You may be pleasantly surprised to notice how friendly and helpful it is. From the main page, you can click to get an Employment Identification Number (an "EIN," explained below), check the status of a refund, and download forms, among other things. (When you know the number of a form or publication, just type it into the main search box on the top-right of the page.) Click the "Businesses" tab toward the top-left of the screen to reach the "Tax Information for Businesses" page. Here, you'll find a wealth of articles, tips, helpful links, and other resources that will help you understand your tax obligations as a landlord.

> TIP
>
> **Read Publication 527 for good tax advice.** Perhaps the most relevant IRS publication for residential landlords is Publication 527, *Residential Rental Property*, which covers how to report rental income and expenses on your tax return, and more. You can access this document on the IRS website.

After bookmarking www.irs.gov (and resolving to return regularly), your next stop should be your state tax agency's website. If you don't know the name of your state's agency or its website, visit http://public.findlaw.com. Using FindLaw's search feature, type "state tax agencies" and choose the resulting link. Once there, you'll find useful resources, such as mailing addresses for your returns, state forms you can download, answers to frequently asked questions, tax-saving tips, and more.

Do You Need an Employer Identification Number (EIN)?

When filing your taxes, you must identify yourself (or your business) with a number, which may be either your Social Security number (SSN) or an employer identification number (EIN). You'll need an EIN to use on your tax returns if at least one of the following characteristics applies to your business:

- you have at least one employee
- you have a 401(k), profit-sharing plan, or other "qualified retirement plan" that meets legal requirements for special tax benefits
- your business is a corporation, partnership, multimember LLC, or single-member LLC taxed as a corporation, or
- you file returns for employment taxes or excise taxes.

If you determine that you need an EIN and don't have one, take action today. You can apply for an EIN by visiting www.irs.gov/businesses/small, calling 800-829-4933, or mailing or faxing IRS Form SS-4, *Application for Employer Identification Number*, which is available for download at www.irs.gov/pub/irs-pdf/fss4.pdf.

If you need to file a tax return or other tax forms soon and don't yet have your EIN, don't sweat it. Simply write "Applied For" followed by the application date in the space provided on the form.

For more information about EINs, read IRS Publication 1635, *Understanding Your EIN*, which you can download from the IRS website.

Keep good records

Keep records as if your business depends on it, because indeed it does. Hopefully, you won't ever need to refer to most of your records. But if records go missing when you need them, you could be in for some trouble. As much as an auditor might want to believe you, the government just won't take a taxpayer's word in place of supporting documentation. Instead, an auditor is legally permitted to estimate your income or expenses (don't expect generous estimates), and can impose a separate penalty for your failure to keep needed records.

Audit Alert

What can happen. Last year, you upgraded the computers in your office, replaced the furniture in your lobby, and bought new equipment for your property's fitness center. You claimed deductions for these expenses on your tax return but didn't keep receipts or other documents that would show how much you paid and when you incurred these expenses. The IRS randomly chooses to audit your return and, upon discovering that you can't back up your deductions, denies them.

How you can avoid it. Even though these expenses are legitimate business deductions, it's risky to claim them if you can't prove what they are and when you paid for them. Without careful records, you'll risk losing those deductions—and will take the chance that the IRS will impose interest and penalties.

What should you keep?

The records you need to keep are those that an auditor would ask for. Suppose an auditor asks for written documentation to satisfy him that a landlord is entitled to take a deduction he claimed, or accurately reported income on his return. The result is a collection of supporting documents that will include bank statements, receipts, cancelled checks, credit card statements, and the like. (See "Back It Up," below, for an outline of what you should keep.)

As these documents pile up over the year, it's easy to lose track of them. If you misplace just one receipt, you risk having to forgo a valuable deduction. Commit to staying organized by keeping a folder for each deduction, expense, or item of income, stored in a secure filing cabinet that you can easily access through the year. When the calendar or fiscal year ends and you've paid your taxes (or gotten your refund), transfer these files to long-term storage and set up folders for the new tax year.

Back It Up

Your tax returns list income and expenses. To substantiate the amount of tax you owe, you'll need proof of both. Here's an outline of the supporting documents you need to keep.

To document ...	You should keep ...
Income	Bank statements, deposited checks, Forms 1099-MISC (from independent contractors).
Travel expenses	Receipts from hotels, gas stations, travel agencies, and other businesses showing the dates and destinations of trips, mileage, and lodging. Also, note the relevance of the trip to your business in your records (for example, to interview a new management company).
Entertainment (including meals)	Receipts and credit card slips that show what you purchased and from whom, along with the price and date. Also, note the relevance of the trip to your business and the identities of people who accompanied you in your records.
Other expenses	Receipts, cancelled checks, credit card statements, or other appropriate supporting documents that identify the expense, the seller, the cost, and the date.

How long should you keep your business records?

You should keep documents that back up the figures you enter on your tax returns—such as your receipts and canceled checks—for as long as you can, but for a minimum of six years. The IRS usually has up to three years to audit your tax return, starting from the deadline for filing the return (or, if you filed late, from the actual filing date). If you underreported your gross income by more than 25%, the IRS has six years to audit your return. Finally, if the IRS suspects a taxpayer is committing fraud, there's no limitation.

 TIP

Use your computer for storing your business records. The IRS will accept a scanned version of your business records as evidence of the income and expenses you report on your tax returns. If you scan your records, consider keeping an extra copy of your digital file collection on a portable electronic storage device, such as a CD-ROM or a USB flash drive.

How long should you keep your tax returns?

The IRS doesn't require you to keep tax returns for a specific amount of time. But it's in your best interest to keep your returns for as long as you can, to cover the "just-in-case" scenario of an audit down the road. Since tax returns take up very little space, it's best never to get rid of them.

Follow the tax rules when using independent contractors or hiring employees

As you grow your rental business, sooner or later you'll need to hire help. Help comes in the form of employees or independent contractors, and special tax rules apply to both situations. Not knowing the rules, or applying them incorrectly, can attract the unwanted attention of IRS auditors. Here are the basics.

Independent contractors

The people you hire to perform certain tasks at your property, who have significant control over what they're doing and don't get benefits, are independent contractors (ICs). For example, if you hire a lawyer to help evict an unruly tenant, or a plumber to replace a leaky pipe, you're dealing with ICs. Taxwise, you must take two key steps with this type of worker.

- **Get the IC's taxpayer identification number.** A person's taxpayer identification number is his Social Security number (SSN) or his employer identification number (EIN, explained above in "Do You Need an Employer Identification Number (EIN)?"). You'll need these numbers for the second step.
- **File IRS Form 1099-MISC to report how much you paid the IC for the year.** Completing this form is easy. In most cases, you'll just identify yourself (the "payer") and the IC (the "recipient") in the spaces provided on the left side of the form, and then include the total amount you paid the IC in box 3. Each year,

you must give Copy B of this form to the IC by the end of the following January, and file Copy A with the IRS by the end of the following February (or March, if filing electronically).

Filing the 1099-MISC helps the IRS keep track of how much income ICs earn, making it difficult for ICs to hide it. There's also a risk-avoidance benefit behind filing accurate and timely 1099-MISCs: Many audits, known as "follow-up audits," are triggered by another taxpayer's audit. For example, if the IRS suspects that your janitorial service is underreporting its income, you may find the IRS at your door too, sniffing around for information or evidence of collusion.

Some ICs aren't covered by the 1099-MISC requirement. If you hire an IC that's a corporation (that doesn't perform legal services), or if you pay an IC less than $600 in one year for the IC's services (including corporations that perform legal services), you don't have to file a 1099-MISC. Also, if your rental activity doesn't qualify as a business (that is, you're really just an investor), you're off the hook. As a rule of thumb, rental property ownership qualifies as a business if, in addition to having a profit motive, you work at it regularly, systematically, and continuously (by yourself or with hired help).

Employees

If you hire a resident manager, maintenance staff, or other employees for your business, you must withhold some of their pay and periodically send it to the IRS and your state tax agency. This withholding and payment routine is known as payroll taxes (or employment taxes), and it ensures that employees and employers pay their tax liability little by little throughout the year, rather than chalk up a hefty sum on April 15. Federal payroll taxes have three components:

- **Social Security and Medicare taxes (FICA).** These taxes are commonly known as FICA, the acronym for the Federal Income Contributions Act. FICA taxes are a 12.4% Social Security tax on wages (up to an annual wage ceiling), and a 2.9% Medicare tax on all employee wages paid. The total FICA that must be paid is 15.3% (subject to the wage ceiling). As an employer, you're responsible for coming up with half this amount (7.65%), but you may deduct it as an operating expense.

- **Unemployment taxes (FUTA).** FUTA stands for the Federal Unemployment Tax Act, the law that established unemployment taxes. The proceeds go toward administering each state's Unemployment Insurance and Job Service programs. If you must pay FUTA taxes, you're responsible for the entire amount, which you can deduct as an operating expense. You must pay these taxes if you pay at least $1,500 to employees during any calendar quarter, or at least one employee worked for at least part of one day in any 20 or more (not necessarily consecutive) weeks during the year.

The official FUTA tax rate is 6.2%, but with a 5.4% credit for paying the applicable state unemployment tax on time, the actual rate should be 0.8%. Also, the taxable wage base for each employee is only the first $7,000 paid in wages each year. This means that the total FUTA tax per employee per year is $56 ($7,000 x 0.8%).

- **Federal income tax withholding (FITW).** Don't worry—you're not responsible for paying taxes on income your employees earn working for you. But you are responsible for making sure their income tax gets sent to Uncle Sam on a regular basis. To do this, you must calculate and withhold federal income tax from all employee paychecks.

State payroll taxes similarly require you to withhold certain amounts from your employees' paychecks and send them to your state tax agency throughout the year. All states require unemployment compensation taxes (to contribute to their unemployment insurance fund), most states require income taxes, and a handful of states require disability insurance taxes (to cover employees for non-work-related injuries or illnesses). For information about workers' compensation insurance, which covers employees for work-related injuries, see Step Nine.

States differ in the types of payroll taxes they require and what your obligations are as an employer. Visit your agency's website for help (see "Familiarize yourself with IRS and state tax agency websites," above). For more detailed information about federal payroll taxes, see IRS Publication 15, *Circular E, Employer's Tax Guide*, available on the

IRS website. And for more information about dealing effectively with employees and ICs, see Step Nine.

Audit Alert

What can happen. You've been running your rental property business on your own, but things are starting to pick up. So, you hire a friend to help with maintenance, tenant relations, and general office matters 20 hours a week. You run a legitimate business and want to do everything "on the books," so every other week you pay your friend with a check for the full amount of her services. On your next tax return, you claim the salary you've paid your friend throughout the year as a deduction. This prompts the IRS to audit your return, with your state tax agency close behind. Both agencies want to know why you haven't been paying federal and state payroll taxes for your employee all year.

How you can avoid it. Know what your tax obligations are before hiring employees. Doing things "on the books" is noble, but doing things right is also important.

Hire the right tax professional

As your business grows, your taxes are likely to get more complicated and require more time to manage. Even if you keep your business small, you may tire of preparing your returns each year and decide it's a task you'd happily pay someone else to accomplish for you.

Fortunately, landlords and other business owners today have a range of options when it comes to getting professional tax help (see "Go With a Pro," below). As with any other type of contractor or service provider, it's always best to follow a recommendation or get a referral. So, talk to colleagues for their recommendations or contact your local apartment association for suggestions. If any leads you get don't pan out, just search for the type of tax professional you need (such as "tax attorney" or "tax preparer") on the Internet. To search directly for an enrolled agent (defined just below), visit the National Association of Enrolled Agents' website at www.naea.org.

Go With a Pro

Many landlords use outside help to prepare their tax returns or handle other tax issues. Here's a rundown of the four main types of tax professionals available to you and the services they offer.

Tax pro type	What they do	Pros	Cons
Tax preparers	Prepare tax returns	Lower cost Several to choose from	No licensing requirement May lack proper training and experience for landlord business
Enrolled agents (EAs)	Prepare tax returns, give tax advice, represent taxpayers	Licensed by the IRS Completed training requirement	May be inadequate for large landlord businesses
Certified Public Accountants (CPAs)	Prepare tax returns, give tax advice	Licensed and regulated by states Completed rigorous training requirement Able to tackle sophisticated tax issues	Probably too expensive and sophisticated for most small landlord businesses
Tax attorneys	Prepare tax returns, give tax advice, represent taxpayers	Licensed and regulated by states Ideal for tax defense work and tax-related legal advice, such as applying for a revenue ruling (this is a written IRS opinion covering a taxpayer's specific circumstances)	Tax advice may be too expensive for small landlord businesses

Know how your choice of business structure affects your taxes

The way you've structured your rental business has a direct effect on your taxes, from the forms you must file to the amounts you'll owe. Because tax treatment is so important to any business, savvy owners factor it in when choosing (or changing) their business's structure. Tax treatment can be quite complex, especially when you own property with others. This is one area where it almost always makes sense to spend some time and money with a tax pro, to get the right advice.

You have a good handful of options when it comes to choosing a structure for your rental property business. You may choose to own your property as an individual (in which case you're known as a "sole proprietor"), or through a business entity (a partnership, LLC, or corporation). Below is a brief description of these various types of business structures, along with their pros and cons.

You can learn much more about this subject by reading *LLC or Corporation? How to Choose the Right Form for Your Business*, by Anthony Mancuso (Nolo).

Business Entities to Choose From			
Business structure	**Description**	**Pros**	**Cons**
Sole proprietorship	An individual owns and runs the business in her name, without creating a special entity	Easy to form, operate, and dissolve	Personal liability for debts and lawsuits
General partnership	Two or more partners contribute money, property, or services to a partnership, which they jointly manage	Easy to form and operate (no written agreement or state filings required)	Personal liability for debts and lawsuits
Limited partnership	General partners manage the partnership while limited partners act as passive investors	Limited partners have limited personal liability for debts and lawsuits	General partners have personal liability for debts and lawsuits You must file formation documents with your state More expensive to create than general partnership
C corporation (also known as a regular corporation or just a corporation)	Its own legal entity; a corporation's owners are known as shareholders	Shareholders have limited personal liability for debts and lawsuits	Business is taxed as separate entity You must file incorporation documents with your state Comparatively expensive and time-consuming to form and maintain
S corporation (also known as a small business corporation)		The business's income and loss "pass through" to the shareholders	You must file incorporation documents with your state Comparatively expensive and time-consuming to form and maintain
Limited liability company	One or more owners, known as "members," manage the business and share in the profits.	Limited personal liability from debts and lawsuits Although the business is a separate legal entity, its income and loss "pass through" to the members	You must file formation documents with your state More expensive to form and maintain than sole proprietorship or partnership

Choose your accounting method wisely

Every business owner must choose an accounting method for reporting income and expenses each tax year. The two most popular types of accounting methods are the cash method and the accrual method. If you're reading this and wondering which method you've been using, then you're probably using the cash method (and if so, you probably don't want to switch).

The cash method is straightforward. You report income in the year you receive it (regardless of when it was earned), and you deduct expenses in the year you pay them (regardless of when you incurred them). For instance, if you get a rent check on December 10, 2008, it counts as income on your 2008 return. If you pay a plumber in January 2009 for work he did in December 2008, this is a 2009 tax year expense.

With the accrual method, you report income in the year you earn it (even if you haven't yet received it), and you deduct expenses in the year you incur them (even if you haven't yet paid them). So, for example, rent that was due in December but not paid until January counts as income for December; and the plumbing job that was finished in December but not paid for until January is a December expense.

If the accrual method sounds a little complicated, that's because it is. Many landlords don't choose the accrual method because they find it's too tricky to account for income and expenses. But there's an advantage to this approach—under the accrual method, you can take a tax deduction for an expense before you actually have to lay out the cash (which could be several weeks or even months later). For example, if you purchase supplies and furniture for your leasing office in December, you can deduct them for that year—even if you don't actually pay the bill for these items until January.

Sound good? Well, here's the downside: Because you must count your tenants' rent as income when it's due (and not when they pay it), you'll have to list late rent as income even though you don't have it in hand. This means that if you don't get the rent payments until the following year, you'll still owe taxes on these payments now (while under the cash method, you would have an additional 12 months to pay these taxes). If you wind up *never* getting rent that you had to report as income, your only solace under the accrual method is to take a deduction the following year for the never-received income as a bad debt. Before you think this is an advantage of the accrual method, take a moment to realize that this bad debt deduction merely cancels out the never-received income that you paid taxes on a year ago. Under the cash method, you wouldn't have claimed this income—and had to pay taxes on it—in the first place.

Your choice of accounting methods is a matter for you and your tax professional to decide. The vast majority of landlords choose the cash method, because it's easier and makes more sense to them, and there's usually no compelling reason to switch. But if your tax professional gives you a good reason to switch to the accrual method, make sure you're square on how the calculations you've been doing will be different going forward.

Regardless of the accounting method you choose, you'll need to indicate your choice when filing your first tax return. If you choose a method and later consider switching, read the relevant section in IRS Publication 538, *Accounting Periods and Methods*, available on the IRS website. Then, discuss your ideas with an accountant or other tax professional. If you decide to switch, you usually must file IRS Form 3115, *Application for Change in Accounting Method*, along with your tax return for the year you want the switch to take effect. You can download a copy of Form 3115 at the IRS website.

Audit Alert

What can happen. You began your business using the cash method of accounting. A couple of years later, you decided to switch to the accrual method of accounting to take advantage of some late-in-the-year deductions for big-ticket items for which you were billed but hadn't yet paid. The next year, it's back to the cash method, followed by two more years under the accrual method, all the time never communicating your intentions to switch methods to the government. Finally, Uncle Sam tells you he's had enough and sends an IRS agent to audit your recent returns.

How you can avoid it. Understand the pros and cons of the cash method versus the accrual method of accounting, and decide which one's best for your property. If you start using one method and later want to switch, consider talking to a tax professional. Then, file Form 3115 with the IRS.

Think Twice Before Choosing Your "Tax Year"

Every business operates using a 12-month accounting period, your "tax year." The tax year can be the calendar year, which runs through the end of December, or a fiscal year, which runs through the end of any other month. Using the calendar year probably makes the most sense for your business.

Businesses that choose a fiscal year often do so because their profits and expenses are seasonal and wouldn't be grouped together properly in a calendar year. For instance, say you own a few houses near a ski lodge that you fix up in November and December and rent from January through March. Choosing a fiscal year ending with March would more accurately reflect your annual income and expenses than the calendar year.

If you decide you want your business to have a tax year other than the calendar year, it's a good idea to consult with an account to confirm that you can. Be aware that there are several limitations and requirements to consider, based on your business's structure. Also, if you decide to switch your tax year in a later year, after your business has already been established, you must first apply to the IRS for permission. For more information, read IRS Publication 538, *Accounting Periods and Methods*, available on the IRS website.

Don't miss a deduction

The IRS has given landlords several deductions. Although some, or even most, of these deductions may not be applicable to your business in a particular year, you should be on the lookout and claim all the deductions you're entitled to. Here's a snapshot of the common types of deductions landlords claim.

Start-up expenses

Most landlords spend money when starting up their rental businesses, for items ranging from license fees, advertising and marketing costs, professional fees, travel expenses, and office supplies. You can deduct up to $5,000 of your start-up expenses for the year in which they're incurred. You can deduct any excess through "amortization," which in this case means equal installments spread over the first 180 months of your business. (Unfortunately, you can't deduct for the actual cost of buying your rental property.)

Operating expenses

As you know well, your business costs money to run. The payments you make on a regular basis—such as for mortgage interest, utilities, employee salaries, supplies, travel expenses, repairs, and maintenance—are deductible in the year you pay them.

Capital expenses

All landlords have at least one capital asset: the building they rent to their tenants. Capital assets are items that have a useful life of more than one year, and also include equipment, vehicles, furniture, and appliances. The costs associated with capital assets are called capital expenses, and you can deduct them through a process known as "depreciation." In short, this means you deduct capital expenses a little bit over time. For example, you can deduct your residential rental building over 27.5 years, shrubbery and other landscaping over 15 years, and automobiles and office machinery over five years.

CAUTION

Only your building—and not the land it sits on—is a capital asset.
So, while you may deduct the expenses for your building over its depreciation
period, you must wait to sell the land to recover its cost.

Making sense of all the deductions that may be available to you
can be complicated. But it can make the difference between earning a
profit and losing hard-earned money. For a helpful, thorough discussion
of deductions along with a rundown of rules and strategies, read *Every
Landlord's Tax Deduction Guide,* by Stephen Fishman (Nolo).

Time tax filings to maximize revenue

If you owe money on your taxes, pay it by the deadline—but don't
rush to pay it extra early. Acting diligent in this case won't do you
any good—the IRS won't cut you any slack and you'll still owe the
same statutory penalties if your payments are based on mistaken
calculations or assumptions. Paying very early means parting with cash
that could be in your bank account earning interest, rather than in the
government's coffers.

Unnecessarily paying early is one thing; preparing your tax return
in plenty of time is quite another. Finishing your tax return well
before the deadline relieves the stress of having to work last-minute,
which can lead to sloppiness, the temptation to take shortcuts, and the
likelihood of careless errors. But wait until the deadline nears before
actually filing your return and paying what you owe. Filing your return
before most other businesses have filed theirs makes it stand out from
the crowd, which could increase the chances that the IRS or your state
tax agency will look more carefully at your return than they otherwise
would.

If you determine that Uncle Sam owes you a significant amount of
money on your tax return, it may be worthwhile to file early (despite
the potential for increased scrutiny). The sooner the IRS and your state
tax agency get your returns, the sooner you'll get your refund and start
earning interest on it.

The Brave New World of eFiling

The IRS, along with many state tax agencies, has strongly promoted filing tax returns electronically over the Internet, known as "eFiling." eFiling is touted as a way for individuals and businesses to more efficiently file their returns, pay taxes, or get refunds.

If you haven't set up eFiling, you might need to do so for your next tax filing. It's now a federal requirement for large and midsize corporations. Several states have also begun requiring it from certain types of taxpayers. For example, in New Jersey, partnerships with at least ten partners, and individuals who use tax preparers with at least 200 returns under their belt must file electronically. As eFiling catches on, you can expect more mandates from the IRS and state tax agencies.

If you're not required to eFile, you may want to consider it the next time around for its ease and efficiency. To start with, eFiling is secure and, unlike the case with filing paper returns, the IRS will acknowledge receipt of your electronic return within 48 hours. If you owe money, you can schedule the funds to get automatically deducted from your account on or just before the deadline, rather than have to send your returns along with checks through the mail several days earlier (and pay for services such as certified mail, return receipt requested). If you expect a refund, you can enjoy the convenience of waking up one day to notice the funds have already been deposited into your account (and are earning you interest), while other landlords may spend the next week or so looking for a check in their mailbox, which they'll then have to deposit at their bank.

On the flip side, some tax experts believe that a return is more likely to be audited if it's filed electronically, because the IRS can more easily search the return and archive the data. So, although eFiling is faster and easier than paper filing, and it will get you your refund more quickly, it's important to weigh this potential risk. Ultimately, as long as no federal or state mandate applies, you should choose the type of filing that you feel most comfortable with—even if it's not what your tax preparer recommends.

For more information about setting up electronic filing and payment with the IRS, visit www.irs.gov/efile. To find out the options available to you with your state tax returns, visit your state tax agency's website.

Get an extension, if you must—but pay on time

If you can't file your tax return on time, you can get an automatic six-month extension from the IRS. But don't get too excited—be aware that this extension only postpones the deadline for *filing* your tax return. If you owe money with your return, you must still pay it by the deadline. Whether you must file your return now or later, paying later will trigger the same interest and penalties.

Of course, you probably won't know exactly how much you owe until you complete your tax return. You must calculate your estimated liability based on the information you have and pay that amount. The IRS offers some leeway here: if that amount turns out to be at least 90% of the amount you actually owe (and you pay the remainder by the new deadline for filing your return), you'll owe interest but no penalties.

If you're due a refund, you can get an extension without having to worry about paying anything by the deadline. But this situation isn't so rosy, either. Keep in mind that the IRS won't start processing your refund until you've filed your return, so an extension will just add unwanted time until you receive the money you're owed.

The IRS has a fairly simple process for letting businesses get extensions for filing their tax returns. To file for an extension, use Form 7004, *Application for Automatic 6-Month Extension of Time to File Certain Business Income Tax, Information, and Other Returns*, which you can download from the IRS website. (Landlords who are sole proprietors and file individual returns should use Form 4868, *Application for Automatic Extension of Time To File U.S. Individual Income Tax Return.*) Check with your state tax agency to find out what form you must use to get an extension for filing your state tax return.

Audit Alert

What can happen. April takes you by surprise, and you know you need more time to file your tax return. You apply to the IRS and get an automatic six-month extension. Four months later, you file your return and pay what you owe. Although you feel relieved, you soon learn that Uncle Sam isn't too pleased and tells you to cough up interest and penalties to boot.

How you can avoid it. If you apply for an extension, realize that it's an extension only to *file* your tax return. If you believe you'll owe any taxes along with your return, you must still pay them (making your best estimate, based on the information you have) by the deadline to avoid penalties and interest.

Amend your return, if needed

If you discover that you've made a mistake, take action. The sooner you rectify it, the less you'll ultimately have to shell out in interest and penalties. Also, correcting your mistake on your own will make you look much better to the IRS or state tax agency than you will if they discover a mistake and bring it to your attention. If you're later audited for any reason, your record of taking steps on your own to correct mistakes will help paint you as honest and professional. This will give auditors reason to offer you the benefit of the doubt, should issues arise.

What about mistakes that cost you—not the government—money? You're not required to amend your return to correct these mistakes (and, if the difference is slight, it's probably not worth the bother). But if you discover a mistake that cost you a significant amount of money, you should certainly amend your return to get back what you deserve. If you don't uncover the mistake until several months later as you're preparing the next year's tax return, you may find it more convenient to amend your return when you file your new one. But be aware that you generally must amend your return within three years from the original return's filing deadline or within two years from the date you paid your taxes, whichever is later.

If you notice a mistake and used a tax professional to prepare your return, check whether incorrect or missing information on your part led to this mistake. If it did, you shouldn't expect your tax pro to pay for it. But, if you did your part and your tax pro was responsible for the error, don't pay additional fees for the mistake (and take the experience as a cue to start looking for a new tax pro).

Use your tax returns as a diagnostic tool for your business

Whether you prepare your taxes yourself or have a professional accomplish this for you, don't be quick to shove your completed tax returns in a drawer and forget about them until tax season comes around again. Instead, while the information in the return is fresh in your mind, take a moment to review the return and think about the underlying figures. Also, compare the current year's return to your returns from the last year or two. As you study the returns, look for answers to the following basic questions. The answers should reveal a lot about the healthiness of your business:

- **Is your business profitable?** You can determine whether your business is profitable by checking line 26 of Schedule E to your most recent Form 1040 (or line 21 of Form 8825, if you own your rental business through a partnership, limited partnership, LLC, or S corporation). This figure represents your total rental income (or loss) for the year.

- **Did your business earn more than it did last year?** You can determine whether your business is growing by comparing the figure on the current year's Schedule E (or Form 8825) to the corresponding figure on last year's form.

- **Do you owe more taxes than last year?** It's not hard to answer that one—just look at the ending figure on your return. But it's another thing to figure out why. Study the expenses section of Schedule E (or Form 8825) to see if anything is different compared to last year's expenses. For example, all things being equal, a significant drop in advertising costs could explain a rise in your tax liability.

After you answer these questions, use them to modify your business plans if appropriate. For example, if you notice that you spent much more money on advertising this year than last year, yet had a harder time finding good tenants, it's probably time to lower your advertising budget or rethink your marketing strategies. Also, if your tax liability was much greater than last year's, take a moment to consider what this means. Don't jump to the conclusion that owing more taxes is a negative sign. On the contrary, it's quite possible you owed more taxes because your business earned much more revenue, in which case the increased tax bill is a sign of a positive development.

Cooperate with auditors

Something in a tax return you filed may trigger an audit by the IRS or your state tax agency. For example, the amount of deductions you claimed may be unusually high for a business of your size, or you may have forgotten to file a key supplemental tax form with your return. It's also possible you may become the subject of a "random audit." In this case, you can rest a little easier because you know that auditors aren't coming after you to investigate a possible mistake they found. (Of course, it's still nerve-wracking to have your books open for scrutiny under any circumstances.)

In either situation, letting anxieties get the better of you is counter-productive. Instead, cooperate and be courteous and professional during audits. Organize your files so that your accountant and the IRS can easily sort through and read them. Not only will auditors appreciate your having made it easy for them to do their job, but you'll add to the image you wish to convey—that you're a careful, structured businessperson who follows the rules. Plus, the less time auditors need to spend sifting through your files, the sooner they'll leave.

If you've done nothing fraudulent or criminal, then you needn't go into an audit worried that auditors will claim that you did. If auditors do find something fishy with your return, it's probably because you mistakenly omitted something that would have increased your tax liability. If so, you'll likely owe what you should have paid to begin with, plus interest and penalties. Major problems await unscrupulous landlords who knowingly try to beat the system by defrauding the government.

Finally, as you await your audit, keep in mind there's a high probability that the IRS or your state tax agency will leave your office at the end of the day, thank you for your time, and tell you that they found no problems. Although, even in this situation, you'd still prefer to have avoided the experience, you can feel that much more assured that you're on the ball when it comes to your taxes, and you can proceed with newfound confidence.

Before heading into an audit, be sure to do some homework, even if your accountant will be the one meeting with the IRS. Read *Stand Up to the IRS,* by Fred Daily (Nolo), for proven strategies for weathering an audit.

Step Ten, Taxes: My To-Do List

Step Ten took you through the process of managing your approach to taxes so that you don't invite an audit. It also showed you how you can avoid giving hard-earned money to Uncle Sam in excess of your actual tax liability. To put the lessons of this chapter into practice, follow these pointers.

☐ **Homework:** Look at the IRS website, and the site maintained by the tax agency in the state where my property is located. Check back now and then for new information.

☐ **Record keeping:** Establish a good record-keeping system, and aim to keep every record that will substantiate the income and expenses I claim on my returns.

☐ **Independent contractors:** Obtain taxpayer identification numbers from independent contractors and have them complete a 1099-MISC.

☐ **Employee withholding:** Withhold the proper amounts from employees' pay, and make timely tax filings on their behalf.

☐ **Tax help:** Find and hire the right tax pro for my business.

☐ **Structure my business right:** Understand how the choice of business structure, and tax year, affects my taxes.

☐ **Deductions:** Discover what deductions I'm entitled to claim, and claim them with confidence.

☐ **Tax timeliness:** Pay attention to when I file my returns, and understand the consequences of a late or amended return.

☐ **Use the returns:** Learn from my returns—compare successive years for evidence of positive trends or issues to resolve.

☐ **Audits:** If faced with an audit, prepare carefully and consider hiring a tax pro to represent my interests.

State Landlord-Tenant Statutes

Here are some of the key statutes pertaining to landlord-tenant law in each state. In some states, important legal principles are contained in court opinions, not codes or statutes. Court-made law and rent stabilization—rent control—laws and regulations are not reflected in this chart.

State Landlord-Tenant Statutes	
Alabama	Ala. Code §§ 35-9-1 to 35-9-100; 35-9A-101 et seq.
Alaska	Alaska Stat. §§ 34.03.010 to 34.03.380
Arizona	Ariz. Rev. Stat. Ann. §§ 12-1171 to 12-1183; 33-1301 to 33-1381; 33-301 to 33-381
Arkansas	Ark. Code Ann. §§ 18-16-101 to 18-16-306; 18-17-101 to 18-7-913
California	Cal. Civ. Code §§ 1925 to 1954, 1961 to 1962.7
Colorado	Colo. Rev. Stat. §§ 38-12-101 to 38-12-104; 38-12-301 to 38-12-302; 13-40-101 to 13-40-123
Connecticut	Conn. Gen. Stat. Ann. §§ 47a-1 to 47a-74
Delaware	Del. Code Ann. tit. 25, §§ 5101 to 5907
District of Columbia	D.C. Code Ann. §§ 42-3201 to 42-3610; D.C. Mun. Regs., tit. 14, §§ 300 to 311
Florida	Fla. Stat. Ann. §§ 83.40 to 83.682
Georgia	Ga. Code Ann. §§ 44-7-1 to 44-7-81
Hawaii	Haw. Rev. Stat. §§ 521-1 to 521-78
Idaho	Idaho Code §§ 6-201 to 6-324; 55-208 to 55-308
Illinois	735 Ill. Comp. Stat. §§ 5/9-201 to 321; 705/0.01 to 742/30

State Landlord-Tenant Statutes (continued)	
Indiana	Ind. Code Ann. §§ 32-31-1-1 to 32-31-9-15; 32-31-2.9-d to 2.9-5
Iowa	Iowa Code Ann. §§ 562A.1 to 562A.37
Kansas	Kan. Stat. Ann. §§ 58-2501 to 58-2573
Kentucky	Ky. Rev. Stat. Ann. §§ 383.010 to 383.715
Louisiana	La. Rev. Stat. Ann. §§ 9:3251 to 9:3261; La. Civ. Code Ann. art. 2668 to 2729
Maine	Me. Rev. Stat. Ann. tit. 14, §§ 6001 to 6046
Maryland	Md. Code Ann. [Real Prop.] §§ 8-101 to 8-604
Massachusetts	Mass. Gen. Laws Ann. ch. 186, §§ 1 to 22
Michigan	Mich. Comp. Laws §§ 554.131 to .201; 554.601 to 554.641
Minnesota	Minn. Stat. Ann. §§ 504B.001 to 504B.471
Mississippi	Miss. Code Ann. §§ 89-7-1 to 89-8-27
Missouri	Mo. Rev. Stat. §§ 441.005 to 441.880; 535.150 to 535.300
Montana	Mont. Code Ann. §§ 70-24-101 to 70-26-110
Nebraska	Neb. Rev. Stat. §§ 76-1401 to 76-1449
Nevada	Nev. Rev. Stat. Ann. §§ 118A.010 to 118A.520; 40.215 to 40.280
New Hampshire	N.H. Rev. Stat. Ann. §§ 540:1 to 540:29; 540-A:1 to 540-A:8
New Jersey	N.J. Stat. Ann. §§ 46:8-1 to 46:8-50; 2A:42-1 to 42-96
New Mexico	N.M. Stat. Ann. §§ 47-8-1 to 47-8-51
New York	N.Y. Real Prop. Law §§ 220 to 238; Real Prop. Acts §§ 701 to 853; Mult. Dwell. Law (all); Mult. Res. Law (all); Gen. Oblig. Law §§ 7-103 to 7-109
North Carolina	N.C. Gen. Stat. §§ 42-1 to 42-14.2; 42-25.6 to 42-76
North Dakota	N.D. Cent. Code §§ 47-16-01 to 47-16-41
Ohio	Ohio Rev. Code Ann. §§ 5321.01 to 5321.19
Oklahoma	Okla. Stat. Ann. tit. 41, §§ 101 to 136
Oregon	Or. Rev. Stat. §§ 90.100 to 91.225
Pennsylvania	68 Pa. Cons. Stat. Ann. §§ 250.101; 399.18
Rhode Island	R.I. Gen. Laws §§ 34-18-1 to 34-18-57

State Landlord-Tenant Statutes (continued)	
South Carolina	S.C. Code Ann. §§ 27-40-10 to 27-40-940
South Dakota	S.D. Codified Laws Ann. §§ 43-32-1 to 43-32-30
Tennessee	Tenn. Code Ann. §§ 66-28-101 to 66-28-521
Texas	Tex. Prop. Code Ann. §§ 91.001 to 92.354
Utah	Utah Code Ann. §§ 57-17-1 to 57-17-5; 57-22-1 to 57-22-6
Vermont	Vt. Stat. Ann. tit. 9, §§ 4451 to 4468
Virginia	Va. Code Ann. §§ 55-218.1 to 55-248.40
Washington	Wash. Rev. Code Ann. §§ 59.04.010 to 59.04.900; 59.18.010 to 59.18.911
West Virginia	W.Va. Code §§ 37-6-1 to 37-6-30
Wisconsin	Wis. Stat. Ann. §§ 704.01 to 704.50; Wis. Admin. Code §§ 134.01 to 134.10
Wyoming	Wyo. Stat. §§ 1-21-1201 to 1-21-1211; 34-2-128 to 34-2-129

Index

Get the Latest in the Law

Nolo's Legal Updater
We'll send you an email whenever a new edition of your book is published! Sign up at **www.nolo.com/legalupdater**.

Updates at Nolo.com
Check **www.nolo.com/update** to find recent changes in the law that affect the current edition of your book.

Nolo Customer Service
To make sure that this edition of the book is the most recent one, call us at **800-728-3555** and ask one of our friendly customer service representatives (7:00 am to 6:00 pm PST, weekdays only). Or find out at **www.nolo.com**.

Complete the Registration & Comment Card ...
... and we'll do the work for you! Just indicate your preferences below:

- -

Registration & Comment Card

NAME   DATE

ADDRESS

CITY   STATE   ZIP

PHONE   EMAIL

COMMENTS

WAS THIS BOOK EASY TO USE?   (VERY EASY)   5   4   3   2   1   (VERY DIFFICULT)

☐ Yes, you can quote me in future Nolo promotional materials. *Please include phone number above.*

☐ Yes, send me **Nolo's Legal Updater** via email when a new edition of this book is available.

Yes, I want to sign up for the following email newsletters:

    ☐ **NoloBriefs** (monthly)
    ☐ **Nolo's Special Offer** (monthly)
    ☐ **Nolo's BizBriefs** (monthly)
    ☐ **Every Landlord's Quarterly** (four times a year)

☐ Yes, you can give my contact info to carefully selected partners whose products may be of interest to me.

RISK1

Nolo
950 Parker Street
Berkeley, CA 94710-9867
www.nolo.com

YOUR LEGAL COMPANION